The Prophetic Element in the Church

As Conceived in the Theology of Karl Rahner

David Lowry

UNIVERSITY
PRESS OF
AMERICA

Lanham • New York • London

Copyright © **1990** by
University Press of America®, Inc.
4720 Boston Way
Lanham, Maryland 20706

3 Henrietta Street
London WC2E 8LU England

Library of Congress Cataloging-in-Publication Data

Lowry, David, 1948-
The prophetic element in the church : as conceived in the theology
of Karl Rahner / David Lowry.
p. cm.
Includes bibliographical references and index.
1. Prophecy (Christianity)—History of doctrines—20th century. 2. Rahner, Karl, 1904-
I. Title.
BR115.P8L68   1990   231.7'45'092—dc20   90–39158 CIP

ISBN 0–8191–7857–8 (alk. paper)

 The paper used in this publication meets the minimum requirements of
American National Standard for Information Sciences—Permanence
of Paper for Printed Library Materials, ANSI Z39.48–1984.

Contents

Preface

The topic of the prophetic element in the church as conceived in the theology of Karl Rahner has brought together a number of concerns that I have had including the lively ministry of the Word, kairotic proclamation, the socio-critical task of the church, and the guidance of the Spirit. Addressing this theme from within the methodology of Rahner has meant demonstrating the fruitfulness of an anthropological approach, especially with a subject which can appear so nebulous. It has meant further confirmation to me of the crucial position of a "transcendental" method (or something like it) within the theological task. I believe that, understood correctly, theology, in its pursuit of clarity on the human reality before God, cannot escape discussions of a transcendental, metaphysical, or foundational nature. Protestant theology, with certain exceptions (Søren Kierkegaard, Paul Tillich, Wolfhart Pannenberg, and process theology), has been weak in this area of ontological reflection. Roman Catholic philosophy and theology have something to offer here, particularly in its history of grappling with the thought of Thomas Aquinas. Karl Rahner writes from within and out of this tradition. In a sense, he continues the ontological discussion of Thomas with a new direction and new questions raised by such modern philosophers as Kant, Hegel, and Heidegger. The ontological questions are deepened and sharpened by attention to and movement from the existentiell[1] reality of the human subject. This approach offers much for the theological task of conceiving the multifaceted nature of Christianity within human experience, not as a foreign element but as explanatory of that experience. My hope is that the following pages on prophetic reality as conceived by Rahner bear out the benefits of a 'transcendental' approach for a subject which, for a number of reasons, does not easily lend itself to clarity.

This work which is a revision and expansion of a doctoral dissertation did not 'just happen'. Nor was it simply a matter of my individual self-determination and activity. As Rahner points out, there are 'spheres' in which human decision and operation take place. I would like to express my gratitude for some of those individuals who have made up that social sphere, without whom this book would not have come into being. My gratitude goes out to the students and faculty of the Lutheran School of Theology at Chicago and the Chicago Cluster of Theological Schools; to Carl Braaten, for asking crucial questions at appropriate times and giving pointed direction which has brought sharpened focus to the theological task and to this work at its dissertation stage; to James Bresnahan, for his wise counsel, encouragement, and insightful discussions on Rahner's method and thought; and to John Szura, who first suggested I look into this area of the dynamic element in the church in the thought of Karl Rahner, and who shares a particular interest in this subject. There are certainly many others among faculty and students who could be mentioned; the list would be long. One other person: I remember with gratitude Joseph Wulftange whose classes at the Jesuit School of Theology helped me into a fuller understanding and appreciation of Thomistic

---

[1]'Existentiell' is a term Rahner uses, following Heidegger, to refer to the lived-out existential experience of the human being. 'Existential' refers to the ontological structures or operations in being human. 'Existentiell', therefore, refers to the experience or appropriation of those existentials in being human. I have followed this terminology throughout this work.

philosophy, 'neo' and 'transcendental'.

Special thanks goes to Maggie Newman who gave great care to the typing of the final manuscript and the work of indexing. I am also thankful for the people of St. Thomas Lutheran Church and the South Cluster Churches for their support in this as in so many things. They are partners in the prophetic ministry of the gospel.

I am especially grateful for my parents and family, for their support and encouragement. And my children, Justin, Joanna, and Elizabeth, who wondered many times out loud when their dad was going to get through with this work, and who overall patiently endured it. I can only barely begin to acknowledge the importance of my wife, Elly, to this undertaking. With deep gratitude I recognize here her steadfast encouragement through the ups and downs of this project, her active listening, her supportive presence, her partnership.

Acknowledgments

Extracts taken from Karl Rahner, *Foundations of Christian Faith: An Introduction to the Idea of Christianity* (1978); originally published as *Grundkurs des Glaubens: Einfürung in den Begriff des Christentums* (Freiburg: Verlag Herder, 1976); are reprinted by permission of the Crossroad Publishing Company, New York and by Darton, Longman and Todd, Ltd., London.

Extracts taken from Karl Rahner, *Theological Investigations*, Vol. 2, (Darton, Longman & Todd, 1963; Seabury Press, 1975); Vol. 9 (Darton, Longman & Todd, 1972; Seabury Press, 1973); Vol. 10 (Darton, Longman & Todd, 1973; Seabury Press, 1977); Vol. 18 (Darton, Longman & Todd, 1983; Crossroad, 1983) are reprinted by permission of the publishers: Darton, Longman and Todd, Ltd. and the Crossroad Publishing Co. Selections from *Theological Investigations* are translations of material originally published in *Schriften zur Theology*, Vols. 1-8 (Zurich: Benziger Verlag, 1954-83).

Extracts from *Encyclopedia of Theology: The Concise Sacramentum Mundi*, edited by Karl Rahner (1982), originally published by Freiburg: Herder (1975), are reprinted by permission of the Crossroad Publishing Co., New York and Search Press, Ltd., Tunbridge Wells.

Extracts from Karl Rahner, *Quaestiones Disputatae*, Vol. 12: *The Dynamic Element in the Church* (1964), originally published as *Quaestiones Disputatae*, Vol. 5: *Das Dynamische in der Kirche* (Freiburg: Herder, 1958); are reprinted by permission of the Crossroad Publishing Co., New York.

Introduction

For thus says the Lord to the house of Israel:
"Seek me and live; but do not seek Bethel,
and do not enter into Gilgal
  or cross over to Beer-sheba;
for Gilgal shall surely go into exile,
  and Bethel shall come to naught."
      Amos 5:4-5

Thus says the Lord concerning the prophets
  who lead my people astray,
who cry "Peace"
  when they have something to eat,
but declare war against him
  who puts nothing into their mouths.
Therefore it shall be night to you, without vision
  and darkness to you, without divination.
The sun shall go down upon the prophets,
  and the day shall be black over them; . . .
      Micah 3:5-6

While they were worshiping the Lord and fasting,
the Holy Spirit said, "Set apart for me Barnabas
and Saul for the work to which I have called them."
      Acts 13:2

For all the differences between them in material content and
Sitz im Leben, these three biblical passages have one thing in
common. They each claim to be a divine message; they are (or
include) a divine oracle or utterance. In the first text there is an

1

admonition of a political nature; in the second, a word of judgment directed to false prophets; and in the third, a directive. These types of prophetic utterance by no means exhaust the kinds of prophetic messages that are present in Scripture. As we shall see, there is an indefinite range of forms of content to prophetic utterances. Nevertheless, we shall see also that the one thing that identifies a prophetic word as prophetic, whatever its content, is its claim to divine origination.

In addition to this fundamental feature of prophetic utterance we will also note two other features. One has to do with the specificity, concreteness, and timeliness of the message. In the above prophetic examples the messages are given as the word that is necessary for the particular moment, and not as a carefully reasoned out implication of a more general presupposition applicable to all times. They are proclaimed as messages of a provisional nature which God has given to human recipients to speak to her people in their present unique historical situation.[1] The third feature of these prophetic utterances has to do with their being other-directed. They are 'revelations' *for others*. They are not merely 'private revelations' but have to do with other persons or groups or societies. The definition of prophecy that I am using in this work contains these three features:

> Prophecy is (1) a timely message or call to action (2) originating from God and (3) directed to others.

This definition, which I arrived at after a study of the phenomenology of biblical prophetism, forms the basis for the framework of my treatment of Karl Rahner on the prophetic element in the church. Prophetic reality is clearly of high importance in

---

[1]In order to avoid impersonalizing or further distancing by grammatical constructions the God who has come near, and also in order to recognize feminine as well as masculine metaphors for God, I have chosen a particular approach to pronouns related to God. Throughout this work I alternate between feminine and masculine pronouns by chapter.

Rahner's thought. My thesis is that Rahner demonstrates the intelligibility and necessity of prophecy in human and ecclesial reality. Rahner's own treatment of prophecy, however, other than an encyclopedic article, is not of a particularly systematic nature. The *framework* for my treatment of Rahner on prophetism, therefore, was suggested not so much by Rahner, but by what I discovered in the study of prophetic phenomenology. The first chapter, therefore, is an overview of scholarship in the field of biblical prophetism, as to its dynamic or formal nature. I seek to lead the reader to an understanding of the basis for the above definition. The three features of prophecy as so defined become the essential elements in the description of prophecy in Chapter II and the discussion of the anthropological foundation of prophecy in Chapter III, in which the paramount question for Rahner is addressed; namely, what in being human makes possible these features of the prophetic? I seek to demonstrate what in human consciousness, for Rahner, can be described as a prophetic kind of knowing, and how this prophetic knowledge, namely, a timely knowledge 'from the Lord' directed to others, is both intelligible and necessary to human being and community. The intelligibility and necessity of prophecy is something that, in the time in which we live, cannot simply be assumed.

Problems with Prophecy

The description of prophetic phenomena found in the many scholarly studies on the subject creates little problem for a modern Christianity and contemporary human experience, as long as it is seen as referring to a particular phenomenon in the history of religions, a phenomenon that can be explained by reference to the subconscious, to stereotypical behavior, to an ancient world view. However, as soon as we assume a prophetic reality in a modern context, and include belief in the divine origin claimed in prophetic messages, and further ask about the prophetic element in the church today, a host of questions and problems is raised. Predominant among them is the question of how an obviously human word can also be a divine word. That is, if prophetic reality means the communication of God to human beings, we are faced with the problem of what this actually means and even how this is possible; this at least is the problem for many Christians of the modern era. The "Thus says the Lord" and "the Holy Spirit said" are not forms of speech generally present in today's church. When we hear of people speaking in this manner many of us are suspicious, and our suspicions are not merely the result of a narrow rationalism, but rather are the quite necessary questioning of a humanity 'come of age', a humanity much less inclined to mystification. The prophetic phenomena of an earlier age (as well as our own) can appear to us as nothing more than the overflow of a subconscious trying to deal with the existential *Angst* of the human condition. For the modern person it is easy to understand the thoughts in the mind of the prophet as his or her own thoughts, and the quite natural result of the peculiarities of his or her own very *human* condition. It is not so easy to conceive of these thoughts as being, at the same time, divine.

This problem with prophetic phenomena is further exacerbated by the way the church has traditionally and historically thought of the prophetic figure. The impression has been given of a 'supernatural' and therefore 'unnatural' reality assigned to some specially selected individuals whose divine empowering was something added on to what otherwise would be considered 'normal' (or natural) human reality. This conception of prophecy and the prophetic figure has been subjected to a certain amount of de-mythologization; and one can wonder, with that demythologization relatively accomplished, whether there are still grounds left for prophecy understood as a 'word of the Lord', or whether what remains is a conception of prophecy as a word of quite human origins, of a psychological and sociological nature.

In addition to this fundamental question above, further problems are raised by the many images conjured up in the popular mind by the term 'prophetic'–everything from foretelling the future to social-activist ministers. There is the association with parapsychological and paranormal phenomena which has been almost universally present wherever there have been explicit prophetic expressions in the past. In fact, certain kinds of extraordinary behavior have often been the means by which a social group has identified a prophet. In our own day, prophecy in a form similar to its practice in the early church has arisen in pentecostal and charismatic movements in the churches. Such phenomena have raised fresh questions about the root causes of such experiences. The term 'prophetic', however, has also been used to describe critical activity of a social and political nature. This certainly has been its predominant meaning in much theological literature. With such an abundance of images it is not always clear to the average Christian (and the theologian) what is meant by 'prophecy', and what importance prophecy holds for the church.

Signs of the Prophetic

Many (including Christians) may entertain suspicions about the root causes of prophetic phenomena as they appear in the biblical literature and contemporary movements; nevertheless, we are faced with the fact (as represented in the above texts) that the church has its origins in a prophetic movement, and that its 'founder' can be termed 'the eschatological prophet'. Furthermore, we are aware of a history of prophetism in the church. While Christian prophecy as an explicit, recognizable phenomenon may have declined substantially toward the end of the second century; nevertheless, there has always been a prophetic element to the church expressed in inspired teachers and preachers, in reformers, in monastic and renewal movements.[2] Throughout the history of

---

[2]The decline of prophecy as an explicit phenomenon in the second century has been attributed to certain social developments, to the institutionalization and hellenization of the church as the emphasis increasingly fell on the rationality of the faith. For discussions on the decline of Christian prophecy see Hans von Campenhausen, *Ecclesiastical Authority and Scriptural Power in the Church of the*

the church there has been a tension between faith as *fides quae* and *fides qua*, between faith in its material nature and faith in its formal or dynamic nature. There has always been the necessity to pass on the traditions of faith as well as to be open in trusting obedience for the fresh, new word. There has also been the danger of becoming closed to the new direction, to the call and impact of God's reign which is always arriving. In other words, there has been in the life of the church a tension between the official structure of the church (and its teachers), which seeks to preserve the treasury of the faith, and the prophets or reformers who seek to bring the 'new' word for the new situation.

This tension continues into our own day. There are a number of movements of our times which are existing in tension with the 'established' order of both society and the church. Signs of the prophetic in our contemporary situation have been associated with movements toward peace and justice, socio-critical actions (often of a symbolic nature) of individuals and ecumenical groups and communities, calls to radical Christian discipleship and action, Christian base communities, charismatic communities, and the charismatic movement.

A 'Searching' Prophetism

Also within the life of the church there is an explicit and implicit search for the prophetic dimension. We often sense something is missing in the way of a prophetic reality. Many of us express frustration with church social statements which seem far too general and lacking in a message which really addresses, in a specific and concrete manner, the situation of our times. We experience the eclipse of the prophetic in the tendencies of official

---

First Three Centuries, trans. J. A. Baker (Stanford, CA: Stanford University Press, 1969), especially chap. 8, pp. 178-212; David E. Aune, *Prophecy in Early Christianity and the Ancient Mediterranean World* (Grand Rapids, MI: William B. Eerdmans, 1983), p. 338; and David Hill, *New Testament Prophecy* (Atlanta: John Knox Press, 1979), pp. 186-92.

church documents to be locked into prescriptions for our times that go little beyond a social analysis and rational deduction from general theological principles, and which, therefore, speak with inadequate specificity to the unique situations of our time. In the same way theology often seems far removed from the real needs of the world. In its preoccupation with and captivity to general abstractions, and its desire to see all sides of the question, it seems unable to offer anything truly concrete and timely to the historical situation in which it operates. This is, at least in part, the criticism liberation theology has leveled at the way theology has traditionally been done. In addition to these experiences of the eclipse of prophecy we can also include the discomfort many of us feel with aspects of the 'prophetic' movements in our midst. We feel the eclipse or distortion of the prophetic in pentecostal and charismatic movements where there are tendencies to view the prophetic dimension solely in terms of the charismatic element without sufficient regard for the historical and political dimension. On the other hand, it is not clear that socio-critical action or critique is, in and of itself, prophetic either, that is, without regard for a charismatic grounding (even when it is grounded in a 'solidarity' with the poor and the victims).

Consequently, at the same time that signs of the prophetic can be recognized in our midst, we also experience an eclipse of the prophetic. The fact that there has been an increased interest in discerning the 'signs of the times' and with reflection on the prophetic dynamic, particularly on the part of liberation and political theologies, reveals our sense that something is lacking in the way the church operates and reflects on its life.

This experience of the eclipse of the prophetic reveals what may be termed a 'searching prophetism'. Karl Rahner has used the term 'searching Christology' to indicate that in human existentiell reality (at least where an implicit faith exists) there is an implicit fundamental search for the 'absolute saviour', a search which culminates in the encounter with Jesus of Nazareth.[3] In regard to prophecy, we can say that there is inherent in the reality of being the church (and in being human) an implicit 'searching prophetism' which must find explicit expression in order for the church to be the church. The church which has its origins in the 'eschatological prophet', Jesus, in whom God is revealed, must throughout its history bear witness to and be sustained by this revelation of God. While the church sees in Jesus the final and definitive self-revelation of God, it is apparent that it also seeks (although often implicitly) an ongoing revelation. The church believes it is guided by the Spirit, that God continues to speak. The church must preserve the Word of God, the self-revelation of God in Jesus, in ever-new historical situations. History, as Rahner reminds us on many occasions, is one-way directed. We can never simply repristinate the past or simply deduce from past revelation the specific directives for today's situation. This is clear from the nature of history and human self-determination and decision making. We cannot simply take the gospel message or an abstract concept of human nature and deduce the specific actions necessary for the present moment. Rahner's position is that we do not, in fact, operate this way. As Rahner sees it there is a dynamic element operative in which truly *human* decisions have the character of divine direction. Consequently, it can be said that there is an implicit or searching prophetism within Christianity and the church which is necessary to human community and which must find expression.

This recognition of an implicit prophetism and the need for an explicit prophetism, an explicit expression of the prophetic element in the life of the church, raises questions for theology which theology has hardly addressed. For one thing, the question can be raised as to what position prophecy holds in the church's

---

[3]Karl Rahner, *Foundations of Christian Faith: An Introduction to the Idea of Christianity*, trans. William V. Dych (New York: Seabury Press, 1978), p. 295 (hereafter cited as Rahner, *Foundations*).

theology. It is somewhat difficult to see where it belongs dog-
matically. Prophecy is a revelatory knowledge, yet the church sees
in Jesus the final and definitive revelation which has brought an
end to the history of revelation. This has led some theologians to
assume the end of prophecy.[4] Nevertheless, the issue of prophecy
has been present in discussions of the theology of the Spirit, the
theology of the three offices of Christ, in Catholic mystical
theology, in Protestant dialectical theology, in liberation theology,
and in discussions on discerning the 'signs of the times', particularly
in Catholic thought.[5] It is beyond the scope of our study to
examine historically the ways theology has addressed the question
of prophecy. It would be a difficult history to write. Rahner has
noted that the history of the theology of the charismatic movement
in the church has yet to be written and, furthermore, that fundamental theology has hardly taken up the question of the dynamic
nature of prophecy.[6] Some of the places one would have to look
to find some treatment related to our topic would include the
medieval analysis of prophetic knowledge, the theology of mystic-

---

[4]Wolfhart Pannenberg, *Faith and Reality*, trans. John Maxwell (Philadelphia:
Westminster Press, 1977), pp. 123-38.

[5]Roman Catholic thought has given particular attention to the question of the
"discernment of spirits": see Casiano Floristan and Christian Duquoc, eds.,
Discernment of the Spirit and of Spirits, Concilium, vol. 119 (New York: Seabury
Press, 1979).

[6]Rahner notes that "The history of the theology of the charismatic movement
in the Church and in the service of the Church is still to be written. It has not yet
been written because the theology has remained relatively undeveloped. The
medieval theology of charisma cannot be regarded as fully developed except in
limited areas. Ignatius of Loyola constructed a logic of the existential recognition
of God's charismatic impulses, but it has not yet been properly assimilated."
(*Encyclopedia of Theology: The Concise Sacramentum Mundi*, ed. Rahner [New
York: Crossroad, 1982], s.v. "Charism," by Karl Rahner, pp. 185-86 [hereafter cited
as *ET*].) In his article, "Prophetism," Rahner recognizes that "In contrast to
medieval theology, the present-day theology of the schools pays relatively scant
attention to prophetism." (*Sacramentum Mundi: An Encyclopedia of Theology*
[New York: Herder & Herder, 1968-70], s.v. "Prophetism," by Karl Rahner, p. 112
[hereafter cited as *SM*].)

ism, the theology (and philosophy) of practical reason and decision making, and the theology of biblical prophecy.[7]

---

[7]Certain Protestant theologians come readily to mind when considering theologically related themes and emphases, although where their thought touches on the area of the prophetic it remains generally undeveloped. Søren Kierkegaard's thought, with its emphasis on the individual and decision making, is conducive to a theology of prophecy. For his use of a (somewhat insane) priestly figure of his times who has 'revelations', and who becomes a figure of the times to which Kierkegaard addresses himself, as well as addressing the significance of 'revelation' and 'revelations', see *On Authority and Revelation: The book on Adler, or a Cycle of Ethico-Religious Essays*, trans. with an introduction and notes by Walter Lowrie (Princeton: Princeton University Press, 1955). Karl Barth also takes up the question of 'special ethics' and a 'practical' and 'active casuistry', a 'casuistry of the prophetic ethos'. See his *Church Dogmatics*, 4 vols., ed. G. W. Bromiley and T. F. Torance, trans. W. T. Thomson, Harold Knight, G. W. Bromiley, et al. (Edinburgh: T. & T. Clark, 1936-69), vol. 3, pt. 4, no. 52, pp. 3-31. Dietrich Bonhoeffer's ethical contextualism is concerned with perceiving the will of God in the specific situation. See his *Ethics*, ed. Eberhard Bethge, trans. Neville Horton Smith (New York: Macmillan, 1955). Also, James T. Laney, "An Examination of Bonhoeffer's Ethical Contextualism" in *A Bonhoeffer Legacy: Essays in Understanding*, ed. A. J. Klassen (Grand Rapids, MI: William B. Eerdmans, 1981), pp. 294-313. Paul Tillich was concerned with 'prophetic criticism' as a reality of revelation, although the concept remained relatively undeveloped. See his discussion of revelation in his first volume of *Systematic Theology*, 3 vols. (Chicago: University of Chicago Press, 1951-63). Also see "Part V; History and the Kingdom of God," in vol. 3, pp. 297-423, where Tillich notes that prophecy does not live by the past but by anticipation of the future. Rudolf Otto in another line of approach, takes up the question of a "faculty of 'divination.'" See his *The Idea of the Holy: An Inquiry into the Non-Rational Factor in the Idea of the Divine and Its Relation to the Rational*, trans. John W. Harvey (New York: Oxford University Press, 1958), pp. 143-54. There is another strand in Protestant and Catholic theology, however, which tends to reject or overlook this dynamic element. Rahner is critical of the textbook theology in Roman Catholic thought which treats ethical decision making as if it were *solely* a matter of rational casuistry. In Protestant theology an example of the devaluation of the dynamic element of prophecy can be seen in an essay by Wolfhart Pannenberg. He asserts that "prophetic proclamation must be replaced by an interpretation of what has now become history through Jesus" (Pannenberg, *Faith and Reality*, p. 128).

There have also been some attempts in biblical prophecy to understand the formal structure of prophecy: Abraham Heschel's prophetic 'pathos' (Abraham J. Heschel, *The Prophets*, 2 vols. [New York: Harper & Row, 1962]); James A. Saunders's hermeneutics of monotheizing ("Hermeneutics in True and False Prophecy," in *Canon and Authority: Essays in Old Testament Religion and Theology* [Philadelphia: Fortress Press, 1977], pp. 21-41); and Robert Carroll's theory of

The Need for a Theology of Prophecy

The fact that the church has its origins in a prophetic movement and is the community of the 'eschatological prophet', that it has a history of prophetism, and that there are prophetic movements present today, that there is the experience of the eclipse of the prophetic, and a lack of theological reflection on the subject, point to the need for a theology of prophecy. As Bernard Cooke has pointed out in his historical and theological study on the *Ministry to Word and Sacraments*:

> Charismatic prophecy is not restricted to Old Testament times; though we have largely lost sight of the fact, prophecy reaches its fulfillment in Christ and in the Christian period of history. Genuine prophets there have been, there are, and there will be in the church. The problem the Christian community always faces is to discover and nurture them, to distinguish the genuine from the false, to accept them despite the challenge they always present. In our own day there is a critical need to reinstate the prophetic voice in the counsels of the church, but to do this, we must understand more accurately what Christian prophetism is, and here the theologian can be a support to the authentic prophet.[8]

There have been directions in recent theology in which the prophetic theme can be recognized. Vatican II assumes the need for a theology of the discernment of the 'signs of the times', and the subject of discernment has become the topic of a number of essays as well as a particular concern of liberation theologies which have sought to bring the Word of God to bear upon the concrete

---

'cognitive dissonance', at least as an element of the formation of the prophetic message (Robert P. Carroll, *When Prophecy Failed: Cognitive Dissonance in the Prophetic Traditions of the Old Testament* [New York: Seabury Press, 1979]). This latter attempt may be an example of a social theory overwhelming the biblical text and completely leaving out the theological question of prophecy. There may be other attempts at theological explanation of prophecy but for the most part biblical scholars are reticent about venturing into this area of discussion.

[8]Bernard Cooke, *Ministry to Word and Sacraments: History and Theology* (Philadelphia: Fortress Press, 1976), p. 330.

situation of our time.[9] Also, Roman Catholic theology has shown a renewed awareness of the socio-critical function of the church.[10] This is true also of Protestant theology, especially eschatological theologies which have seen in the absolute future of God the critique of all utopian futures.[11] There has also been a reworking of the Lutheran two-kingdoms doctrine in which a corrective has been offered to the tendency to separate 'worldly affairs' from 'religious affairs' thereby giving room for the socio-critical role of the church.[12] Nevertheless, to my knowledge, a substantial and

---

[9]Austin Flannery, ed., *Vatican Council II: The Conciliar and Post Conciliar Documents* (Northport, NY: Costello Publishing, 1975), p. 912; Floristan and Duquoc, *Discernment of the Spirit and of Spirits*.

[10]At Vatican II the Roman Catholic church sought, in a significant way, to unburden itself of the role of teacher and guide of the nations, in a recognition of the autonomy of the world. Recent Roman Catholic theology has expanded this recognition, embracing the positive aspects of secularization. One of the significant developments of this positive acknowledgement of secularization is a renewed awareness of the socio-critical function of the church. For some particularly insightful theological assessments of secularization in Roman Catholic theology, see Johann Baptist Metz, *Theology of the World*, trans. William Glen-Doepel (New York: Herder & Herder, 1969); Edward Schillebeeckx, *World and Church*, trans. N. D. Smith (New York: Sheed & Ward, 1968); Rahner, "Theological Reflections on the Problem of Secularization," in *Theological Investigations*, 20 vols. (1961-83), vol.s 1-6 (Baltimore: Helicon); vols. 7-10 (New York: Herder & Herder); vols. 11-14 (New York: Seabury); vols. 15-20 (New York: Crossroads); 10:318-48 (hereafter cited as Rahner, *TI*). In "Theological Reflections on the Problem of Secularization," Rahner views secularization as setting the church free for its socio-critical or prophetic role: "In its situation of pluralism and secularism the Church leaves society to develop along its own lines. Now precisely because she is incapable of shaping the course of society in its concrete sense, the Church herself has a quite new task in relation to this society, a task which might be characterised as 'prophetic' " (p. 330).

[11]The significance of the eschatological dimension for the relation of the church and society can be seen in the theology of Jürgen Moltmann. See, for example, his *Theology of Hope: On the Ground and the Implications of a Christian Eschatology*, trans. James W. Leitch (New York: Harper & Row, 1967), and *The Crucified God: The Cross of Christ as the Foundation and Criticism of Christian Theology*, trans. R. A. Wilson and John Gowden (New York: Harper & Row, 1974).

[12]For reformulations of Luther's two-kingdoms doctrine see, among others, Pannenberg, *Ethics*, trans. Keith Crim (Philadelphia: Westminster Press, 1981),

focused theology of prophecy has yet to be developed.

Karl Rahner and the Grounds
for a Theology of Prophecy

I am not attempting in this work to develop a theology of prophecy nor do I assume Karl Rahner developed such a theology. What I do seek to show is that Rahner has given us a foundation upon which a theology of prophecy can be built and has raised the issue of prophecy's significance for the church. My thesis is that Rahner has demonstrated the necessity and intelligibility of prophecy for the life of the church by showing that the prophetic dynamic is constitutive of being human and of human community. Rahner approaches the question of prophecy from an anthropological starting point, thus responding to the predominant question suggested above (at least on the part of the Western post-enlightenment human being) as to the possibility of a human word being a divine word. By showing the a priori conditions for the possibility of revelation and prophecy in human reality, Rahner provides an anthropological basis for developing an understanding of the nature of prophecy and its position in human community and the church. Before indicating more fully the significance of Rahner's thought for a theology of prophecy, it seems in order, first, to make some general observations about Rahner's method.

---

chap. 6, pp. 112-31; Carl E. Braaten, *The Future of God: The Revolutionary Dynamics of Hope* (New York: Harper & Row, 1969), chap. 5, pp. 141-66; and his *Principles of Lutheran Theology* (Philadelphia: Fortress Press, 1983), chap. 7, pp. 123-39; Eric W. Gritsch and Robert W. Jenson, *Lutheranism: The Theological Movement and Its Confessional Writings* (Philadelphia: Fortress Press, 1976), chap. 13, pp. 179-90; and for a recent Reformed critique of the two-kingdoms doctrine see Moltmann, *On Human Dignity: Political Theology and Ethics*, trans. with an introduction by M. Douglas Meeks (Philadelphia: Fortress Press, 1984), chap. 4, pp. 61-78.

Rahner's Method

Rahner has been particularly concerned to make the Christian faith intelligible within the modern world situation by relating the content of the Christian faith to the experience of being human and being Christian. Rahner has observed that in the pluralistic situation of our times, which is characterized by a kind of "intellectual concupiscence" in which traditional formulations of faith seem far removed from modern expression and experience (How does the physicist understand transubstantiation, or the historian the self-understanding of Jesus as historically demonstrable?), there is a need to understand the Christian faith from its center and to understand it within the foundational experience of human beings. God's revelation, for example, cannot be understood only by recourse to its objective, historical content, but must also be appreciated through a grasp of the human being as the recipient of God's revelation. Rahner recognizes that this has always been at least implicitly a part of theological method, but its significance has only been explicitly realized in recent years through the influence of philosophical movements beginning with Descartes and Kant. Rahner is concerned to point out, however, that the Christian faith can never be deduced from the a priori or transcendental structures of the human subject, but rather that these a priori conditions in the subject for receiving God's revelation illuminate the a posteriori and historical actuality of God's revelation.[13]

The turn to the subject is not a turn to 'subjectivism'. It is a turn to what is uniquely *human* experience, to human existentiell reality. Rahner does not reject Christian dogmas or the Bible as

---

[13]Rahner, "On the Situation of Faith," *TI* 20:13-34, and "Theology and Anthropology," *TI* 9:35: "This anthropological approach does not entail a rationalistic and unhistorical reduction of man to the status of an abstract transcendental being in his merely formal structure as such, as if what is historical and not deducible and what is experienced concretely a posteriori had no significance for salvation. It means that everything of significance for salvation is to be illuminated by referring it back to this transcendental being (which is not the same as *deducing* the significance *from* the transcendental being)."

starting points for doing theology and he views the work of historical criticism and the development of a Christology from below as
crucial for modern theological work. His concern for the subject
does not exclude historical, objective revelation. On the contrary,
Rahner believes neither the subjective nor objective side of revelation can be understood without the other. Furthermore, our
contemporary situation in which the authority of the Bible and the
church is in question (whose authority can never, in any case, be
established within themselves) calls for a theology which takes
seriously the experience of the subject of God's revelation.

This human subject can be characterized by both a transcendental and historical dimension. The human being cannot escape
his or her dependence on history as the place of salvation. On the
other hand, salvation (or revelation or God's self-communication)
as received by human reality can be understood in terms of the
human subject's transcendental openness for God's salvation.
Rahner's concern with the subject *as subject* is an emphasis on that
which is most fundamental to being human and therefore most
likely to be overlooked. Rahner is particularly concerned to stress
that in our experience we do not only experience ourselves as
objects, as products of our environment, socialization, and genetic
potential; but as subjects, persons, individuals who conceptualize,
who decide, who act upon our world and upon ourselves. It is in
the structure of this 'subjective' experience, in which the uniqueness of human reality may be perceived, that Rahner discovers the
transcendental dynamic of the human being which grounds all
knowing, including the knowledge of God. It is both the transcendental and historical aspects of human reality that form the a priori
conditions for the kind of knowing that is human knowing and
therefore also the conditions for the possibility of knowing God.[14]
Rahner's attention to human subjectivity does not include the
rational deducing of the Christian faith from something like the
religious consciousness of the human being. Rather, this turn to

---

[14]Rahner, *Foundations,* pp. 1-89.

the subject seeks to grasp the Christian reality (of God's self-communication) from within human experience, and therefore be able to direct the modern person to his or her own experience as a way of providing direction and an understanding of the essence of Christianity. Assumed in this is that God's gracious self-communication is not something merely external to human experience, a declaration or series of doctrines that remain outside human reality, but rather that the reality of God herself is to be discovered within human experience (and human history), and therefore inherent to human reality understood ontologically.

This turn from a focus on and starting point with particular dogmas and doctrinal positions to the starting point of the subject has been characterized as a movement from a cosmocentric to an anthropocentric (or from a cosmological to an ontological) approach.[15] Rather than ask, first of all, concerning the nature of particular theological truths, the question is asked concerning the nature of the human subject who grasps these truths (and is grasped by them), and who must make sense out of them from within his or her own experience. An anthropological and ontological approach begins with the human being as the subject of God's self-communication. Rahner believes there is strong theological support for such an anthropological method in the doctrine of the union of God and humanity in the incarnation, in the 'hypostatic union'. By attending to our experience of being human and by seeking to objectify that unthematic transcendental openness that is essential to our experience we cannot escape the question of God.[16]

Rahner believes that, not only is this anthropological approach necessarily a part of theological method (although only really explicitly recognized in recent times); it is crucial for theology done today. Rahner has characterized the contemporary

---

[15]*ET*, s.v. "Church and World," by Karl Rahner.

[16]Rahner, "The Human Question of Meaning in Face of the Absolute Mystery of God," *TI* 18:89-104.

situation as undergoing a process of secularization which in one respect can be viewed as an outgrowth of Christianity, and as necessary for the diaspora nature of the church to be seen. He has characterized the world as coming to a kind of maturity and autonomy, of becoming anthropocentric, as no longer being under the care of nature but given over more radically to its own freedom. Today's situation is also one in which the overwhelming mass of knowledge and the pluralism and relativity of viewpoints is acutely experienced, which contributes to an 'intellectual concupiscence' particularly in regard to traditional formulations of the faith.[17]   In such a situation, within the existential and intellectual experience of the contemporary human being, neither the church's magisterium nor the Bible is perceived as the starting point of faith and the obvious court of appeal. "Today it is the credibility (that is, the meaningfulness and existential assimilability and human unrenounceability) of the fundamental dogmas of Christianity that makes credible the existence of a supernatural revelation (rightly understood) and not vice versa."[18]

Therefore theology and proclamation must be apologetic. Such an apologetic approach must begin with the experiential reality of the human being today. It must concern itself not only with faith as *fides quae* but as *fides qua*. And it must see the various dogmas of the Christian faith from their center in the foundational mysteries of Christianity (which Rahner identifies as the Holy

---

[17]Rahner's views on the church-world relationship will be further elaborated in Chapter 2. Significant essays include: "Theological Reflections on the Problem of Secularization," *TI* 10:318-48; "The Experience of God Today," *TI* 11:149-65; "Thoughts on the Possibility of Belief Today," *TI* 5:3-22; "The Man of Today and Religion," *TI* 6:3-20; and "On the Situation of Faith."

[18]Rahner, "On the Situation of Faith," *TI* 20:21, and "The Theological Dimension of the Question about Man," *TI* 17:55: "We cannot confront the people we have to do with today with the Scriptures, assuming, simply and from the very outset, that these have formal authority as the Word of God. What the Bible says, what it tells us about ourselves, what the truly central thing is in this statement and promise about us men and women must convince us through its *inner* truth . . ."

Trinity, the incarnation, and grace [as an existential reality]).[19]

The anthropological turn does not necessarily mean the reduction of Christian revelation.

If one is aware from the start of the complementary relationship existing between the anthropological starting point and the theological answer, then one should not permit any further attack on the proposed point of departure. A man can say that he is only interested in answers for which he has a question; so God can only communicate with a person on a level which concerns that man's innermost core of existence. Why should this lead of necessity to an abridgement of Christian faith? Man is essentially a questioner, indeed he is an absolute question which does not stop at any given point. An objective curiosity is part of his nature, for a person is endowed, even before he begins to ask questions, with the grace of the Holy Spirit, which is rooted in the centre of his personal being. He is given the capacity to ask for infinity and to lay himself open to the infinity of God. If we do not hold back our questions, needs and desires from this natural right and this horizon of meaning, then we experience ourselves in the concrete situation of salvation as a question which can only find an answer in the self-communication of God in the Holy Spirit and in Christian revelation.[20]

Rahner's anthropological approach is particularly conducive to a theology of revelation and prophecy, for it is concerned with the capacity in the human being for receiving a revelation. Rahner has directed much attention to the question of the conditions for the possibility of humankind being a 'hearer of the word'. He has distinguished the transcendental and predicamental, historical aspects of revelation (their difference and unity) in such a way as to steer a course between an 'immanentism' which has God as so inherent in creation that revelation is little more than the necessary expression of humanity's religious needs, and an 'extrinsicism' in which revelation is conceived as solely coming from the 'outside' by God's intervention, and therefore is something of an add-on or afterthought to the real ontological make-up of the human being.

---

[19]Rahner, "The Concept of Mystery in Catholic Theology," *TI* 4:36-73.

[20]Rahner, "The Foundations of Belief," *TI* 16:9.

Rahner distinguishes between the 'official' history of revelation (the salvation history of the Old and New Testaments) and the history of revelation (salvation history) that is coextensive with the history of humankind (which is also codetermined by guilt). Rahner conceives God's self-revelation as always and everywhere present to humankind (at least as offered). God's gracious self-communication is inescapably present to human freedom and knowing (at least implicitly), and therefore to be human is to live in response to God's revelation (at least implicitly). This revelation which is present to every human mind can find words, and therefore can be prophecy.[21]

Rahner on Prophetism

In addition to his anthropological starting-point and its importance for a theology of prophecy, Rahner's significance for this subject can be recognized in the attention he has given to the dynamic element in the church. Among his many writings related to this subject there are *The Dynamic Element in the Church*, *Visions and Prophecies*, "On the Question of a Formal Existential Ethics," "On the Theological Problems Entailed in a 'Pastoral Constitution,'" "Reflections on a New Task for Fundamental Theology," "The Function of the Church as a Critic of Society," and "Prophetism."[22] Rahner has directed our attention on many occasions to the 'dynamic element', to 'charismatic' or 'prophetic instruction', to the 'logic of practical reason', to 'individual concrete knowledge', all of which are related to this prophetic dynamic. As a means of achieving some understanding of the way Rahner

---

[21]For a brief treatment of 'revelation' see Rahner's articles in *SM*, s.v. "Revelation."

[22]Rahner, *The Dynamic Element in the Church*, trans. W. J. O'Hara (Freeburg: Herder, 1964); "On the Question of a Formal Existential Ethics," *TI* 2:217-34; "On the Theological Problems Entailed in a 'Pastoral Constitution,'" *TI* 10:293-317; "Reflections on a New Task for Fundamental Theology," *TI* 16:156-68; "The Function of the Church as a Critic of Society," *TI* 12:229-49; and *ET*, s.v. "Prophetism."

approaches the question of prophecy we turn to his article on
"Prophetism" in *Sacramentum Mundi*. This (coupled with our
study of biblical prophetism in the next chapter) will provide us
with some direction for developing the procedure we will follow in
our reflections on the foundations of prophecy.

Rahner begins this essay with the phenomenon of prophecy
in the history of religions and notes the characteristics of the
prophetic figure. The prophet is the bearer of a timely and unique
word, the new word which puts the prophet in the position of a
critic of society and religion. This word is not the word of the sage
which has a timeless character but the word for the moment which
makes demands on its listeners. Furthermore, the prophet claims
to bring a word from God; the prophet is a bearer of revelation,
and the prophet's actual nature and vocation is "intrinsically
connected with his message, with his 'concept of God'." In other
words, the prophet does not merely reflect or report on the events
of his or her time but is "an intrinsic element of these events,"
interpreting them in such a way that they are given "their real
depth and truth and [are allowed] to exert their full force." This
means also that the prophet brings a message "primarily for others
–for those to whom he is sent with a mandate."[23]

It is possible to summarize the above remarks by saying that
the prophet is the bearer of:
1. A word of God
2. A timely and unique word
3. A word for others

Following this characterization of the prophetic figure,
Rahner addresses the position of prophetism in church dogma. He
recognizes that prophecy is constitutive to a religion grounded in
revelation and therefore "is essential to the history of OT and NT
salvation." This recognition does not exclude the existence of
genuine prophecy outside 'official salvation history' for, as we
noted earlier, there is also a universal salvation history, the self-

---

[23]*ET*, s.v. "Prophetism," p. 1286.

communication of God to all human beings "by virtue of his universal salvific will." Since this self-communication of God and 'transcendental' revelation is present to all human beings as an existential, as a condition of their being, it must also find categorial expression; that is, be 'objectivated in words'. Consequently, the *possibility* is there in every human being for prophecy. This does not, of course, exclude the possibility of false prophets and quite distorted objectifications of this revelatory dimension in the human being. The relationship of prophets outside the Old and New Testaments to the prophets of the Bible (and 'official salvation history') is that the latter are the acknowledged historical precursors of Jesus Christ who "is the vehicle of the pure and eschatologically unsurpassable revelation of God, present in him as event, and in his words as going to constitute that event."[24]

After recognizing some of these concerns which Christian teaching has traditionally had in regard to prophetism, Rahner then takes up the need for a theology of prophecy, and mentions the elements such a theology would need to consider.

> Points to be discussed would include the prophetic vocation, the coming of revelation to the prophet himself, the growth of his inner certainty that he is uttering and must utter the divinely revealed truth, the various types of the prophetic word–imagery, apocalyptic discourse, promise, threat of judgment, etc. Here grace, the self-communication of God, would have to be considered as revelatory by its very nature. The unity and the difference between such revelation and revelation in words would have to be treated expressly. One would have to consider the circular process in the prophet himself, in which the mission and content of the message legitimate each other.[25]

Of particular significance for our concern with the a priori conditions for the possibility of prophecy is Rahner's assertion that the experience of grace is "revelatory by its very nature." It is because of this understanding of grace that he can see "no absolute

---

[24]Ibid., p. 1287.

[25]Ibid., p. 1288.

opposition between mystical and prophetic experience." As we shall see, Rahner seeks to show how grace as God's self-communication must be considered to be an existential of being human, and as such provides an answer to the question of the conditions of possibility in the human being for the coming of revelation to the prophet. If we add to this Rahner's concern with the ontology of the individual, we have the basis also for prophetic vocation, inner certainty, and the 'circular process' in which vocation and message legitimize each other.[26]

The next aspect of prophecy from a dogmatic standpoint which Rahner takes up in this article is the question of the relationship of prophecy to Jesus, the eschatological prophet. Jesus is the eschatological prophet because in him the reign of God comes, and in his resurrection it is victorious. Consequently, he does not merely proclaim and point to the salvation of God, but brings God's salvation in his own person: "his task and his person are identical." Jesus does not merely proclaim the particular word for a particular age; he is the Word for all ages. Therefore only those persons are prophets after Jesus "who strive to uphold his message in its purity, who attest that message and make it relevant to their day."[27]

In the final section of this essay, Rahner makes a number of observations about the church and prophecy. He points to the sacramental aspect of the church as an indication of its prophetic dimension. The church continues the presence of the incarnate Word of God in the world, for there, in the church, the "word effects what it signifies." The sacraments are "the supreme actuation of the efficacious word" and thus the church in its sacramental aspect is a prophetic word. This fundamental prophetism includes within it the spontaneous charisms and charismatic prophecy which are essential to the life of the church, making "the message of Jesus new, relevant and actual in each changing age."

---

[26]Ibid.

[27]Ibid.

Rahner makes the point that it is of little importance whether or not the bearers of this message are called prophets. He recognizes, furthermore, that the prophetic voice can be repressed, and that the "defence of genuine prophecy against a conservative establishment . . . can itself be a prophetic mission." He concludes with the practical note that the official priestly ministry should be seen "in the light of the prophetic [rather] than the cultic element."[28]

I have briefly outlined Rahner's article on "Prophetism" in order to see how he develops the discussion of this topic. I believe it gives some direction for proceeding with this subject, which in fact is in keeping with the conclusions of the next chapter on biblical prophetism. We have seen that Rahner begins with the phenomenon and experience of prophecy and then takes up the dogmatic issues with a concern, at least, to point in the direction of the conditions for the possibility of the prophetic. He believes a theology of prophecy must show what in being human and being the church makes this prophetic experience intelligible and necessary. This is, in fact, our predominant concern. Beyond this, he relates prophecy to Jesus Christ and the church.

The Plan of This Work

We begin as Rahner has done in the essay summarized above, with the phenomenology of prophecy. Then we take up the question of the anthropological grounds for prophecy. We will be seeking an answer, in Rahner, to this question: What about being human is sufficient to explain the experience of prophecy? An answer to this question addresses our concern for intelligibility and will further demonstrate the *necessity* of prophecy for human and communal becoming. Following these foundational concerns we will consider Rahner's treatment of prophetic witness in the church, its necessity, and implications for church and theology.

The first two chapters deal with the experience of prophecy.

---

[28]Ibid., 1289.

The first chapter addresses the question of the dynamic character of prophecy as it appears in the biblical sources. I begin here because I recognize the need to see the continuity between the prophetic dynamic in the church today and the original expression of biblical, Christian, and ecclesial prophecy. We will find basic clues in this chapter for the fundamental characteristics of the prophetic word. Chapter I concludes with the recognition of the essential features of prophetic knowledge which then provide the basic framework for communicating Rahner's conception of the prophetic element in the church. In Chapter II we will seek to understand the kind of perception within Christian (and human) experience as Rahner has articulated it which corresponds to these fundamental characteristics of prophetic knowing. We will do this by directing our attention in particular to Rahner's analysis of 'individual concrete knowledge'.

In Chapter III we will seek the transcendental reality in being human which grounds all historical and categorial (and therefore provisional) modes of being, and which also forms the basis for the correlation between the biblical phenomenology of prophecy (Chapter I) and the experience of human perception today (Chapter II). The phenomenology of prophecy (Chapter I) will suggest the framework for the main arguments of Chapter III. As we saw, Rahner portrays the prophetic figure as the bearer of the divine word, a timely and unique word, a word for others. Our phenomenological analysis will also suggest these characteristics of the prophetic word. Chapter III will seek the *conditions* in being human, as Rahner has formulated them, which make possible these three aspects of the prophetic word. Thus, Chapter III is concerned with the anthropological and ontological foundations of a unique and timely word and decision of divine origination directed to others. The relationship of Chapter II to Chapter III is significant. Chapter II is essentially descriptive, Chapter III explanatory.

In the next three chapters we develop the implications of the preceding chapters for the life of the church. Chapter IV is concerned with the question of the discernment of genuine prophecy, Chapter V with the prophetic dynamic in relation to the eschatological prophet Jesus Christ and the church, and Chapter VI with further implications for church and theology today.

The treatment of Rahner's thought in the following pages will not involve a cataloging of what Rahner has said on the subject. It will be much more concerned with his method and its applicability to this subject. We will follow his method where it is used in the explicit treatment of our subject, and where he has not explicitly treated a concern of ours we will seek to draw out the implications of his method for our task, as well as drawing upon the implications of similar themes that he has taken up. In this way we will see how Rahner demonstrates the intelligibility and necessity of a Christian and ecclesial prophetism.

Chapter I

Biblical and Phenomenological Studies on Prophecy

The church has its origins in a prophetic movement. We have already suggested that this is one of the reasons theology must concern itself with the nature of prophecy. Since the church has its origins in a prophetic movement, and since it is concerned to remain in continuity with its origins, our considerations on prophecy begin with a brief overview of biblical scholarship on the phenomenology of prophecy. Furthermore, since we are concerned with the anthropological grounds for prophecy (that is, the transcendental conditions in being human which make prophetic perception possible), we must have some sense of what has been involved in prophetic phenomena and experience. In the following discussion we are concerned with the dynamic nature of prophecy (rather than its material content), particularly as it appears in the biblical literature. By attending to the work of biblical scholars on this subject we will help ensure that the dynamic we are dealing with (at least on a foundational level) is in fact the dynamic associated with biblical prophecy and the church's origins. Furthermore, a summary of phenomenological studies on prophecy will provide the reader with a clearer grasp of the definition of prophecy that I am using, as well as the basis of the format for my treatment of Rahner on this subject.

Psychological Characteristics
of Prophecy

Prior to J. Wellhausen, the Old Testament prophet was viewed as a preacher of the Mosaic law. Following Wellhausen the conception was reversed, the prophet being seen as the precursor of the law. This view stimulated an emphasis on the individuality and originality of the prophet. For the past half century Old Testament scholarship, beginning with G. Hölscher's *Die Profeten* (1914), has taken a psychological approach to the subject of prophetic phenomena.[1] Hölscher believed all prophecy was ecstatic, and scholars following him have responded to questions concerning the extent to which ecstasy played a part in Old Testament prophecy. Most scholars have viewed ecstasy as being a part of the Hebrew prophetic experience as it is in cultures universally. There are exceptions, such as Abraham Heschel, who believes the notion of ecstasy is completely inappropriate for understanding the prophet of Israel. His concern is that the notion of ecstasy conjures up the conception of psychological aberrations, and also he is particularly concerned to stress the uniqueness of the Hebrew prophet. For Heschel the prophet of Israel is *sui generis*.[2]

---

[1] Gustav Hölscher, *Die Profeten: Untersuchungen zur Religionsgeschichte Israels* (Leipzig: J. C. Hinrich, 1914).

[2] See Heschel, *The Prophets*, esp. 2:87-253. Claus Westerman also stresses the uniqueness of the biblical prophets. See his work, *Basic Forms of Prophetic Speech*, trans. Hugh Clayton White (Philadelphia: Westminster Press, 1967). For a survey of biblical scholarship on prophecy see O. Eissfeldt, "The Prophetic Literature," in *The Old Testament and Modern Study: A Generation of Discovery and Research*, ed. H. H. Rowley (Oxford: Clarendon Press, 1951), pp. 115-61. Eissfeldt identifies two strands of scholarship on the question of ecstasy in classical prophecy: those who believe it played a significant role, and those (the minority) who believe it played little or no role in the prophet's experience. See also James L. Crenshaw, *Prophetic Conflict* (New York: Walter de Gruyter, 1971). Crenshaw gives an excellent introductory survey of biblical scholarship on prophecy. And see W. McKane, "Prophecy and the Prophetic Literature," in *Tradition and Interpretation: Essays by Members of the Society for Old Testament Study*, ed. G. W. Anderson (Oxford: Clarendon Press, 1979), pp. 163-88.

Nevertheless, the general consensus seems to be that connections of a psychological nature can be drawn between the prophets of Israel and prophets or intermediaries of other cultures. There are at least striking similarities. J. Lindblom, in his classic work *Prophecy in Ancient Israel*, has recognized a wide range of types of prophetic experience and has drawn heavily from the comparative study of prophetic phenomena.[3] He derives an understanding of prophetic experience from such diverse phenomena as the prophecy of Mohammed, prophecy in Greece and the Ancient Near East, the sleeping preachers in Finland, St. Bridget of Sweden, and medieval Christian mystics. He makes the point that prophecy is a universal human phenomenon: "The prophetic endowment is deeply rooted in human nature; what may be borrowed from other quarters is the behaviour and forms, in a word, the external manifestations."[4] Lindblom, however, is more cautious than many earlier scholars in his estimation of the importance of the ecstatic element. He believes that prophetic experience ranges from the nonecstatic to the ecstatic, and he has viewed the ecstatic experience of Israel's prophets as being generally an ecstasy of concentration "in which one is so intensely absorbed by one single idea or one single feeling, or by a group of ideas or feelings, that the normal stream of physical life is more or less arrested."[5]

In addition to ecstatic visions and auditions, Lindblom also perceives in the classical prophets 'symbolic perceptions' in which an object in the material world takes on, in the state of inspiration, a spiritual significance and 'literary visions' which are imaginative or intellectual visions consisting in thoughts and ideas which come into the mind of the inspired prophet. Lindblom uses the distinction made by medieval mystics among corporeal, imaginative, and

---

[3]J. Lindblom, *Prophecy in Ancient Israel* (Philadelphia: Fortress Press, 1962). For a discussion of his comparative approach and general conclusions see pp. 29-46.

[4]Ibid., p. 32.

[5]Ibid., p. 4.

intellectual visions as a helpful means of understanding visionary experience. In corporeal visions the visionary believes he or she perceives the vision by ordinary senses; in imaginative visions he or she sees with the 'eye of the soul'; and in intellectual visions there is a kind of spiritual perception, a 'formless word', a spiritual sense of things.[6] What is significant for our discussion is the range of psychological experience involved in prophetic experience. There is conscious process and spontaneous insight; there is ecstasy and also meditation, reflection, and even normal mental abstraction. It would seem that prophecy cannot be identified or defined simply by a particular psychological experience for it operates within a full range of psychological experiences which correspond to other human activity.

The Sociological Approach
to Prophetic Phenomena

In recent years biblical scholarship has taken up a sociological approach to the phenomenology of prophecy. Robert R. Wilson in *Prophecy and Society in Ancient Israel* takes up the question of prophetic phenomena from within a sociological perspective, concerning himself with the role of society in the formation of the prophet.[7] In contrast to Lindblom, who gives psychological definitions to possession and nonpossession types of prophetic experience, Wilson gives a sociological definition. 'Possession' and 'nonpossession' are cultural theories that explain divine influence

---

[6]Ibid., pp. 36-39. I have followed Evelyn Underhill's interpretation of the third type of visionary experience. See Evelyn Underhill, *Mysticism: A Study of the Nature and Development of Man's Spiritual Consciousness* (New York: E. P. Dutton, 1961), pp. 282-85. Lindblom understands the third type as abstractive in nature.

[7]Robert R. Wilson, *Prophecy and Society in Ancient Israel* (Philadelphia: Fortress Press, 1980). For recent articles incorporating a sociological approach see *Semeia 21: Anthropological Perspectives on Old Testament Prophecy* (Chico, CA: Scholars Press, 1982).

(i.e., the divine takes up residence in the intermediary's body or the intermediary's spirit goes outside the body to the divine). Wilson emphasizes the role of society in the validation and legitimation of the intermediary, in the formation of central and peripheral intermediaries, and in the significance of stereotypical behavior. Society plays an important role in the behavior of the prophet by recognizing the kind of behavior deemed appropriate to an intermediary, that is, in the recognition of the identifying marks of mediation. Consequently, societies may have contrasting ways of identifying prophetic behavior. Lindblom has also noted this; that while prophecy is a universal human phenomenon it may have many different manifestations depending on its societal formation.

This is apparent in the relationship of Christian prophecy to Hellenistic and Judaic prophecy and oracular traditions. The prophetic phenomena (and manifestations of the Spirit generally) were given form by the conceptions and stereotypical behavior derived from the Hebrew Scriptures, from Rabbinic traditions, and from Greek prophetic experience. It may be assumed that there were, on the one hand, examples of ecstatic phenomena of an orgiastic type among early Christian congregations influenced by Hellenist philosophies and experience and, on the other, examples of more 'sober' expressions of the prophetic. Paul (with his "Rabbinic sobriety") viewed the Christian prophet as one who had full consciousness and exercise of will in the reception and delivery of a prophetic utterance.[8] Paul's letter to the Corinthian church indicates the tension present early in the church between Hellen-

---

[8]For the Rabbinic influence on Paul's understanding of the Spirit see W. D. Davies, *Paul and Rabbinic Judaism: Some Rabbinic Elements in Pauline Theology* (New York: Harper & Row, 1948), especially chap. 8, pp. 177-226. Although Paul had ecstatic experiences, he gave them secondary importance, as was true of the Rabbinic tradition generally in which "ecstatic 'spiritual' experiences which some Rabbis claimed were looked upon as more dangerous than welcome . . . " (p. 213). For Paul's view of prophecy and the importance of conscious control see James Reiling, "Prophecy, the Spirit and the Church," in *Prophetic Vocation in the New Testament and Today*, ed. J. Pangopaulos (Leiden: Brill, 1977). Prophecy in early Judaism is discussed by Aune, *Prophecy in Early Christianity*, pp. 103-52.

istic pneumatic experience and Rabbinic and Christian conceptualities. Later on the Montanist movement shows the influence of Hellenistic oracular experience and behavior which conformed to a conception of divine possession that envisioned the prophet as being overwhelmed by the divine in an utter loss of control. Following the rise of the Montanist movement, and in reaction against it, ecstatic manifestation (of an orgiastic type) became viewed by many in the church as a sign of false prophecy.[9]

The point is that various societal factors and fundamental anthropological conceptualities give formation to the stereotypical behavior of prophets and to their acceptance, whether that is the behavior of Corinthian pneumatics, or the Montanist prophets, or that of those who prophesied along the line of a more Pauline (and possibly Rabbinic) conception. It must be recognized that the nature of prophecy cannot be determined (nor its truth or falsity) solely on the basis of its particular form of manifestation.

Identifying Prophetic Utterances

Among the kind of identifying behavior of prophets perhaps the most significant is the use of particular formulaic features in the prophetic utterance which identify the utterance as prophecy for the hearers. David Aune, in *Prophecy in Early Christianity and the Ancient Mediterranean World*, isolates six general formulaic features of ancient Israelite prophecy, namely, the messenger formula ("Thus says Yahweh"); the commission formula ("Say to X . . ." or "Go and say to X . . ."); the proclamation formula ("Hear the Word of Yahweh . . ."); the divine oracle formula ("An oracle of Yahweh"); oath formulas ("Yahweh has sworn by . . ."); and revelation formulas ("Thus the Lord God showed me" or "The Lord said to me").[10] Early Christian prophecy has similar features.

---

[9]Von Campenhausen, *Ecclesiastical Authority*, pp. 189-92.

[10]Aune, *Prophecy in Early Christianity*, pp. 89-91.

In addition there are certain compositional features or tendencies of prophetic speech; for example, the prophetic oracle is often brief and poetic. However, prophetic speech may also be lengthy and prosaic, and compositional features are not reliable indications of prophecy.

Furthermore, scholars have recognized a broad range of literary forms and subject matter in prophetic speech.[11] Aune has identified various major forms of prophetic speech in ancient Israel, early Judaism, and early Christianity. For example, basic forms of Christian prophecy include oracles of assurance, prescriptive oracles, announcements of salvation, announcements of judgment, legitimation oracles, and eschatological-theophany oracles as well as several complex forms involving combinations of the above or explanatory amplification.[12] On the whole, such subject matter is not peculiar to prophecy but can be found in other forms of Christian witness.[13] The significant point for our concerns is that prophecy cannot be identified by a particular literary type or subject matter. Prophetic oracles, rather, are identified in the New Testament by particular formulaic features similar to those given above of Old Testament prophecy. Accord-

---

[11]"A great many rhetorical and literary types are represented in the utterances of prophets in accordance with the different themes which are dealt with. There are exhortations to repentance, reproaches, announcements of judgments, threats against the apostates in Israel and against pagan nations, words of consolation and promises for the future. There are woe and satire, scorn and lamentation, hymns and prayers, monologues and dialogues, judicial debating, utterances formulated after a ritual pattern, descriptions of visions and auditions and confessions of personal experiences of different kinds. There are letters and messages, short oracles and extended sermons, historical retrospects, confessions of sin, decisions in cultic matters, parables and allegories, similes and sententious phrases of wisdom, lyric poetry of various kinds, and discussions of religious and moral problems" (Lindblom, *Prophecy in Ancient Israel*, p. 155).

[12]Aune, *Prophecy in Early Christianity*, pp. 32-27.

[13]In ancient Israelite prophecy, the judicial speech form has a unique place, although it is one of a number of prophetic speech forms. See Westermann, *Basic Forms of Prophetic Speech*.

ing to Aune, this "suggests that the distinctive feature of prophetic speech was not so much its content or form, but its *supernatural origin*."[14] In other words, the prophet was perceived as one whose special message was from God.

One further perception of the prophetic phenomenon is particularly significant for our concern with characterizing the dynamic nature of prophecy, and that is the problem of discernment of true and false prophecy, the question of criteria for recognizing true prophecy.

Prophetic Conflict

James Crenshaw, in *Prophetic Conflict*, gives an overview of types of criteria that have been identified in the Old Testament for distinguishing true from false prophecy.[15] He distinguishes three major categories: message-centered criteria, prophet-centered criteria, and chronological criteria. Under the category of message-centered criteria he identifies the criterion of fulfillment or nonfulfillment (Deut 18:22, Isa 30:8, Ezek 33:33, among other passages). The problem Crenshaw sees with this criterion is threefold: the vagueness of many prophecies, the conditional character of prophecy in which what is predicted is governed by the response to the message, and most notably the fact that the predictive element in prophecy plays a relatively minor role–therefore for much prophecy this criterion is not applicable.

Another message-centered criterion is that of the promise of weal or woe (such a criterion seems to be indicated, for example, by Ezek 13:10). True prophets proclaim doom, false prophets proclaim peace. The difficulty with this criterion is that there are indications of 'false prophets' who declare woe (Deut 18:22 and Mic 3:5b) and 'true prophets' who promise weal (most noted example, Isaiah). The form of the revelation (i.e., ecstasy, dream)

---

[14]Aune, *Prophecy in Early Christianity*, p. 338.

[15]Crenshaw, *Prophetic Conflict*, pp. 49-61.

has also been cited as a criterion, but it is apparent that both false and true prophets had ecstatic and other kinds of similar psychological experiences. Faithfulness to Yahweh or Baal is a criterion (Deut 13:1-3) which has only a narrow application to prophecy outside the Yahwistic cult.

Prophet-centered criteria include the prophetic office, conduct, and conviction of call. The notion that professional cultic prophets are necessarily false is untenable. The question of immoral conduct has problems considering some of the questionable behavior of 'true prophets' and the seeming absence of immoral conduct among 'false prophets'. The criterion of conviction or being 'called' lacks any objective foundation for testing a prophet.

The chronological criterion assumes that all prophecy outside the period between Moses and Ezra is false. Such a criterion, however, has little to provide for the problem of Old Testament prophecy. Crenshaw's conclusion is that there is no absolute valid criterion for distinguishing true and false prophecy.

The problem of discerning between true and false prophets and prophecy continues in early Christianity. David Aune gives Paul's criterion as a criterion of message: the content of a prophecy must conform to Christian teaching and is to be judged by the congregation in a rational manner.[16] (In contrast, G. Friedrich views Paul's method of discernment as spiritual and nonrational; one must have the gift of discernment.[17]) 1 John gives the criterion of content also (namely, that Jesus Christ has come in the flesh). The means of testing is not entirely rational for there is an 'anointing' that makes discernment possible. Aune also identifies the criterion of behavior in Matthew ("You will know them by their fruits"). The development of criteria in response to specific situations can be seen in the criteria of the Didache (for example, if any apostle stays more than three days or asks for money, he is

---

[16] Aune, *Prophecy in Early Christianity*, pp. 219-22.

[17] *Theological Dictionary of the New Testament*, s.v. "προφητης," by G. Friedrich.

a false prophet). The Shepherd of Hermas also designates behavior as the criterion (the true prophet is meek, gentle, humble; the false prophet is impudent, impertinent, lives in luxury). There are difficulties, however, with such criteria as the conduct of the prophet and the content of the message, as already indicated above. Aune views prophetic conflict as arising essentially between prophets and other prophets or leaders, and the criteria that developed as a response of one group toward the other. In other words, a particular sociological dynamic can be perceived.

There remains the problem of an absolute valid criterion. The problem of discernment is not only a matter of distinguishing that call or message which conforms to Christian teaching or behavior. The community of faith that must evaluate two contrasting 'prophetic' calls to action may find itself confronted with two choices, both of which conform generally to Christian teaching. How does the Christian community recognize that one is the call of the Lord for this moment and the other therefore 'false' or that neither are to be followed? This question moves the problem beyond one of prophetic conflict to the question of evaluating the message. The question becomes not so much one concerning the prophet's motivations or whether or not the prophet is true or false, but rather a question of whether the message is from the Lord or from some other spirit or subconscious tendency.

Defining Prophecy

As the above discussion would indicate, there are problems with developing a working definition of prophecy. The following points can be made concerning the development of a working definition:

1. It is difficult to define prophecy by a particular psychological manifestation. Prophetic experience incorporates a broad range of psychological phenomena and behavior, and shares these psychological experiences in common with other forms of human activity (i.e., poetic inspiration, meditation, normal abstraction). At

least prophecy cannot be identified simply with one kind of psychological experience peculiar to itself. This does not, however, diminish the significance of the psychological study of prophetic phenomena. The fact that prophecy can take on the character of more common psychological experience makes an understanding of it more accessible, particularly to those of us who have not experienced the more extraordinary manifestations of some prophetic phenomena. Also, while prophecy may reveal many elements of common human psychological experience it is important to recognize those elements which are characteristic of prophetic experience (though not necessarily unique to it).

2. Prophecy cannot be defined by its form or content since it expresses itself in an indefinite range of literary forms and subject matter. Prophecy shares with other forms of human communication a common variety of concerns and modes for expressing those concerns. What makes prophecy prophecy is not that it is concerned with this or that particular theme, or that it is expressed in this or that way. Prophecy may be a word of consolation, of challenge, of judgment, of salvation, a call to action. The content of such messages cannot be the defining element of prophecy.

3. There is no absolute objective criterion for discerning true from false prophecy which might provide us with *the* defining characteristic. From a sociological and psychological perspective there may be questions regarding conflicts between prophets and other prophets and leaders (and therefore the relativity of viewpoints), and the experience of conviction on the part of the prophet, but from a theological perspective there is the question of identifying the 'word of the Lord'. There can be a general objective criterion (i.e., Christian teaching or behavior) but such a general criterion cannot discern between, for example, two mutually exclusive specific 'prophetic' calls to action, both of which may conform to the general criterion. The discernment that one of the two calls to action is the more timely and necessary word and therefore the word of the Lord for this particular situation cannot be realized by any objective criterion in an absolute way. Nevertheless, this fact

indicates the unique and timely nature of the prophetic word. (It is not a universal and timeless word of wisdom or general Christian teaching.)

4. The one thing that makes a prophetic utterance identifiable (whether it is true or false), however, is the indication given by the prophet that what is being communicated is a 'revelation' or 'word of the Lord'. Such an indication is made by certain formulaic features or stereotypical behavior. On the side of the prophet, there is the conviction that this is a word of the Lord (regardless of the particular form of psychological experience). A definition of prophecy must, at least, incorporate this claim of being a divine message.

Biblical scholars have sought in one way or another to come up with a definition of prophecy. David Hill in *New Testament Prophecy*, drawing upon the attempts of other scholars (including David Aune), gives this 'functional' definition of the Christian prophet:

> A Christian prophet is a Christian who functions within the Church, occasionally or regularly, as a divinely called and divinely inspired speaker who receives intelligible and authoritative revelations or messages which he is impelled to deliver publicly, in oral or written form, to Christian individuals and/or the Christian community.[18]

David Aune objects to the substantive nature of this definition; that is, he objects that it is couched in terms that designate the essential nature of the prophet and prophecy and therefore is more of a theological and normative definition than a functional or phenomenological one. A more functional definition (by functional is meant the functional characteristics of the prophet) would include something on the order of the following: The Christian prophet is one who *claims* to be a "divinely called and divinely inspired speaker. . . ." Aune points out that Hill generally does not make a careful distinction between the historical or phenom-

---

[18]Hill, *New Testament Prophecy*, pp. 8-9.

enological and theological dimensions of his subject. Furthermore, Hill's definition of the prophet as divinely called and inspired creates a problem when he deals with the relationship among prophets, teachers, and other leaders in the church. He has difficulty distinguishing them because it can also be said of them that they are divinely inspired, and that they also communicate divinely inspired messages.[19] This is a significant point for our own discussion, for we are concerned with the theological dimension of the subject. From a theological perspective we will have to recognize that Christian teaching, counseling, leadership, and prophecy, have in common a charismatic (and divinely inspired) element.

Let us, however, attempt our own working definition of prophecy with the above observations in mind. We have noted in the foregoing discussion that a prophetic utterance is identified as such for its hearers not by its form or content, but by formulaic features or stereotypical behavior which present it as being of divine origin. As Aune notes: "Christian prophetic speech . . . is Christian discourse presented with divine legitimation, either in the absence of more rational structures of institutional authority, or in conflict with them."[20] The first thing we must recognize is that prophecy is assumed to be a message from God.

The last phrase, however, in the above quote in which prophecy is contrasted to "more rational structures" is also significant for defining prophecy. Although rationality is certainly an element in prophetic perception and discourse, nevertheless, the prophetic word is presented not as a rational deduction from an overarching theological perspective, but rather as a 'revelation'. Although, as we have seen, not all prophecies come to the prophet through visions and auditions; nevertheless, there is often a 'directness' to prophetic perception, as is indicated by the psychological aspects of prophetic phenomena, which can be contrasted to the more discursive nature of *theoretical* reason. (In fact, prophetic insight, as

---

[19]Aune, *Prophecy in Early Christianity*, p. 10.

[20]Ibid., p. 338.

we shall see, can be viewed as an aspect of *practical* reason.) Nevertheless, 'directness' of an insight cannot in and of itself designate it as prophetic, for the experience of having an insight of any kind (theoretical or practical) has the quality of 'directness'. This 'directness' of a prophetic insight, however, arises from the encounter with the uniqueness of the historical situation in which the prophet must recognize his or her call and the proclamation or unique message of the moment, which because of its specificity cannot be merely the expression of a rational deduction from theological principles, but is perceived in a more or less 'direct' manner. A rational deduction from general theological principles and an analysis of the social context can do no more than provide the general moral or doctrinal boundaries in which the more specific call or word is perceived. This specificity and uniqueness or timeliness of the prophetic word as we have noted can be seen in the nature of prophetic conflict. As we have indicated, the criterion of Christian teaching or morality cannot distinguish between two 'prophetic' calls to action when they are mutually exclusive in their content, but morally permissible in terms of Christian teaching. However we might further define the nature of this specificity and timeliness of the prophetic word, it must be recognized as a second feature of prophecy. Finally, the third essential feature of prophetic perception is that it is directed to others. The prophetic word or vision is not of a private nature. It is experienced as a word that is given to be communicated to others, whether to individuals or the community. With these three characteristics of the prophetic word in mind, namely, divine origination, timeliness of the word, and other-directedness, I offer the following 'working definition': *Prophecy is a timely message or call to action originating from God and directed to others.*

In Chapter III, where we take up the question of the conditions of being human which make prophecy possible, this definition will guide our format. We will consider the anthropological grounds for the divine origination of the prophetic message, for its timeliness and uniqueness, and for the other-directed orientation of the message.

Before we take up the conditions in the human being for the possibility of prophecy, which forms the subject matter of Chapter III, I will give a more careful analysis of prophetic experience in the way Rahner has developed it. In the next chapter we seek to recognize in human and Christian experience that kind of perception and communication which indicates a timely message to others, originating from God.

Chapter II

Prophetic Perception

In this chapter we will look at Rahner's conception of those aspects of human cognition which bear the marks of prophetic perception; that is, we will examine a mode of knowing which grasps a unique and timely word whose origination (at least implicitly or unthematically) is experienced as coming 'from God'. We are seeking to answer the question, What in human knowing can be described as a prophetic kind of knowing, as Rahner has formulated it? This will mean looking at the experience of transcendence and two fundamental aspects of practical reason, namely, a *general* moral faith-instinct and *individual* concrete knowledge, and the latter's acute expression in the experience of 'direct revelations'. Some preliminary remarks, however, are in order.

Existentiell Reality
and Reflection

Rahner distinguishes between 'original self-possession' and reflection, though not in such a way that they can be conceived in reality as existing apart, but rather as a 'unity in difference'. There is no self-possession without reflection and vice versa. The human being in being present to himself or herself is aware of an original reality that is more than the reflection which is initiated by and is a moment of that reality.

> When I love, when I am tormented by questions, when I am sad, when I am faithful, when I feel longing, this human and existentiell reality is a unity, an original unity of reality and its own self-presence which is not *totally* mediated by the concept which objectifies it in scientific knowledge.[1]

This original reality must, however, be conceptualized if it is to be known and communicated. This is done more or less adequately partly depending on the concepts that lie ready at hand within one's culture, although one may also have numerous concepts with little sense of the original reality which gave rise to them. (Rahner believes this is particularly true of theology in which we can acquire "a very great skill in talking and perhaps not have really understood from the depths of our existence what we are talking about."[2]) Furthermore, there are varying degrees of reflectedness. Not everyone has the same level of reflected awareness of their experience, nor has everyone entered into the same kinds of experience. Consequently, any communication of an analysis and conceptualization of human experience is dependent, in part, on the experience, reflection, and good will of the hearer. (This is certainly the case when addressing the question of prophetic perception as an aspect of human cognition.) The reflections of this chapter are reflections on aspects of human cognitive experience. Consequently, we need to make ourselves aware of this existentiell reality of our own cognitive experience, that is, we need to reflect on this lived-out experience of cognition.

By reflection we can recognize the polymorphic nature of human consciousness, the various kinds of psychological and emotional states that make up human experience, as well as the behavior patterns, values, and societal influences which have an

---

[1]Rahner, *Foundations*, pp. 14-23, 15-16.

[2]Ibid., p. 16.

impact on human knowing.[3] Human knowing operates in the midst of this polymorphic character of consciousness and can be identified as such. This is what Bernard Lonergan attempts to do in *Insight*; he seeks to distinguish the operations that are involved in knowing in the human subject.[4] Rahner also, particularly in his early works *Spirit in the World* and *Hearers of the Word*, grapples with the dynamics of human knowing.[5] In the following pages we are concerned with these cognitive and volitional aspects of human experience which can be reflected on in our conscious awareness. We are, in fact, interested in a particular kind of cognitional experience. It is an experience in which a unique and timely word is perceived as, in some sense, originating from God and directed to others, although we can leave aside for now the "directed to others" since the orientation of the word (whether to ourselves or others) does not alter the origins and timeliness of the word.

Therefore, at least initially, we are interested in a cognitive and volitional experience in which the word or imperative for action appropriate to the historical moment is recognized as

---

[3]Bernard J. F. Lonergan, *Insight: A Study of Human Understanding* (New York: Harper & Row, 1957). On the polymorphic nature of human consciousness see pp. 385-87. For a discussion of cultural bias and its impact on human knowing see pp. 222-42.

[4]Lonergan's method is didactic; he seeks to lead the reader through his or her own experience of sensibility, understanding, reasonable affirmation. In other words, he involves his reader in a reflection on what he or she is doing when he or she is knowing. The resulting identification of cognitive operations in the human subject becomes the basis for his development of method in *Method in Theology* (New York: Herder & Herder, 1972). This "transcendental" approach is similar to Rahner's and is essentially the approach of this chapter in which we seek to identify those operations in human consciousness that can be described as a prophetic kind of knowing.

[5]Rahner, *Spirit in the World*, trans. William Dych (New York: Herder & Herder, 1968); and "Listening to the Word," trans. Joseph Donceel, parts of which are in *A Rahner Reader*, ed. Gerald A. McCool (New York: Seabury, 1975), pp. 1-65, the rest in unpublished form. This translation of *Hörer des Wortes* is much to be desired over the Michael Richard translation, *Hearers of the Word* (New York: Herder & Herder, 1969).

coming from God (or, at least, has the divine origination as an implicit aspect of the experience). It may not be surprising, therefore, that we seek an understanding of prophetic perception as an aspect of conscience or practical reason.

Practical Reason

Moral knowing, as Rahner sees it, is one of those realities "which have many layers."[6] It involves a knowledge of the situation which gives rise to the moral question and the prudential judgment which recognizes the concrete means by which the moral good can be achieved. It involves a synthetic judgment which is the unity of what is and what ought to be. Certainly the knowledge of moral principles or laws (the ten commandments, Christian teaching, evangelical principles) and the rationally deduced implications of such principles form an aspect of moral reasoning. Of particular interest to us, however, are two fundamental aspects of conscience to which Rahner has given special attention. These two basic aspects include the above-mentioned elements, but are themselves the two basic functions of practical reason which correspond to the human being's experience of common human reality and his or her unique individual humanity. These two aspects have to do with a *general* and *individual* moral sense. Rahner refers to these aspects of conscience early in his career in "Der Einzelne in der Kirche" (first published in 1946), which has since been translated in *Nature and Grace*: ". . . we must distinguish two functions of conscience; the one which tells a man's subjective self the universal norms of ethics and moral theology and applies them to his "case," and the one by which the individual hears God's call to him alone, which can never be fully deduced from universal norms.[7]

---

[6]Rahner, *Foundations*, p. 216.

[7]Rahner, "Der Einzelne in der Kirche," *Stimmen der Zeit* 139 (1946): 260-76. This article later was published in *Gefahren Im Heutigen Katholizimus* (Einsiedeln:

These two aspects of practical reasoning (general and individual moral knowledge) make up the one activity of moral decision making as that expresses the human being's immutable essence, as well as individual uniqueness (as these are realized in self-awareness). It is with these aspects of moral reasoning that we are particularly concerned in this chapter, at least to the extent that they elicit a grasp of the dynamic of prophetic perception. What we will seek to show is that in both functions of conscience there is a charismatic or dynamic element. Special attention will be given, however, to *individual* concrete knowledge as especially descriptive of a kind of prophetic perception. We will see that this individual knowledge in its most acute expression involves cognitive experiences of a 'direct' character to which the term 'revelations' has traditionally been applied.

The question may be raised as to whether prophetic knowledge can be subsumed under the category of 'practical reasoning', since the material nature of prophecy has not always involved imperatives or calls to action, but many other kinds of messages (words of salvation, judgment, comfort, warning). Prophecy, however, is future-oriented. The prophet perceives the word which *ought* to be proclaimed, the *new* word which is not simply a re-pristination of the word of the past but which connects to the past as it comes to be in the present. The word may not be an explicit call to action, but it will be a word that is necessary in the present moment for the further self-determination and realization of a people or community. (The message, "Do not be afraid!", for example, may be the necessary word in a particular situation for a community to move forward in concrete action.) Consequently, as we shall see, human freedom and decision making play an important role in prophetic knowing.

One further observation must be made. Since the content of

Johannes Verlag, 1950), pp. 11-38. It can be found in translation in Rahner, *Nature and Grace: Dilemmas in the Modern Church* (New York: Sheed & Ward, 1964), pp. 9-38.

prophetic perception is understood as originating from God, we must give particular attention to that aspect of prophetic experience which can be recognized as being grounded in divine reality. This will mean that we must give particular attention to the experience of transcendence and the significance of this experience for all forms of knowledge, and in particular its significance for moral knowing. In fact, it will be seen to play an important role in these two modes of practical reason which we will be examining. We must see how, in Rahner's thinking, human self-transcendence in its infinite openness is a receptivity for the infinite God which, in other words, means the condition for the possibility of God's self-communication in human being. This self-transcendence must find categorial expression, and when it is borne by the self-communication of God it is the basis for the possibility of a categorial word of prophecy. We will be giving particular attention to this transcendental reality in Chapter III. However, since in this chapter we will be recognizing the significance of human self-transcendence in prophetic perception it seems important to provide a general description of the experience of transcendence before taking up those modes of knowing which have a prophetic character.

Our concern at this point, therefore, is with Rahner's descriptions of transcendental experience. We are assuming in all of this, with Rahner, that human existential reality is not only transcendental, but that it is also historical; and that, in fact, the historical mediates the transcendental dimension. Nevertheless, what makes the human being uniquely human being as over against other created historical reality is this transcendental dimension, and what makes human history not merely the cyclical phenomenon of nature but uniquely history (with direction and an ultimate goal) is again this transcendental dimension, so that in fact history can also be understood as the history of transcendentality.[8]

---

[8]Rahner uses the term 'transcendental' in both a vertical and horizontal sense. It can mean the infinite openness of the human being which transcends all categorical objects and as such is the basis for categorical knowledge. It is also used, therefore, to refer to the a prior condition for the possibility of categorical

The Experience of Transcendence

The experience of transcendence is the experience of subject-ivity (or 'subjectiveness'), the experience of being a subject.[9] It is the experience in all acts of knowledge and freedom of always being open beyond those finite acts for the more, for the infinite horizon of those acts.

> What is present in our ordinary and academic consciousness is no more than a tiny island (even though it is large enough in itself and continually and increasingly enlarged by our objectifying knowledge and action) in a boundless ocean of the nameless mystery which grows and becomes clearer the more precisely we know and will in detail.[10]

It is the experience, as Paul Tillich has put it, of 'standing out' of one's world, so that one is not simply immersed in the world but *has* a world. The grasp of finite objects, the 'having' of a world is possible only against the backdrop of a boundless horizon. That I grasp a limit is because I already have moved beyond that limit.

---

knowledge. It is in this latter sense that Rahner uses the term as a way of connecting his theology to transcendental philosophy (and Kantian usage). Transcendental method and philosophy begins with the foundational or tran-scendental conditions in the human subject that ground the possibility of all knowledge. Human transcendence, for Rahner, is that fundamental transcendental which uniquely makes human knowing possible. For an excellent discussion of Rahner's terminology see Karl-Heinz Weger, *Karl Rahner: An Introduction to His Theology*, trans. David Smith (New York: Seabury, 1980). See also Rahner's article on "Transcendental Theology," *SM* 6:287-89.

[9]Rahner is concerned to point out that the human being is not merely an object among other objects, but is a subject experiencing, desiring, acting, inquiring, understanding, judging, deciding. I cannot turn inward and find this subject, this self, this "I," who does these things; I will only, as Hume did, "stumble on some particular perception or other," and not on this perceiving self. That is, the human being as subject can never be objectified (and remain subject) and become a datum for empirical science, and yet we are conscious of ourselves as subjects in our acts of subjectivity. To be a subject is to be not merely acted upon but to self-consciously act upon one's world, and even more so to decide about oneself, to determine oneself.

[10]Rahner, "Experience of the Holy Spirit," *TI* 18:196.

The experience of transcendence is discovered in the very act of
questioning, in that openness to being which arises from being (I
must already know something in order to even ask a question), and
in the fact that there is no end to my questioning. I can always ask
more questions. Transcendental experience is the experience of
being borne by the infinite depth of being, of being open to the
totality of being.

It is that unthematic, unobjectified knowing (or experience)
that is always present which grounds and makes possible my
thematic and objectified categorial knowledge. It can be made
thematic also, and in so doing pushes the limits of language, always
requiring an analogical kind of communication. As oriented to
boundless mystery, as infinitely open, this transcendental experience is the unthematic experience of God, so that this
transcendental experience of God grounds the possibility of our
knowing, willing, loving.

> He whom we call God dwells in this nameless and pathless expanse of our
> consciousness. The mystery purely and simply that we call God is not a
> particular, especially peculiar, objective piece of reality which we add to the
> realities named and systematized in our experience and fit in with the latter;
> he is the encompassing, never encompassed ground and precondition of our
> experience and its objects.[11]

Furthermore, this transcendental experience of God is not
only the experience of God as the asymptotic goal of our transcendentality which is never reached, but it is also the experience
of God as realized goal (through the 'incarnation' or 'hypostatic
union'), or at least as the *offer* of God's nearness: that is,
transcendental experience is also the experience of grace (as
offered, as received, or as rejected). This infinite openness of the
human subject is an openness for the self-communication of God
which is always present at least implicitly or unthematically, and
which in our acts of knowledge and freedom is being responded to

---

[11]Ibid., p. 197.

in one way or another, at least implicitly. This responsiveness to God's self-communication is mediated by the historical and predicamental, by the objects of our world, and most of all by our relationship to our neighbor. It is not itself a historical or objective, finite datum of our experience in the sense of one particular experience among others, but rather is the sustaining ground of all our experiences and the taking up of ourselves as a whole. Nevertheless this self-communication of God (which includes our lived-out response) takes objective, concrete form.[12]

This transcendental experience, when it is the experience of grace as realized (God's self-communication as accepted), can be described as the experience of the Holy Spirit. In his essay "Experience of the Holy Spirit," Rahner gives concrete examples of experience of the Spirit, a kind of phenomenology of the Spirit (or at least examples of what the experience of the Spirit may be like; although he recognizes that because one can never objectify adequately one's own transcendental experience, one cannot know with certainty that this or that experience in oneself or in another is an experience of the Spirit). I quote at some length from this essay because it provides a sense for the experience of the Spirit in ordinary everyday life as Rahner conceives it, in those instances which are pushed to the fore of our consciousness.

> When, over and above all individual hopes, there is the one and entire hope that gently embraces all upsurges and also all downfalls in silent promise,
> when responsibility is undertaken and sustained, even though no evidence of success or advantage can be produced,
> when someone experiences and accepts his ultimate freedom, of which no earthly constraints can deprive him,
> when the fall into the darkness of death is accepted with resignation as the dawn of incomprehensible promise,
> when the sum total of all life's accounts, which we cannot work out

---

[12]See, among other essays by Rahner, "Experience of Self and Experience of God," *TI* 13:122-32; "Experience of Transcendence from the Standpoint of Christian Dogmatics," *TI* 18:173-88; "Religious Enthusiasm and the Experience of Grace," *TI* 16:35-51; "Reflections on the Experience of Grace," *TI* 3:86-90.

ourselves, is seen as good by an incomprehensible 'other,' although this cannot be 'proved,'

when the fragmentary experience of love, beauty, and joy is felt and accepted as promise of love, beauty and joy purely and simply, and not regarded with deep cynicism and scepticism as facile consolation in the face of ultimate bleakness,

when the bitter, disappointing, and fleeting monotony of ordinary life is borne with serene resignation up to its accepted end out of a strength whose ultimate source cannot be grasped and so cannot be brought under our control,

when we venture to pray into a silent darkness and know that in any case we are heard, although there seems to be no response from there about which it would be possible to reason and argue,

when we get away from ourselves unconditionally and experience this capitulation as the true victory,

when falling becomes standing firm,

when despair is accepted and mysteriously experienced as assurance without any easy consolation,

when man entrusts all his knowledge and all his questions to the silent and all-sheltering mystery which is loved more than all our individual perceptions that turn us into petty lords,

when we practise our death in the course of ordinary life and then attempt to live in the way that we wish to approach death, calmly and with resignation,

when . . . (as we said, it would be possible to go on for a long time),

then God is present with his liberating grace. Then we experience what we Christians describe as the Holy Spirit of God; then an experience occurs that is inescapable in life (even if it is suppressed) and is offered to our freedom with the question of whether we want to accept it or to barricade ourselves against it in a hell of freedom to which we condemn ourselves. The mysticism of everyday life is there, God is found in all things; here is that sober intoxication of the Spirit of which the Church Fathers and the early liturgy spoke, which we may not reject or despise simply because it is sober.[13]

What we will seek to show is that it is this same 'ordinary' experience of the Spirit, of a graced transcendentality, which also finds expression in words and historical actions of a prophetic nature where this transcendental experience is mediated categorially in a more or less adequate way. This is what we will seek to recognize in the following pages and in Chapter III where we will

---

[13]Rahner, "Experience of the Spirit," *TI* 18:202-03.

consider this transcendentality as the a priori condition for the possibility of a human word being a divine word. At this point, however, we take up that aspect of conscience which Rahner has referred to as a "general moral faith-instinct." We will have opportunities to return to this notion of transcendence in the following discussions.

The General Moral Faith-Instinct

The notion of a general moral faith-instinct is related in Rahner's essay, "The Problem of Genetic Manipulation," where he takes up the question of the method by which the problem of the morality of genetic manipulation is addressed. He recognizes certain difficulties that arise when this problem of genetic manipulation is approached in the traditional natural law manner. The traditional approach is legitimately concerned to demonstrate what is appropriate or inappropriate to the nature of being human. However, the possibilities of a rational-deductive kind of demonstration are limited. The difficulties that Rahner sees include, on the one hand, the general observation that the nature of human freedom means that humankind must necessarily manipulate itself (therefore, Why not genetic manipulation?) and, on the other, the moral sense or intuition that certain concrete examples of genetic manipulation are morally questionable. Consequently, the question is raised as to how we move from certain general observations concerning human nature (i.e., the observation that humankind necessarily manipulates itself) to specific ethical guidelines related to new developments in a field of the natural sciences (i.e., ought human beings to manipulate themselves genetically). There is the additional problem of knowing exactly what the unchangeable nature of the human being is, considering its conditional expression in variable historical forms. History is one-way directed, giving expression in ever new ways to essential human reality. Genetic manipulation is an example of the historically new situation which confronts the human being, for which there are no

clear previously formed abstractions of essential human nature that
can easily be applied in a rational manner to this case. Furthermore, there is a problem of relating that abstract human nature to
the specifics of concrete forms of genetic manipulation when one
considers the naïveté of the ethicist in regard to the more technical
aspects of genetics. It is in the context of these epistemological
problems that Rahner raises the question of a "*moral* mode of
knowing."[14]

In particular he directs our attention to that element in
practical reason which he calls the "general moral faith-instinct,"
which he distinguishes from an "individual existential moral
knowledge."[15] It can be termed an "instinct" in the sense that it is
pre-conceptual and prior to (or foundational to) the rational
reflection that springs from it. Consequently, this "'instinctive'
judgment cannot and need not . . . be adequately subject to
analytic reflection."[16] This general sense of right and wrong is not
nonrational, but rather "wherever the judgment of this moral faith-
instinct attempts to express itself in words regarding a particular
issue, it naturally and inevitably works with the categories of
rational analysis, 'reasons,' conceptual arguments, etc. . . ."[17] But
it cannot be reduced to rational analysis. Rahner is particularly
concerned that ethical discourse not proceed as if a moral position

---

[14]Rahner, "The Problem of Genetic Manipulation," *TI* 9:225-34.

[15]I have chosen to translate *global* as "general" rather than follow the
translation in *TI* 9, which renders it as "universal." "Universal" tends to give the
sense merely of an essential and therefore universal structure of knowledge,
whereas Rahner's conception of a general moral faith-instinct (*globalen sittlichen
Glaubensinstinkt*) has to do with the general nature of the knowledge arising from
a general sense of things and not with the universality (in the essential structure
of the human subject) of this mode of knowing (although it is universal in this
sense also). Rahner is concerned with a *general* moral faith-instinct as over against
what can be termed an *individual* moral faith-instinct, although a general (*global*)
sense of oneself can be said to be involved in individual concrete knowledge
(*Dynamic Element*, p. 166).

[16]Rahner, "Genetic Manipulation," p. 238.

[17]Ibid.

could be demonstrated solely by rational proofs deduced from an abstract conception of the nature of the human being. He notes that

> . . . a merely 'rational' scrutiny of moral theological 'proofs' will often reveal–initially to one' great surprise–that, looked at purely 'logically,' they already presuppose what they claim to be 'proving,' or else they have recourse to Holy Scripture or the Church's magisterium as a final court of appeal, in spite of the fact that they are supposed to be dealing with questions of natural law, requiring an *inner* justification. What is really behind these 'proofs'? Under certain circumstances they are not as bad as they seem. They are ultimately an expression of the [general] faith-instinct, which is by no means identical with its objectivisation in analytic terms.[18]

Rahner recognizes that there is a danger in any appeal given purely to this kind of "instinct" since it can become an "argument" for "historically conditioned prejudices, whether those of tradition, society or class ideology."[19]   Consequently, there must be accompanied with this approach a critical stance. Nevertheless, the fundamental reality of something like a general moral faith-instinct in human decision making must be recognized. To ignore it and operate as if we could simply produce specific moral guidelines from a rational deduction from general principles would be to relegate ourselves to a moral blindness and to generalities. Rahner gives, as an example, the response of German theologians to the question of the production and use of the napalm bomb in Vietnam. In short it shows clearly

> that whenever a moral theologian merely dissects such a particular 'case' into a thousand aspects and individual problems and has the courage only to make abstract deductions from more general principles, merely engaging in 'casuistics'; whenever he fails to react simply and plainly from the instinct of faith to the single totality of the 'case,' he arrives at 'solutions' which are simply blind to concrete reality; in plain language, they are *false*. Such 'solutions' do not exhibit the uncompromising simplicity of decisions which

---

[18]Ibid.

[19]Ibid., p. 239.

are truly Christian and human, and only reveal their own impotence.[20]

Consequently, this fundamental faith-instinct must not be ignored. Rahner refers to this instinct as a *faith*-instinct, for it is the "instinct" or perception derived from one's "fundamental option." The fundamental stance or position of one's existence determines one's horizons and such a stance is 'prior' to the reflections that spring from it.[21] Rahner also calls this instinct the "general moral instinct of reason and faith" (*globaler moralischer Vernunft- und Glaubensinstinkt*), thereby expressing the unity of faith and reason as grounded in the transcendental reality of the human subject.[22] Rationality is an element in this mode of knowing, and yet a moral decision cannot wait until all conceptual and rational analysis is performed before it is made. The moral decision "demands that one should enter into the darkness of reality (which is never completely transparent) and have the courage to take the step from theory to practice."[23] This step must always be taken with the self-critical awareness

> that its judgments contain unreflected elements which are, as such, contingent, subject to change; and that consequently a *different* judgment may be shown to be correct at a later time. All the same, a particular contingent judgment of this kind can still be the only correct one *in its situation.*[24]

The taking of the step, the making of the decision involves the

---

[20]Ibid., p. 241.

[21]Rahner, "Zum Problem der genetischen Manipulation," *Schriften Zur Theologie* vols. 1-13 (Einsiedeln: Benziger Verlag, 1954-78), 8:304 (hereafter cited as Rahner, *ST*): "This mode of knowing is also at work in human life overall, wherever one is 'committed' [*engagiert*] to a particular stance [*Haltung*]. . . ." Consequently Rahner recognizes this mode of knowing even in a rationalistic skeptic who operates from a rationalistic stance (p. 305).

[22]Ibid., p. 305.

[23]Rahner, "Genetic Manipulation," p. 239.

[24]Ibid.

synthetic judgment in moral knowing which resolves the dialectic between the knowledge of the existential situation and the knowledge of moral obligation. It means the perception of the general moral principle or norm and how it applies to *this* situation. In the self-awareness of the human subject and as a perception arising from one's fundamental stance in faith, the action fitting to essential human nature for this new historical situation is grasped.

Rahner does not go into a detailed analysis of this general moral faith-instinct. Nevertheless, what we can recognize is that there is, in addition to an individual mode of knowing of a 'charismatic' nature, also a general kind of knowing that is grounded in this charismatic and transcendental dimension of the human subject. That is, the knowledge of what is generally fitting to *common* human nature in its immutable essence is not merely a matter of rational deduction from the abstract concept of human nature but involves the transcendental experience of the human being who in self-awareness can have a fundamental and general sense not only of his or her individual unique essence, but of that which he or she has in common with humankind (or with what may be called the human being's immutable essence).[25] It ought to be mentioned at this point also that such a knowledge which is concerned with what is general and 'in principle' includes also a general knowledge of the existential situation and can never be divorced from the conditions of the historical moment. We gain our moral sense of things within the world and in our attention to the world, although at the same time always before God.[26]

---

[25]Rahner's distinction between mutable and immutable, unique and universal essence will be treated below, pp. 100-103.

[26]In his essay on "Genetic Manipulation," Rahner limits the discussion to a particular form of genetic manipulation and then proceeds to give the "reasons" for this kind of manipulation which constitute an "appeal to, and the inadequate objectifying of a humane and Christian 'instinct'" (p. 251). He pursues, in particular, the motive, the subjective act from which springs the objective activity of genetic manipulation as a way of determining its morality in terms of its origins in human intention.

At this point it may be helpful to connect this general moral faith-instinct with the dynamic of prophetic knowing. Although much remains to be developed in terms of this prophetic knowing, nevertheless, we can begin to recognize how this element of practical reason can be viewed as an aspect of prophecy. There is much, for example, in the biblical phenomenon of prophecy that can be conceived in terms of this general moral faith-instinct, for there is in much prophetic preaching a general moral knowledge (often with reference to God's previous actions and promises) which is applied to a specific set of circumstances, but it cannot be said that such an application follows a narrow rational-deductive method. After all, 'false' prophets also appealed to the knowledge of God's commandments and the history of her acts. Rather, there is involved in these prophetic utterances a perception, a "faith-instinct" grounded in a fundamental stance.[27] It is this fundamental existentiell position which provides the horizons within which the knowledge (and memory) of God's workings with her people is seen in its applicability to the specific set of circumstances. Consequently, when the prophet sees the emptiness of the ritual sacrifices in the face of injustice and the oppression of the poor and calls for a very specific kind of repentance, this perception and imperative arise from an existentiell fundamental stance or faith-instinct. After all, other 'prophets' saw other things and applied the knowledge of God's actions and promises in other ways.

As another example, we can cite the preaching of Jesus whose proclamation of the reign of God took on different dimensions and very specific applications depending on whether he was addressing the Pharisees or the tax collectors and prostitutes. Certainly, rational explanations can be given (and can be expected) as to why the essential message of the gospel of the reign of God took on different applications according to the different situations and people. There may be occasions when such reasons are explic-

---

[27]Something like this seems to be what Abraham Heschel has in mind when he writes of the prophet's pathos (*The Prophets*, 2:1-11, 27-47).

itly given, and yet it cannot be assumed that the decision to apply the message of the gospel in a particular manner to a specific situation was reached by an exhaustive rational-deductive method, as if everything could somehow be taken into account in advance. This general faith-instinct cannot be used to explain prophetic reality in its entirety, but it does provide an aspect of it and, as we shall see, an element of that 'from God' to which prophecy points as the basis for its authority. We now direct our attention to the second aspect of practical reason which is significant for understanding the dynamic of prophetic knowledge.

The Logic of Concrete Individual Knowledge

In addition to a general knowledge of right and wrong (and its application to the particular situation) which can arise from a moral faith-instinct, and which also can be elaborated in an "essential ethics" that is rationally and logically deduced from an abstract concept of the nature of the human being, there is a concrete individual knowledge which also arises from something like a moral faith-instinct, but which cannot be rationally deduced from an abstract concept of human nature, for it has to do with what is individual and unique. Rahner is concerned that we recognize that there is a personal and spiritual individuality, that there is a difference between individuation and individuality, between the 'uniqueness' that comes as a result of what has been historically fated to us (our heredity, socialization, environment), and the unique call and destiny which comes from God. Corresponding to this personal and spiritual individuality is a mode of knowing appropriate to it, a concrete individual knowledge. The analysis of this second function of conscience is what Rahner calls for in his essay "On the Question of a Formal Existential Ethics," and what he gives us in his essay, "The Logic of Concrete Individual

Knowledge in Ignatius Loyola."[28]

In his essay "Reflections on a New Task of Fundamental Theology," Rahner calls fundamental theology to a new task involving the analysis of the "logical structure of the practical reason operating in matters of faith, and the grammar of existential commitment."[29] He believes that the beginnings of an analysis of the structure of a graced practical reason and the "grace of faith" are found in Ignatius Loyola's theology of decision. In his essay "The Logic of Concrete Individual Knowledge" (first published as "Der Logik der existentiellen Erkenntnis bei Ignatius v. Loyola" in *Das Dynamische in der Kirche* in 1958), he has developed this epistemology of the individual as he discovers it in Ignatius.[30] This essay is foundational for understanding much of what he has written subsequently on this subject and the related concerns of the dynamic, charismatic, and prophetic element in the church (much in the same way that *Spirit in the World* and *Hearers of the Word* are foundational for understanding the epistemology behind Rahner's treatment of the theology of revelation).[31] Therefore we

---

[28]Rahner, "Formal Existential Ethics," *TI* 2:217-34 and "The Logic of Concrete Individual Knowledge in Ignatius Loyola," in *Dynamic Element*, pp. 84-170.

[29]Rahner, "New Task for Theology," p. 164.

[30]Rahner, *Das Dynamische in der Kirche* (Freiburg: Herder, 1964).

[31]In an interview at the age of seventy-five, Rahner was asked what he considered the most important among his writings. He mentioned an early devotional work *On Prayer* and his treatment of "the logic of concrete individual knowledge in Ignatius Loyola" and related themes. See Leo J. O'Donovan, "Living into Mystery: Karl Rahner's Reflections at 75," *America*, 10 March 1979, pp. 177-80. Rahner has made clear elsewhere that this individual concrete knowledge is a 'prophetic' kind of knowing. See, for example, his essay, "Some Theses for a Theology of Devotion to the Sacred Heart," *TI* 3:339:
> "Hence the private revelation as a mission to the Church can be conceived as a heavenly imperative interpretation of the particular situation of the Church at this time; it answers the question as to what is most urgently to be done here and now in accordance with the general principles of faith. A private revelation corresponds accordingly in the sphere of the Church to that first and second moment of choice in the life of the individual of which St. Ignatius speaks, and whose mode of choice can never be grasped

turn our attention to this essay as it provides an analysis of the second function of conscience, an individual concrete knowledge.

Here Rahner is concerned with both a historical treatment of Ignatius's modes of making an election (in particular the second mode) and a theological reconstruction of Ignatius's insights.[32] It is Rahner's theological formulation that is of particular interest to us and we will refer to his historical treatment only as that is needed to clarify this formulation. Rahner views the Ignatian *Exercises* as a guide to recognizing God's will, especially when it has to do with a particular calling or imperative for action which cannot be known simply by attending to "general normative principles." The *Exercises* are particularly fitting for one who is deciding about vocation or making any major decision, although their underlying presuppositions can be applied also to the decision making of ordinary everyday living. What is striking to the modern reader is that Ignatius assumes the existence of psychological impulses arising in the consciousness which come from God. It is to the nature of these "impulses" and their recognition that Rahner gives considerable attention. After all they present a problem, not only theologically, but apologetically since

> . . . a man of the present day with the attitude to life that comes naturally to him will only with the greatest difficulty be prepared to recognize

---

> by purely theoretical considerations alone, because while the universal can circumscribe the relevant individual it can never (at least in principle) precisely pick it out."

[32]The importance of transcendental philosophy, Heidegger, and Thomas Aquinas for Rahner's thought are often noted and clearly apparent. Also of great significance for the spirit and ethos of Rahner's thought is Ignatius Loyola. Among Rahner's writings in which he has directly taken up Ignatian themes, see "The Ignatian Mysticism of Joy in the World," *TI* 3:277-93; "Christmas in the Light of the Ignatian Exercises," *TI* 17:3-7; *Spiritual Exercises*, trans. Kenneth Baker (New York: Herder & Herder, 1965); *Ignatius of Loyola*, with a historical introduction by Paul Imhof, trans. Rosaleen Ockenden (New York: Collins, 1979). For a transcendental theological approach to the Ignatian Exercises, see Harvey D. Egan, *The Spiritual Exercises and the Ignatian Mystical Horizon*, foreword by Karl Rahner (St. Louis: The Institute of Jesuit Sources, 1976).

something that he discovers in his consciousness, as a highly personal influence of God, and to view his states of mind, impulses, his "consolation" and "desolation" as the effect of powers that transcend him. It is much more likely he will think of hormones, effects of the weather, hereditary factors influencing character, repercussions of the unconscious, complexes and innumerable other things than that the idea will occur to him that God, his guardian angel or the devil is at work. He will still admit that all these modes of experience in the inner world of the soul have their religious importance, must be regarded as subject to moral evaluation, and to that extent have something to do with God. But that they could be directly produced by God, will not easily be evident to him today.[33]

As we shall see, the distinction Rahner makes between transcendental and categorial objects becomes important for understanding the nature of these divine impulses.

Also, Ignatius distinguishes among three modes of making an election. Rahner's interpretation of these modes is significant for the development of his own thought on the subject. He believes the second mode is the "normal" mode (as he believes Ignatius conceives it), and that the third mode (the rational-deductive mode) is essentially an element in the second mode and that the first mode (prophetic inspiration and "revelations") is an acute expression of the second mode.[34] Consequently Rahner's treatment

---

[33]Rahner, *Dynamic Element*, pp. 120-21.

[34]Ibid., pp. 95-129. See especially p. 103:
> "The second mode of Election differs from the third not by total disparity but as the large whole differs from a part which is necessarily contained in the whole even though by itself it does not constitute the whole. And the third mode in its turn is rather to be conceived as the deficient form of the second, a way of making the Election which, as we have already said, aspires to be integrated into the greater, more comprehensive whole."

Also pp. 105-06:
> "It follows from that too, that the three modes of making the Election have one and the same nature and are only distinguished by the differing degrees to which they realize that nature. The first method is the ideal higher limiting case of the second method and the latter itself includes the rationality of the third as one of its own intrinsic elements. The third method is the less perfect mode of the second (and must be so regarded) and itself seeks to rise beyond itself into the second kind of Election."

of concrete individual knowledge is an analysis of this second and 'normal' mode of making a decision. We will take up this normal expression of concrete individual knowledge and then consider its more acute expression in 'revelations'. The third mode which deals with the rational-deductive approach will only be considered here as an element in the dynamic of concrete individual knowledge.

Individual Knowledge
(Ignatius's Second Mode)

We are asking about the "method of an individual and concrete ethics of the discovery of that particular will of God which cannot fully be resolved into general principles."[35] In the following discussion we will attempt to boil down to its methodological and theological essence what Rahner has gleaned from Ignatius's "Rules for the Discernment of Spirits" and given us in his subsequent theological formulation.[36]

Rahner notes that Ignatius's divine 'impulse' or motion tests other impulses to determine their origin, to determine if they are 'from God'. This primary divine motion is termed the *consolacion sin causa.* Rahner recognizes that a distinction can be made between the motion and the object which causes the motion. In the case of this primary divine motion or consolation, it is "without cause." What is, in fact, decisive for understanding this divine motion is the absence of an object which lies behind it as its cause.[37]

In order to see the significance of this we need to clarify the meaning of "consolation." Consolation as Ignatius uses this term refers to an "inner frame of mind"; he uses words like peace, tran-

---

[35]Ibid., pp. 116-17.

[36]Rahner's approach consists in a "free movement alternating between the text of the Exercises and theological observations, in which each partly by turns questions or answers" (Rahner, *Dynamic Element*, p. 117).

[37]Ibid., p. 132.

quility, quiet. What he seems to be pointing to is the experience
of the fittingness of a particular decision or action. The key to
recognizing that such a consolation or experience of 'fittingness' is
of divine origin is its absence of cause. In other words, if that
"from which the understanding and will gradually draw their consolation" or experience of fittingness is without cause, then the
experience of fittingness is of divine origin. This experience of the
sin causa, of the objectless cause, is the experience of God herself.
It is, in Rahner's terms, the experience of transcendence, of the
infinite horizon which is the condition of possibility of all acts of
knowledge, but which is itself not a concept or categorial object
but rather the "nonconceptual light" which brings to light the
definite limited object. The *criterion* for distinguishing between the
consolation that has as its cause a definite limited object, and the
consolation that arises from the experience of the infinite being of
God, is grounded "in the essential disparity of the very structure
of the experience itself." That is, the experience of a "consolation
without cause" carries with it its own certainty. We can see this if
we attend more precisely to the nature of this experience.[38]

We recall the distinction that we made earlier between transcendental and categorial experience. As we shall see more fully
in the next chapter, the experience of transcendence, of a *Vorgriff
auf esse*, is the condition for the possibility of conceptual knowledge. This *Vorgriff* (pre-apprehension), however, is not itself an
object of consciousness but the infinite horizon in which objects of
consciousness are experienced and known. This transcendental
openness of the human subject is an anticipatory reaching out to
the totality of being. It is utter receptivity to being. Furthermore,
this transcendental dynamic is "graced"; that is, this transcendental
receptivity to the totality of being (which means a *potentia*

---

[38]Ibid., pp. 129-42, esp. p. 137. What is involved here is not the abstract
conceptualization of a consolation with cause on the one hand and a consolation
without cause on the other, but an experience that has conceptual content, on the
one hand, and a nonconceptual experience, on the other.

obedientialis for God's self-communication) is oriented to the self-communication of God herself. In other words, this transcendental orientation to being in general has been "supernaturally elevated" to participation in the life of the triune God. This human transcendence, therefore, is a synthesis of the anticipatory reaching out to being in general and an ordination to God herself (a synthesis which cannot be distinguished by an act of introspection).

In "The Logic of Concrete Individual Knowledge in Ignatius Loyola," Rahner makes the point that the awareness of this supernatural transcendence can grow and "become more pure and unmixed." There can develop a more focused awareness of this transcendental dynamism, not only as it is experienced as the pre-apprehension of knowledge but as the "pure dynamism of the affirming, receptive will" (*reine Dynamik des bejahenden, sich öffnenden 'Willens'*).[39] That is, the conceptual object which normally is the focus of awareness can become more transparent and the transcendental dynamism of the will can become central in one's awareness and experience. In other words, one can grow in faith, hope, and love, and one can also become more aware of the experience of faith, hope, and love which are expressions for this transcendental dynamic. (Otherwise, how could they become the focus of the kind of attention they receive, for example, in the Scriptures.)

Furthermore, this transcendental dynamic or anticipatory reaching out carries with it its own certainty for it is pure openness, unlimited affirmation, and therefore embraces all being, all truth. Consequently, even in that judgment which affirms what *is*, the unhindered willingness or openness of the will to embrace being is significant. With practical reason, which is oriented not to what is but to what ought to be, it is the transcendental dynamic of the will and therefore love which predominates, although the rational and speculative dimension remains an element. In fact, what Ignatius calls the "consolation without cause" is this free

---

[39]Rahner, *Dynamic Element*, p. 145 (*Dynamische*, p. 127).

transcendence. As such, by its very nature, as "the supernaturally elevated spirit's affirming apprehension" (*die bejahende Inbesitznahme des übernatürlich erhobenen Geistes*) it cannot deceive; it necessarily reaches out to and affirms being, affirms what *is* and what ought to come into being.[40] Since its affirmation is unlimited, reaching out to Absolute *Esse*, to God, it is the condition for the possibility of affirming all finite objects (as they exist before God). For Rahner, God is the one self-evident truth, for this transcendental knowledge of God is the subjective ground of all finite truths. In every act of knowledge God is implicitly affirmed. But this also means that it is this infinite openness to God which grounds the practical judgment which makes the knowledge of the concrete individual decision or action to be made possible. It is within this pure openness to God that such a practical judgment of the individual can be made and a concrete action be recognized as a summons 'from God'.[41]

For Ignatius this means making an experimental test. In a situation involving a number of possible courses of action it means testing the particular courses of action by placing them (by imagination or play-acting) within the experienced awareness of this pure transcendental openness oriented to God and discovering

> whether the will to the object of election under scrutiny leaves intact the pure openness to God in the [experience of supernatural transcendence] and even supports and augments it or weakens and obscures it; whether a synthesis of these two [postures (*Haltungen*)], pure receptivity to God . . . and the will to this limited finite object of decision produces "peace," "tranquility," "quiet," so that true gladness and spiritual joy ensue, that is, the joy of pure, free, undistorted transcendence; or whether instead of smoothness, gentleness and sweetness, sharpness, tumult and disturbance arise.[42]

---

[40]Rahner, *Dynamische*, p. 130.

[41]It follows that the criterion for recognizing the divine motion is not its suddenness or inexplicability, but rather this certainty of divine calling is in the nature of the experience. See Rahner, *Dynamic Element*, p. 158.

[42]Rahner, *Dynamic Element*, p. 158 (*Dynamische*, p. 138).

By way of a test (which takes a certain amount of time) the individual in his or her imagination seeks to bring a possible definite object of decision into a synthesis with his or her "innermost fundamental stance" (*innersten Urhaltung*) as a means of determining its fittingness, as a way of recognizing what is fitting.[43] The "operative principle of choice will be God, or, more precisely, that concrete, unique, intrinsic orientation towards God which constitutes the innermost essence of man . . . "[44] In other words, the "fundamental option" of the individual person, which is his or her faith (or love) in its transcendental origin, is the criterion, not as an abstract concept, but in concrete experience, for whether or not a particular imperative is of divine origin. Rahner (and Ignatius) assumes that this fundamental option or stance is sufficiently pronounced in the experience and focused awareness of the individual to be able to seek its congruence (or incongruence) with a particular object of decision. Rahner recognizes that a good many factors can get in the way or cloud the issue in such an experimental test. We will not take up that concern at this point. Nevertheless, what is being recognized is that individuals discover God's will for themselves as they discover what is congruent with the love of God as that love bears up their lives. The individual experiences a particular course of action as expressive of and sustained by loving openness to God, or as disruptive and constricting of that openness (and therefore, in the case of the latter, a course of action incongruent with the call of God in the individual). Augustine's words, "Love God and do what you please" are appropriate here for they express this sense that we can do what we please, what we sense is fitting as that arises out of (and is experienced as congruent with) our love of God. We must not, however, imagine that this takes place through a rational analysis and comparison of the finite object of choice with the objectification or conceptualization of this transcendental reaching out to God in love. It is

---

[43]Rahner, *Dynamische*, p. 139.

[44]Rahner, *Dynamic Element*, p. 160.

rather the experience of the fittingness of a particular object of decision with our transcendental experience of the love of God (in itself).

It ought to be recognized, also, that such a means of making a decision does not apply to all decision making. There are many things which, for all their material diversity, are congruent with the fundamental tendency of an individual and are not subject to this method of making a decision. There may be, for example, a particular action one feels called to, but a number of possible ways to carry out that action.[45] Nevertheless, Rahner believes that in major decisions people tend to come to a decision in more or less this way, implicitly, whether they know the formal logic of concrete individual knowledge or not, just as people use abstract knowledge regardless of whether they know the rules of logic.

> Consequently in every case he will probably make his decision through a fundamental global awareness of himself actually present and making itself felt in him during this space of time, and through a feeling of the harmony or disharmony of the object of choice with this fundamental feeling he has about himself. He will not only nor ultimately make his decision by a rational analysis but by whether he feels that something "suits him" or not. And this feeling will be judged by whether the matter pleases, delights, brings peace and satisfaction.[46]

We might add that this does not exclude the possibility that one can make a decision, operating out of a fundamental option which is a radical 'no' to the transcendental openness to God. Such a decision will not, however, be based in a *consolacion sin causa*; but yet it will be similar to the formal structure of decision making indicated above, for even in sin the human being cannot operate in any other manner than a human one to the extent that the human being acts at all. Furthermore, there can be a variety of 'impulses' as well as rationales that influence a decision. In any

---

[45]Ibid., pp. 165-66.

[46]Ibid., p. 166.

case the above description is applicable to the faithful insofar as and to the extent that they have entered into the love of God and give expression to that in "doing what they please" or, in other words, in doing what seems fitting.

We can summarize what has been said above by reference to a more recent essay by Rahner entitled "Dialogue with God?," in which he asks the question concerning how it is possible to conceive of God's speaking to us.[47] The method he follows involves, first of all, pointing to our transcendental experience. We have already indicated that, for Rahner, this experience must be understood as "supernaturally" elevated through the incarnation so that this graced transcendental experience is in itself God's Word; it is the self-communication of God. Consequently, the human being can be understood in his or her very being as God's utterance.

> God's most fundamental word to us in our free uniqueness is not a word that occurs as something additional or as a single object among other objects of experience, categorically, at a definite point within the wider field of our consciousness; it is we ourselves in unity, totality, and dependence on the incomprehensible mystery that we call God, the word of God that we ourselves are and that as such is spoken to us.[48]

Consequently the primary and fundamental sense in which prayer is dialogic is recognized in this transcendental aspect, in which "Man hears himself . . . as God's address, which is filled with God's promise of himself by faith, hope, and love, in God's gracious self-communication."[49] There is, however, a second sense in which prayer can be understood as dialogic:

> If, that is, man accepts unconditionally and genuinely this absolute openness toward God, derived from God and his freedom (which is God's original word to man), if it is not concealed, distorted, or misused by man's

---

[47]Rahner, "Dialogue with God?," *TI* 18:122-31.

[48]Ibid., p. 128.

[49]Ibid., p. 129.

prior decision in regard to quite definite categorial contents of his consciousness, then . . . we have what Ignatius of Loyola described in his *Spiritual Exercises* as 'indifference' and (when this indifference is really radically freely achieved and maintained) 'consolation . . . without any preceding cause'. If, within such an ultimate dialogic freedom, a particular individual object of choice is encountered, which, even after long spiritual experience and questioning, does not distort, confuse, or restrict this pure openness to God, if it is experienced precisely as the medium by which this indifferent openness to God is accepted and remains intact in unconditional surrender to him–that is (conversely), in unconditional acceptance of God's word, that we ourselves are–then this categorical object of choice (however intramundane and relative it may be in itself) can and may be understood as a factor in this dialogic relationship between God and man, because and insofar as the chosen object is incorporated into the totality of the dialogic conversation, without imperiling or removing the latter's boundless and absolute openness.[50]

This individual encounter with God's unique concrete word addressed to the individual, the sense of personal direction, of calling, is what we have attempted to analyze. Since this aspect of practical reason involves the apprehension of the concrete will of God in a particular situation we can see that this logic of concrete individual knowledge has particular significance for prophecy.

We have already recognized that this logic of concrete individual knowledge does not apply to all decision making. We have recognized that practical reason has various levels or dimensions to it, including a general moral faith-instinct, the element of discursive reasoning, the formation of conscience by the content of Christian teaching, commandments, principles, as well as in some cases this dynamic of concrete individual knowledge.

In order to begin to clarify the significance of this logic of individual knowledge for prophecy we can briefly relate it to the prophetic dimension. Rahner himself, in discussions dealing with the prophetic or charismatic element, has related this logic of concrete individual knowledge to this dimension. Thus, for example, he points to his essay "The Logic of Concrete Individual

---

[50]Ibid., pp. 129-30.

Knowledge in Ignatius Loyola" as the basis for what he says concerning "charismatic instruction" in "On the Theological Problems Entailed in a 'Pastoral Constitution.'"[51] After all, groups, societies, the church, insofar as they form a unity are individual also, for which this logic of concrete individual knowledge also applies. (This will be developed more fully later.)

At this point we can simply relate this dynamic of individual knowledge to some examples of prophetic phenomena. I will use biblical examples although examples could also be given from the history of charismatic expression in the church. Thus, for example, in Acts we encounter such phrases as "it seemed good to the Holy Spirit and to us," or that they were "forbidden by the Holy Spirit to speak the word in Asia." We do not have to assume that such experiences involve a 'direct revelation'; the dynamic of a concrete individual knowledge is quite applicable here. After all, in a particular situation there would be only so many possibilities for the direction of the evangelical mission and those possibilities could be quite 'naturally' weighed or tested as to their congruence with the apostle's experience of the Spirit (this supernaturally elevated transcendental openness to God and her will). In a similar manner we can understand Paul's and his companions' response to a vision of a man of Macedonia calling out, "Come over to Macedonia and help us": they concluded that they were to preach the gospel there. The vision is, in a sense, neutral; some- one could have suggested the same thing (that they should go to Macedonia) and the dynamic of the decision to act would have been the same. That the vision is recognized as 'from God' (and not merely the result of certain psychological stirrings, although it

---

[51]Rahner, "Theological Problems in a 'Pastoral Constitution,'" p. 297. Also, in *Visions and Prophecies*, trans. Charles Henkey and Richard Strachan (New York: Herder & Herder, 1963), Rahner notes the significance of this individual knowledge for the church's sense of direction: "Now in the life of the Church a divine impulse analogous to this Ignatian election must operate for the Church's election and cannot be replaced . . . by theoretical considerations and the deductions of theologians and moralists . . . " (p. 27).

is that also) implies a discernment of spirits, a testing as to its congruence with their existentially realized, graced transcendental experience. In other words, their conclusion (God is calling us) arises out of the certainty which is inherent to this dynamic of concrete individual knowledge.[52]

Other experiences can be added (Jesus' "setting his face toward Jerusalem" and his contemplation of his death can be understood as an expression of this kind of dynamic of human subjectivity.[53]) These experiences involve primarily the recognition of an imperative or direction to be taken by an individual or a group. We can think, also, of messages which give a directive to a people or nation which may arise as a result of the operation of this dynamic. "Prescriptive oracles" in particular fit this dynamic; after all, this dynamic has to do with the guidance of the Spirit in specific situations as that guidance is quite individual (whether the individual is a group, society, the church, or an individual person). We can also include the *discernment* in given situations as to whether what ought to be proclaimed is a message of assurance, or an announcement of salvation, or an announcement of judgment. The discernment, in other words, of the kind of message and the specific dimensions of it that are appropriate to the given situation and people may be grounded in this kind of dynamic which involves the test of congruence with the reality of faith (experienced in its origins as that infinite and affirmative openness to God's self-communication).

We could add examples from the contemporary experience of the church. When local congregations or the larger juridical church bodies set for themselves specific, concrete goals, we can assume that such goals are not arrived at merely by, on the one hand, an analysis of the historical situation and the needs of the church and, on the other, the rational application of theological principles of Christian mission. Rather, where such goal setting is

---

[52]Acts 15:28, 16:6, 9-10.

[53]Luke 9:51, 53.

undertaken in faith, we can assume this element of "individual concrete knowledge" in which certain goals will be perceived from a faith-stance as 'fitting' to the historical situation and as an expression of Christian mission. Such concrete knowledge will be objectified in a rationale, but will not ultimately rest on that rationale. We can add other examples. We think of the prophetic voices in the church; individuals and groups who call the church to concrete positions and actions that they perceive are demanded by the times. For example, should the church disinvest from any corporation doing business with the apartheid government of South Africa? Positions on both sides of the question can be argued on moral and rational grounds. It may be, however, that the final taking of a position on this issue can only be known through a 'discernment of spirits' or the "logic of individual concrete knowledge," much in the same way as an individual comes to decide about vocation.

Let us briefly contrast this mode of individual knowledge with that of the general moral faith-instinct we have already treated. In the case of a general moral faith-instinct what is being perceived in the light of faith is the rightness or wrongness of a particular action in relation to what is congruent with our common essential human nature. There may be prophetic voices in the church who criticize church statements or actions as weak or self-serving statements or actions, which for all their rationale are simply wrong, given the historical situation. What is being experienced in a prophetic individual's self-awareness is the incongruence of particular positions or actions with our common humanity which the individual shares. In the case of individual concrete knowledge, what is being perceived is something unique to the individual (whether an individual person, group, or nation) in a particular historical situation. There may be any number of morally permissible courses of action for a church to take in expressing its essential Christian mission, but it chooses a particular course of action over others as the one that must be taken for *this* church in *this* historical moment. This particular course of action from the viewpoint of a general and essential morality is no more ethical than other courses of action, and yet it may be perceived as the action that the particular church is summoned by God to take. From these examples and reflections, it may be a little clearer in the concrete as to what is being referred to by the notion of an "individual concrete knowledge" and how this is applicable to prophetic perception. Let us now seek to develop further this dynamic of concrete individual knowing as that finds acute expression in what traditionally was conceived as prophecy in the strict sense, in 'direct revelations'.

Individual Knowledge by 'Direct' Revelations (Ignatius's First Mode)

As we have already noted, Rahner views this "first mode of election" as an acute or ideal expression of the second and normal mode. In both cases we are concerned with essentially the same dynamic, although in the case of the first mode this revelatory dynamic may be characterized as more 'direct'. It is because of this 'directness' that a distinction can be made between these two modes. In directing our attention to 'revelations' of a more 'direct' nature we will not be primarily concerned with their significance as a mode of making an election or decision, but rather in their significance for understanding the prophetic dynamic.

The essential difference between the normal mode of making an election and this mode of direct revelation is the directness of the experience. This revelatory mode is characterized by the lack of a period of testing. Rather, the experience is more of a direct influence of God in propositions or even in images, visions, and auditions which may carry with them the certainty grounded in the experience of their congruence with the fundamental transcendental openness of the prophet, and which are not, therefore, arrived at by testing various options. Rahner notes that the normal mode is not a matter of direct revelation, whereas in the first or directly revelatory mode, that is, in 'direct' revelations

... the fundamental central experience of direct relation to God must be

assumed to be present and of prime importance. But they might be defined
by the fact that in them that experience, by a decisive influence of God,
finds concrete expression in the proposition, judgment, precept and so on,
of the predicamental order. In contrast to this the *experiencia* of the
Second Mode of Election is a "trial," an experimenting at one's own risk
and peril, whether and how the central religious experience coheres with
such and such limited, predicamental objects.[54]

As we shall see, the directness of this experience is not a
result of being more directly related to God in a foundational way,
in the dynamic of a graced transcendental openness, nor in being
less mediated through God's miraculous suspension of the laws of
nature and intervention in the normal cognitive operations of the
human subject. Rather, what has been said above concerning the
transcendental grounding of the experience of congruence in the
normal mode of making an election remains the essential, primary
dynamic in this matter of direct revelations. In fact, in a so-called
'direct' revelation the options for a decision (or the message to be
communicated) are generally available in the material of one's life,
including what is present subconsciously. The implicit (or explicit)
experience of their congruence with this basic existentially realized,
graced transcendental openness to God gives rise to their concrete
expression as a kind of overflow of this basic transcendental orientation operating in the subject's life and consciousness. (In contrast to this, these options for a decision in the normal mode are
consciously present and acknowledged through normal perception,
and then are tested in the manner seen above.) The prophetic
message arises from the perception which flows 'naturally' out of
this lived, graced transcendental openness to God which provides
the horizons in which people and situations are viewed (and consequently as they are seen before God and her will). It can be
seen, therefore, that the difference between the first and second
modes is more a matter of degree than of kind. In the case of the
one, the first mode, the certainty of God's will grounded in the

---

[54]Rahner, *Dynamic Element*, p. 159, n. 42.

experience of congruence and the actual content of God's will form a unity in the subject's experience, whereas in the other, the second mode, they are temporally distinct. That is, in the second mode there are possible expressions of God's will (perceived as the morally permissible possibilities present in a given situation) and then, there follows, through a time of testing, the relative certainty (or sense of congruence) that *this* particular possibility is God's will in this unique situation for this individual (or group). In the first mode, the concrete will of God is simply (and 'directly') known. There may be degrees of directness or indirectness, however, between these two modes.

It is, in any case, this first mode which has been generally conceived as expressing the dynamic operative in prophetic revelation certainly in its more narrow sense. Rahner has concerned himself with this dynamic in various places and has noted that it is essentially the same dynamic whether the revelation is "private" or prophetic. Consequently, what we will be indicating initially concerning this dynamic applies to 'revelations' generally in this somewhat more restricted sense. The only difference between private and prophetic revelations is that one is only directed to the individual receiving the revelation (and therefore is of little concern to the church's life and mission), and the other is directed to others, to the church, and therefore, in particular, raises questions of its genuineness, of whether and how it is 'binding' on the church, of criteria for discernment of its genuineness.[55]

---

[55]Rahner's distinctions are somewhat fluid here. He also distinguishes (following theological tradition) between "mystical" and "prophetic" visions. Both are understood as private revelations; however, the first is solely personal and the second is addressed to others. Rahner notes that in Catholic mystical theology the prophetic element has been devalued in favor of mystical experience. Rahner raises the question as to what extent an imageless, almost purely transcendental experience of God can be considered 'Christian', considering the significance of the incarnation and the word. While there are many dangers and risks to prophetism, prophetic reality is essential to the life of the church. Furthermore, Rahner notes that "orthodox theology has never paid any serious attention to the question whether there are prophets even in post-apostolic times, how their spirit can be

In order to clarify more concretely the kind of phenomena we have in mind when referring to 'direct' revelations, we can recall some of the prophetic manifestations mentioned in the first chapter. We are thinking of 'literary visions', in which words or thoughts come to the mind of the prophet; 'imaginary visions', in which images come to the mind which then need to be interpreted; 'symbolic perceptions', in which a perceived material object takes on special meaning; 'intellectual visions', or a spiritual sense of things; and also 'corporeal' visions and auditions.[56] In each case, we are assuming that these 'revelations' are received in the consciousness of the prophet (or in the case of private revelations, in the mind of the 'mystic') as a message from God.

In order to grasp more fully the nature of this experience of 'direct revelations' we will focus on 'imaginative visions'. By doing so we are able to draw from a work by Rahner, entitled *Visions and Prophecies*, written the same year as the *Dynamic Element in the Church* (and therefore "Individual Concrete Knowledge").[57] On the one hand, it lifts up the importance of the prophetic element in the church and calls for a theology of prophecy; on the other hand, it is a critique of Catholic fundamental and mystical theologies' criteria for recognizing genuine visions as well as a critical assessment of the significance of visions in the life of the church. For the most part, Rahner's concern in this work for recognizing genuine revelations is with the criteria. In addition to this, however, he provides some direction for an understanding of the dynamic nature of visions.

---

recognized and discerned, what their role is in the Church, what their relationship to the hierarchy, what the important of their mission for the exterior and interior life of the Church" (*Visions and Prophecies*, pp. 18-20, 21).

[56]For Rahner's brief treatment of the classical typology of visions, see *Visions and Prophecies*, pp. 31-41; and cf. Underhill's treatment in *Mysticism*, pp. 266-97.

[57]The original German edition of Rahner's *Visions and Prophecies* is *Visionen und Prophezeiungen* (Freiburg: Herder, 1958). *Visionen und Prophezeiungen* was vol. 4 in the *Questiones Disputatae* series (German edition), *Das Dynamische*, vol. 5.

As we previously mentioned, visions have been classified in mystical literature as being of three kinds: the corporeal, the imaginative, and the spiritual. We have already indicated that the corporeal vision is a vision in which the content of the vision is experienced as affecting the senses from the outside as an objective external reality. The notion that the vision is in fact an objective reality, really corporeal, is, as Rahner puts it, a judgment concerning this perception (on the part of the visionary) which we can assume is false.[58] We can assume with Rahner that such corporeal visions are in essence imaginative visions although they can be distinguished from other imaginative visions by their being experienced as objective in an external sense as over against those imaginative visions that are experienced as being an object of the imagination or as being in the 'mind's eye'. Our concerns at this point include both kinds of imaginative visions (understood in the way just indicated).

In regard to these imaginative visions, then, Rahner would have us recognize two essential elements. First, visions must conform to the psychical structure of the knowing subject; they must be acts which "express the laws of the person's ontological structure . . ." Secondly, in order to be genuine visions 'from the Lord', they must be caused by God.[59]

In the case of the first element certain psychological implications can be recognized in a general way. First, a *species sensibilis* or phantasm (image) is produced. This *species sensibilis impressa* can take on many forms as it affects different kinds of senses or all the senses, internal or external (that is, affecting an imaginative

---

[58]The problems with assuming that corporeal visions are in reality corporeal are numerous and possibly obvious enough so that we do not need to go into them here. Rahner lifts up a number of problems with such an assumption in *Visions and Prophecies*, pp. 33-41. While Rahner is cautious with excluding entirely the possibility of corporeality–it cannot be disproved–he nevertheless presumes all visions are imaginative (except, of course, for "spiritual visions" which are not visions in the strict sense). See *Visions and Prophecies*, pp. 122-31.

[59]Rahner, *Visions and Prophecies*, p. 42.

sense of hearing, smelling, seeing, or, in the case of 'corporeal visions', the experience of an audible sound, the physical sensation of smelling, the sight of an external object). What is particularly significant is that this *species sensibilis impressa* is produced, not by an external stimulus, but from within the subject. It is the result of human subjectivity, rather than the external objective world. At this level, limited simply to a *species sensibilis impressa*, we could speak of an imaginative vision in which what is encountered is with the 'mind's eye'. For those visions in which what is encountered has an 'objective' aspect a second dimension must be recognized in which there is an objectification of this *species sensibilis* so that this object of sense consciousness becomes an object which "is felt to be 'perceived' or only 'imagined'" depending "on the character of the psycho-physical stimulus, i.e., of the *species sensibilis*." That is, this objectification of the *species sensibilis* is felt or judged to be an external reality of perception or an objectification (and corpo-reality) in the imagination alone as this is determined by the nature of the *species sensibilis*.[60]

In the case of the second element, namely the divine causal-ity of the vision, Rahner observes, first of all, that the notion that the vision is 'from God' is ambiguous, for everything is 'from God'. A vision, in fact, can be a gift from God and contribute to a person's faith, although it is only 'natural' in the sense that it is not 'directly' caused by God but only the result of various stirrings from one's subconscious. The kind of vision we are concerned with here, however, is one that is 'supernaturally' caused. In *Visions and Prophecies*, Rahner recognizes two kinds of divine, supernatural causality. The first is that kind we have already indicated by the term "graced transcendentality," and which Rahner also called "supernatural existential." The second has to do with "a divine intervention which partly suspends the laws of nature" or, in other words, a miracle (in the strict sense, as Rahner conceives it).[61] In

---

[60]Ibid., pp. 47-54, 49.

[61]Ibid., p. 45.

considering divine causality at this point, and in anticipation of the line of thought of the next chapter, we can limit ourselves to the first notion of supernatural causality. It is also in keeping with the basic thrust of Rahner's thought. His reference, in this work, to the problematic notion of a miracle as the intervention of the laws of nature can be attributed in part to his respect and caution in regard to the tradition and traditional conceptuality. Nevertheless, he does not seem to be entirely comfortable with this formulation. He notes the difficulty in an actual case with recognizing which kind of 'supernatural' causality is involved, and that one is not more significant (religiously or ontologically) than the other.[62] Furthermore, Rahner's own thought develops substantially in this area. In *Foundations* he recognizes the problems involved in the notion of a miracle as the intervention of the laws of nature (while also recognizing the truth that is being pointed to in this concept) and develops a notion of miracle grounded in human subjectivity and, therefore, in this "supernatural existential" or graced transcendentality.[63] Consequently, we can limit our conception of the divine causality of a vision to the graced transcendentality of the human subject.

Rahner takes up the question of divine causality by asking about "the point of contact of the divine action on the visionary."[64] We can assume, with Rahner, that the sense organs are not directly affected by God. (If that were so we would have to conceive of a 'miracle' understood as a suspension of the laws of nature.[65]) "Rather the vision is a kind of overflow and echo of a more

---

[62]Ibid., pp. 45-46.

[63]We will take up the question of the miracle as sign when we consider more fully the question of criteria for recognizing true prophecy. On a subject like this we can see Rahner's respect for the tradition, the truth that is there, and then the movement–a kind of *Aufhebung*–to a higher viewpoint.

[64]Ibid., p. 55.

[65]Ibid., p. 56, n. 52.

intimate and spiritual process."[66] Rahner does not develop further the nature of this more central spiritual dimension in his work. He does point to the fact that the noted mystics of the church have given little significance to visions because they saw in them only a reflex of the real thing that they were after, namely, union with God (who transcends all images).[67]

Although Rahner does not give a detailed analysis of this central spiritual dimension in *Visions and Prophecies*, we already know that it is the graced transcendental aspect of human reality which must find categorial expression. Insofar as this graced transcendental experience in the individual involves a fundamental receptiveness to the self-communication of God (which this graced transcendental reality is), then there is the basis for perceptions, imaginings, dreams, visions, that arise as expressions of this reality. Visions of a paranormal character cannot be viewed, by reason of their paranormality, as being any more expressive of this transcendental dimension than more ordinary activities of perception. Many of the so-called 'mystics' in the history of the church, as Rahner points out, may have simply had a propensity for these psychic phenomena which have the same character as hallucinations and other eidetic phenomena, which in other cases have a merely 'natural' cause.[68] What we are recognizing, at this point, is that it is this graced transcendental dynamic (as accepted in a foundational and existentiell way) which is being expressed in "imaginative visions" (whatever their form) which gives them the character of genuine visions 'from God'.

This can be extended to 'literary visions' also in which words, thoughts, propositions come to the mind of the prophet. There is little to distinguish the literary vision from the imaginative vision, for words, after all, are not imageless. The same essential dynamic

---

[66]Ibid., p. 56.

[67]Ibid., p. 56, n. 53; p. 57.

[68]Ibid., p. 55, n. 51.

is at work. The phenomenon of words and images arising seemingly from the subconscious (for a modern conceptuality) into consciousness (as if from 'nowhere') is an experience everyone can identify with (with some reflection). The experience of coming to an insight which must take on conceptual form is of this nature also. Creative, artistic people often have an abundance of such experiences. We think of the musician who can hardly write down the musical score to keep up with her imagination or the poet who brims over with thoughts and images and impressions.[69] The point that we need to see is that this very 'natural' experience can *also* give expression to the deeper spiritual reality of one's "fundamental option" or, in other words, of faith. When this expression is not merely a private affair but extends to a perception of the historical situation, the church, the world, then that expression can be understood as prophetic.

Summary

In the foregoing discussion we have recognized those aspects of the dynamic element in human experience which Rahner has identified as the general moral faith-instinct and individual concrete knowledge and the latter's acute manifestations in 'direct revelations'. We further saw that these modes of knowing are grounded in a "graced transcendentality" and in faith. We have seen in this human and Christian experience a dynamic element which corresponds to our initial observations of the character of prophetic perception. We have been considering a mode of knowing which arises from a faith-stance and grasps the unique and timely imperative or call to action or word that must be spoken, and therefore can appropriately be called a prophetic word (at least when it is directed to others).

The discussion up to this point has been largely descriptive

---

[69]We can think of William Blake in whom there is a blending of the visionary and poetic, as well as mystical and prophetic.

rather than explanatory. In the following chapter we will expand on our theme by providing an ontological basis for understanding this prophetic experience as Rahner has delineated it.

Chapter III

Anthropological Foundations of Prophecy

We have already noted that the predominant question for many people today regarding the notion of prophecy as a message from God is how an obviously human word can also be divine. We have seen that this divine origination of the message is precisely what the prophets claim; they believe they are bearers of a revelation from God. We have, furthermore, considered in the previous chapter an aspect of cognitive and volitional experience which bears the marks of a prophetic kind of knowing. We may not be able to relate this experience to our own in some of its more acute and intense forms, but nevertheless, we can perceive at least the roots of some of the more extraordinary experiences in the common human cognitive reality we share. In "individual concrete knowledge," as Rahner has described it, Christians and human beings, generally, through reflected self-awareness, can discover an aspect of their own struggles with decision making and self-direction. In this mode of knowing we perceived the importance of a transcendental dimension which seemed to indicate that this cognitional reality was grounded in an unthematic experience of God. It is to this aspect of knowledge that we will give special attention in this chapter.

What we are attempting to see is that, in Rahner's thinking, the prophetic element can be shown to be *intelligible* and *necessary* to being human. Rahner's approach is anthropological.[1] He seeks

---

[1]See especially Rahner's essay "The Theological Dimension of the Question About Man," *TI* 17:53-70. There he notes that "[t]he Christian message which is to be conveyed to men and women does not mean conveying something alien and external. It means awakening and interpreting the inner-most things in man, the ultimate depths of his existence's dimensions" (p. 67).

Rahner is concerned to demonstrate that the essence of Christianity is not by-passed by attending to the question about the human being. Attention to the anthropological problem raises the question of God and God's revelation. This is the case not only from the standpoint of a 'natural theology' but also because of the nature of God's self-revelation. God's self-communication in the human being is an existential-ontological reality. Revelation is not to be understood as a super-structure (on the essence of the human being understood 'naturally'), which never enters into human existential experiences, nor *only* as a past historical event (p. 58). Rather God's revelation is an experienced reality and, consequently, when we attend to our experience and reflect upon it we are confronted with the question of God and his revelation.

In this essay, Rahner moves beyond the traditional (scholastic and ortho-dox) approach which views "revelation as one individual, particular source of knowledge along side others belonging to secular empiricism and the philosophy of man." A theological anthropology that is developed within such a framework asserts "particular facts about man which can be known only through its own source of knowledge and which differ from what the secular human sciences have to say." In contrast, Rahner believes there is a theological dimension to all questions about the human being or, in other words, all anthropological questions when pushed radically enough turn into the "one theological question." It is a matter of seeing the questions (of secular sciences) about the human being in their radical depth (pp. 57, 60).

The question may be raised as to what happens to a Christian anthropology based on revelation if such a theological anthropology is viewed as only the radical development of a secular anthropology. Rahner's answer to this question involves the recognition that revelation as the self-communication of God is an existential for all humanity (at least in the form of offer). The human being's experience (in knowledge and freedom) and orientation to incomprehensible mystery which is God is the basis for the theological dimension of all anthropological assertions. In this view, the experience of revelation is foundational to the human being's experience of self and world. This does not do away with the traditional view of revelation as the explicit, historical event of God's revelation in Jesus Christ (which is now preserved and passed on in the *kerygma* and teaching of the church), but rather this historical event of revelation is the culmination of human self-transcendence which is always also historical; the self-revelation of God is both the end and quasi-formal cause of created reality, and therefore is foundational for the experience of grace (and therefore 'revelation') everywhere and at all times. Consequently, it should be possible for a theological anthropology to begin and to show what there is about being human which is sufficient to explain Christian experience, the experience of God's revelation. He asks about the a priori conditions for the possibility of God's revelation and therefore of prophecy. In other words, his method is one of transcendental reflection in which that which is most foundational to our experience (and therefore transcends the many forms of our experience) is made the object of reflection. In this chapter we are seeking the transcendental conditions in the human subject which are sufficient to explain prophecy, that is, to make intelligible the knowledge of a unique and timely word directed to others and originating from God.

Prophetic perception, as we have seen, is a form of knowledge in which freedom (and therefore practical reason) dominates, for the knowledge involved here is not so much a grasp of what is, but what ought to be, or what ought to be proclaimed for the new realization of God's will to take place. This practical knowledge certainly includes theoretic knowledge, for it works (as does practical reason generally) with images, concepts, abstract logic, both in its necessary grasp of the historical context, of what *is*, and in its perception of what *ought* to be. Critical and theoretical rationality is an element in practical reason and prophetic knowledge. Nevertheless, prophetic knowledge is essentially a kind of practical knowledge and therefore must be understood primarily as an expression of human freedom; and this is our starting point. We begin with an overview of Rahner's understanding of human freedom. We will be able to see what, for Rahner, are the a priori conditions in being human for a human decision to be a divine decision. This will give us the anthropological basis, in Rahner's thinking, for revelation, for grace, and for the divinely inspired word and decision, and therefore a basis for prophecy but by no

---

end with the human being in his or her experience and history, so that the Christian message can be presented "in such a way that it is really nothing other than the interpretative call of the reality which is experienced and present in the listener himself, even if it is not understood" (pp. 65-67).

means only prophecy. To recognize more acutely the basis in human being for a prophetic dynamic which elicits a provisional word to others, we must also consider the a priori conditions in being human for the unique and timely word and for the possibility of speaking such a word to the other. We will do this by attending to the transcendental dynamic of freedom and love as this has bearing on human individuality in a world constituted by others. We will then give particular attention to the dynamic of hope understood as human transcendence directed to the future which opens up the possibilities for a truly *timely* word. Finally, we will consider, at least in summary form, prophetic revelation within the broader framework of Rahner's theology of revelation.

The Transcendental Conditions for a Human Decision Being a Divine Decision

The prophetic word is a word which calls for action or response and therefore for decision. It seeks to bring to realization God's will in *this* historical moment for *this* particular people or community and therefore seeks *this* community's further self-realization. The prophetic word is itself a decision on the part of the prophet who has decided between possible courses of action or, in other words, who wills or affirms, in his or her perception of the community, a particular direction or message. Furthermore the prophetic word also demands from its listeners a decision, an affirmation in action (whether 'internal' or 'external'). Consequently, the question of how a human word can be a divine word is also a question of how a human decision can be a divine decision. In the case of prophecy, it is primarily such a question. How can an act of human freedom also at the same time be an act of God's creative freedom in the realization of God's will?

In the following pages I will show how, for Rahner, human freedom is dependent on the creative freedom of God. We will see that, just as all knowledge, for Rahner, is grounded in the unthematic 'knowledge' of God, so all decision making and valuing is grounded in the unthematic willing of God. We will see that human transcendentality is an inescapable and "necessary willing" whose term is God, and that free acts of self-determination are dependent on this necessary willing; in fact, they are only free to the extent that they are freely dependent on this 'necessary willing'. We will recognize, furthermore, the reality of a *graced* freedom, and therefore the basis for the prophetic dynamic in which a human decision originates in the creative freedom of God as integral to the particular decision itself.

While the question of human freedom is being addressed directly at this point, nevertheless, we must keep in mind that knowledge and freedom form a unity in the one experience of transcendence. Already in *Hearers of the Word* Rahner formulates a conception of freedom that remains basic to further developments of the notion throughout his theological work. In *Hearers of the Word*, Rahner recognizes the *necessity* of human inquiry. We, as human beings, cannot escape inquiring, and therefore in this necessity of our being we are implicitly affirming the luminosity and openness of being. Furthermore, in every act of affirmation of being, in which we also affirm ourselves (in the self-presence of knowing), we affirm ourselves necessarily. We cannot escape affirming ourselves and therefore such an affirmation is experienced as unconditional. (We do not, that is, already have possession of the fullness of being; we must *inquire* after it.) Therefore, in the act of affirming ourselves, we are unconditionally affirming a contingent reality. Such an unconditional affirmation in its ground is what is also meant by will.[2]

The human being experiences himself or herself as contingent and yet as willing absolutely, and therefore experiences his or her contingent existence as borne by unconditional being, as being "carried by the free power of pure Being."[3] In other words, God's

---

[2]McCool, ed., *A Rahner Reader*, pp. 31-35; Rahner, *Foundations*, pp. 75-81.

[3]McCool, ed., *A Rahner Reader*, p. 34. In the following pages, as is the case here, all quotes from or references to *A Rahner Reader* are from the section of

creative freedom is the ground of his creature's freedom. This 'necessary willing', this inescapable grounding of human willing and action is the transcendental experience which Rahner refers to as the *Vorgriff auf Esse*, which may be translated as the "anticipatory grasp of being" recognizing its nature as the pre-grasp of finite reality, not only in knowing but in willing.[4] Consequently, just as God (as Absolute *Esse*, as the "whither" of this anticipatory grasp) is the ground of human knowing, so also is he the ground of human valuing and willing.[5]

The necessity of human willing does not take away from the freedom of human willing. In fact it is this infinite openness of human transcendence which grounds the possibility of choosing between various possible objects of action. We cannot avoid willing something. Rahner is concerned to point out, however, that our willing is never primarily a matter of choosing arbitrarily between this or that action. It is ultimately a choosing and realizing of ourselves before God.

There is, on the one hand, freedom understood in its origins as the self-determination of the human subject, a self-determination grounded in God's own free, creative determination.

---

the *Reader* which gives portions of Joseph Donceel's translation of *Hörer des Wortes*.

[4]Rahner makes much of the notion of *Vorgriff* as the a priori condition for the possibility of apprehending finite objects, of abstraction and conceptualization, and therefore as the condition for the possibility of what we generally call knowledge. Here we are concerned with this concept as it relates to human freedom and practical knowledge. The concept is, however, foundational in Rahner's thought and is present in his early works as the transcendental basis for the possibility of knowledge as well as the pre-apprehension of God in every act of knowing. See Rahner's doctoral dissertation, *Spirit in the World*, trans. William Dych (New York: Herder & Herder, 1968). Also, McCool, ed., *A Rahner Reader*, for Joseph Donceel's translation of *Hörer des Wortes*.

[5]See James Bresnahan's discussion of Rahner on freedom, particularly for his analysis of Rahner's argument in *Hearers* in "The Methodology of 'Natural Law' Ethical Reasoning in the Theology of Karl Rahner, and Its Supplementary Development Using the Legal Philosophy of Lon L. Fuller" (doctoral dissertation, Yale University, 1972), pp. 180-218.

On the other hand, freedom must also be grasped in its categorial and historical objectification. We can speak, therefore, of the "origins of freedom" and the "spheres of freedom." At this point we are particularly concerned with the origins of freedom. Later we will concern ourselves more directly with the spheres of freedom as we discuss the conditions in human being for a "word for others."

Origins of Freedom

. Our concern here is with freedom in its origins, freedom at its heart and center. In the act of knowing one becomes present to oneself.[6] In human decision (included also as an element in knowing) one actualizes oneself.

> Now, a free act is originally not so much the positing of something else, of something external, of some effect which is distinct from and opposed to the free act itself. It is rather the fulfillment of one's own nature, a taking possession of oneself, of the reality of one's own creative power over oneself. Thus it is a coming to oneself, a self-presence to oneself.[7]

For Rahner human freedom is essentially self-actualization (*Selbsttat*). He has an abundance of terms for expressing this: self-realization (*Selbstverwirklichung*), self-fulfillment (*Selbstvollendung*), self-performance (*Selbstvollzug*), self-disposal or determination (*Selbstverfügung*), self-responsibility (*Selbstverantwortung*), self-possession (*Selbstbesitz*). And in that this self-actualization of freedom is before God, freedom is also self-surrender (*Selbst-übergabe*).[8]

---

[6]In *Spirit in the World* and *Hearers of the Word*, Rahner demonstrates that, in the dynamics of knowing, human beings go out of themselves into the material of the world in order to come to themselves, be present to themselves.

[7]McCool, ed., *A Rahner Reader*, p. 39.

[8]Rahner, "Theologie der Freiheit," *ST* 6: 215-37 and *Grundkurs*, pp. 46-50. The variety of terms Rahner uses does not always come out in the English translation. For example, *Selbsttat, Selbstverwirklichung, Selbstvollzug* are at times all translated by "self-realization."

The experience of freedom is the experience of subjectivity. It cannot be discovered by the empirical sciences as one datum among others. The empirical sciences according to their methodology can properly seek and analyze the causal relations that go into making us what we are as human beings. However, human reality cannot be reduced to the sum total of these material causes. Rather the human reality we are is also the reality of being subjects who reflect, analyze, and decide about those finite causes that make up our existence. Freedom is to be discovered in the experience of being a subject. This transcendental experience in its infinite openness to God means that we become what we are, not simply as the result of a series of finite causes, but by the establishing of ourselves in a definitive and final way. It means that in our temporal passage we are establishing our eternal identity (although it remains hidden) as we receive it from God who is the source and goal of our freedom.[9]

Freedom, therefore, is the making of oneself in response to God. It is not essentially a matter of doing this or that but a doing oneself in a definitive and final way.

> Freedom is, so to speak, the capacity for establishing something necessary, something which lasts, something final and definitive, and wherever there is no freedom, there is always just something which by its nature goes on generating itself, and becoming something else and being reduced to something else in its antecedents and consequences. Freedom is the event of something eternal. But since we ourselves are still coming to be in freedom, we do not exist with and behold this eternity, but in our passage through the multiplicity of the temporal we are performing this event of freedom, we are forming the eternity which we ourselves are and are becoming.[10]

God as the Ultimate Ground
for Human Freedom

Freedom therefore is self-actualization understood not as an

---

[9]Rahner, *Foundations*, pp. 35-39.

[10]Ibid., p. 96.

act of self bent upon itself (an act of egotism) but the determination of the self before God and as coming from God. As the ground of human transcendental openness which makes the grasp of finite objects in knowledge and freedom possible, God is the ground of human freedom, of human self-actualization. Rahner likes to make the point that "the radical dependence and the genuine reality of the existent coming from God vary in direct and not in inverse proportion."[11] Human freedom is increased as it lives in dependence on its ground which is the freedom of God. The possibility of freely willing this or that particular object is grounded in the 'necessary willing' which is the human's infinite transcendental openness to God. Furthermore, since God, as the "whither" (*Woraufhin*) of human transcendence, of the anticipatory grasp of being, is the horizon and goal of this infinite openness, therefore God is also the goal of human freedom. Human freedom is always concerned with God in all its acts. In all finite acts of freedom we are saying yes or no to God (and to ourselves).

In other words, we do not only know and decide about something external to ourselves but rather we know and decide about ourselves and God. The world, history, matter is the medium through which we come to ourselves and to God, and in fact welcome ourselves and become ourselves and in so doing welcome God. In our self-transcendence, in our openness to being we welcome being, welcome our own being and since God as the fullness of being is the 'whither' of this infinite openness, God also is implicitly welcomed in every free act, in every welcoming. This welcoming or love of being is also love of God. "This means that at the heart of the finite spirit's transcendence there lives a love for God." (This love for God can even be understood as an 'inner' moment of knowledge.[12])

Being in its fullness is both present-to-itself and possesses itself. Freedom—and therefore love—is a mark of unconditional

---

[11]Ibid., p. 79.

[12]McCool, ed., *A Rahner Reader*, pp. 40-41.

being. Love

> is, in itself, the unifying and absolutely original essence of all reality, and
> therefore there is nothing apart from it except emptiness and nothingness.
> For it has been written: 'But God is love,' and in these two words man finds
> two different ways of expressing the single infinite mystery of his own
> existence.[13]

'God' is a definitionless term pointing to the "nameless one," to incomprehensible mystery. But that incomprehensible mystery is experienced not only as the infinitely distant horizon which grounds the possibility of categorial knowledge, but also as that term of our transcendence which opens this transcendence in its movement in freedom and love. This nameless mystery is present in loving freedom; it is therefore "*holy* mystery." These two words "express equally the transcendentality both of knowledge and of freedom and love." God is known as "incomprehensible mystery"; God is also freely loved in self-surrender and worship and therefore experienced as *holy* mystery.[14]

This freedom of the human being which is a self-actualization before God always includes a yes or no to God; it includes a self-surrender or a self-refusal, toward God. This necessary loving which is ultimately directed to God grounds a "free loving," a free-welcoming of God. (It also grounds the possibility of a radical "no" to God, a "no" which both rejects the source and term of its fundamental decision and at the same time affirms it implicitly as the unconditional ground of its decision.) The decision for God or the love of God is, furthermore, grounded in human transcendence understood not merely as an infinite reaching out toward a goal never achieved, but rather as a *graced* transcendence in which God gives himself in nearness. It is human freedom as graced freedom which grounds the possibility of a human decision being at the same time a divine decision.

---

[13]Rahner, "Unity-Love-Mystery," *TI* 8:229-50.

[14]Rahner, *Foundations*, pp. 44-51, 65-66.

Graced Freedom

Freedom understood as the love of God that welcomes God's creation into his presence, grounds human freedom as the love that welcomes the coming of God in nearness.[15] God, who expresses himself (in his Logos) and welcomes his own expression of himself, grounds the human being's welcoming of God's expression of himself (his Logos) in his creation (in the incarnation). The welcoming of God's self-communication within humanity is grounded in God's own welcoming of himself. Since God expresses himself in our humanity it is God that we affirm and welcome when we embrace ourselves and our neighbor. It is the triune reality of God that grounds human freedom. Rahner makes the point that freedom (as well as knowledge) is a mark of being. It is *Seinsfreiheit*.[16] It is a mark of not only finite being but of infinite being, of the fullness of being. In the triune reality of God, in which God as incomprehensible mystery (God the Father) expresses himself in his Logos (God the Son) and welcomes and loves his expression (God the Spirit as the *welcoming* of God), God both knows himself (is present to himself) and loves himself (in his self-expression).[17] As God has expressed himself into his creation (and therefore having become not only its efficient cause but quasi-formal cause) and welcomes his own expression of himself, so God's welcoming grounds his creatures' welcoming of his Logos. God, who knows and loves himself, who is present to himself and possesses himself and who is the infinite ground of his finite creature's self-knowledge and self-possession, who is the efficient, creative ground of finite being, has also entered his creation as its

---

[15]For Rahner, of course, the Sign (or real symbol) of God's nearness is Jesus Christ. It is through Christ, the Logos or self-expression of God, that humanity's freedom is a graced freedom.

[16]Rahner, "Theologie der Freiheit," p. 222.

[17]See Rahner, *The Trinity*, trans. Joseph Donceel (New York: Herder & Herder, 1970), in which Rahner seeks to show how the "economic" Trinity is the "immanent" Trinity. See also Rahner, "The Theology of Symbol" and "History of the World and Salvation-History."

inner entelechy achieving its graced self-transcendence in which his creation realizes its goal in the knowledge and love of God in his appearing, in his coming to be present.

This self-communication of God within his creation as its quasi-formal cause which has been achieved in the 'hypostatic union', in Jesus Christ, grounds the *potentia obedientialis* (or created human nature) as that to which this obediential potency is directed. Therefore, freedom as self-surrender to God's coming in nearness is grounded in the self-surrender of Jesus Christ which is at the same time the giving over of God in his Logos to that which is other than himself, and the welcoming of that other which is himself in his Logos. The human being who is the "utterance in which God could empty himself" has been welcomed as the other of God's self-utterance by God's emptying himself into the other of his creation, and this also means that God's emptying and welcoming grounds the human welcoming of God in his Logos (and therefore at the same time the welcoming of oneself).[18] The offer and acceptance of God's self-communication is a characteristic of human transcendentality which Rahner refers to as the 'supernatural existential'.[19] It is the transcendental movement of

---

[18]Rahner, *Foundations*, pp. 212-28, 224.

[19]One of the ways Rahner expresses the bestowal of grace upon all human beings as essential to their being is by the term, "supernatural existential." By 'supernatural' he is indicating the graced character of this human reality; that this reality is not only of the order of creation, but of redemption. And yet the order of creation is assumed as an essential factor in it, in that nature has been elevated in *human* nature to a graced reality. It has been elevated by 'uncreated grace'. By "existential" he is indicating that this supernatural element of grace is essential to the being of the human being in human existing. Grace, therefore, is not to be understood as a superstructure upon nature which does not enter into human reality in an existential-ontological sense nor as the supernatural elevating of some while others remain 'natural'. Because of the incarnation there is no merely 'natural' human reality. To be human is to be supernaturally elevated into the holy mystery which is God. Nature is the precondition for the acceptance of grace. The self-transcendence of nature in *human* nature which is open in its infinite orientation for the self-expression of God has been taken up by this Logos of God and therefore 'graced'. With the incarnation, nature has been graced, and this

freedom as self-surrender before God who has come near.

> This antecedent self-communication of God which is prior to man's freedom means nothing else but that the spirit's transcendental movement in knowledge and love towards the absolute mystery is borne by God himself in his self-communication in such a way that this movement has its term and its source not in the holy mystery as eternally distant and as a goal which can only be reached asymptotically but rather in the God of absolute closeness and immediacy.[20]

Freedom is freedom toward God; it is ultimately the loving acceptance of God's gracious giving of himself and at the same time the acceptance of one's own self as it comes from God who is its infinite ground and goal.

Freedom has to do with the human being as a single reality and as a whole. It has to do with his or her "fundamental option." Freedom in this sense has to do with the basic thrust of a person's life before God. The self-realization which is the fundamental task of every human being is a self-realization towards God, or self-refusal which says "no" to God. We have already recognized that in every free grasp of finite reality in concept or action there is the free embrace and welcome of self and God (who is the ground of the experience of the self and finite reality). Freedom is not to be thought of in an atomistic way as dispersed among an indefinite number of finite choices, but rather as the one fundamental disposing of one's existence, a self-disposal which is borne by God's

---

graced reality of nature is an existential for all human beings. See Rahner, *Foundations*, pp. 126-33; *Nature and Grace: Dilemmas in the Modern Church*, trans. Dinah Wharton (New York: Sheed & Ward, 1964), chap. 5, "Nature and Grace," pp. 114-49; *The Christian Commitment: Essays in Pastoral Theology*, trans. Cecily Hastings (New York: Sheed & Ward, 1963), chap. 2, "The Order of Redemption within the Order of Creation," pp. 38-64. In the above essay Rahner distinguishes between grace-nature and order of redemption-order of creation. Grace is distinguished from nature as the reality which is conferred on nature by God as a gift (of himself). The "order of redemption" expresses the concrete actualization of graced nature and as such "includes the order of creation as an essential factor in it" (p. 41). Furthermore, graced nature is divinized *human* nature.

[20]Rahner, *Foundations*, p. 129.

disposal of his creation.[21] All acts of freedom are grounded in the one self-determination of the subject in freedom before God.

This does not mean that all acts contain the same level of commitment or self-disposal. We have recognized that an element of volition exists in knowledge. However, the difference between the knowledge of a mathematical equation and the categorial knowledge of God reveals an aspect of the nature of volition in terms of the commitment involved. That mathematical knowledge may appear to be more certain than the knowledge of God is not because it is more 'self-evident', but because it is peripheral to our lives. It is that reality which is most central to our lives, to the realization of our selves, that requires the greatest commitment, and without that commitment or will, knowledge is unobtainable.[22] We are reminded of the words of Jesus in the gospel of John: "If any man's will is to do his [God's] will he shall know . . ." (For Rahner, God is the only "self-evident" reality for he is unthematically experienced in every act of knowledge and freedom as their ground.) Some acts take on more of the character of self-disposal than others, depending on what finite object or value they are directed to. While all our coming to God in knowledge and freedom is a coming to God through finite reality (and always and everywhere), this 'coming to God' (and to ourselves) is most fully realized in our relation to our neighbor.

We might add at this point that this coming to God or self-disposal before God is always also a being set free from sin. The self-communication of God is a forgiving self-communication. This means for freedom that the grace of God breaks the "bondage of will," setting freedom free.

---

[21]For Rahner's discussion of "fundamental option," see Rahner, "Guilt-Responsibility-Punishment within the View of Catholic Theology," *TI* 6:197-217. See also "The Commandment of Love in Relation to the Other Commandments," *TI* 5:431-59. On the experience of God and self see "Experience of Self and Experience of God," *TI* 13:122-32.

[22]McCool, ed., *A Rahner Reader*, pp. 44-45.

> Even in the Catholic, and not only in the Protestant view of the relation between God and man the freedom of the latter as derived only from himself is guilty and imprisoned egoism; hence as far as he is concerned, this freedom refuses to accept God's self-communication and to let God be God. Hence God's grace, which ultimately means himself, must set freedom free for God.[23]

Freedom, therefore, when it is set free from its bondage to sin is free "to receive God from God through God" so that all of a human being's reality expresses either a being set free by God's grace or a free and yet guilty refusal of God.[24]

What we have been attempting to recognize is that a human decision can be a divine decision, and is a 'divine decision' insofar as it is freely dependent (that is, rather than a dependence in opposition to) on that 'necessary willing', that anticipatory grasp (*Vorgriff*), whose term is God. Since God, as the term of this transcendental reaching out is not merely the asymptotic goal which provides the illimited reach within which objects of value can be perceived but is rather the goal which has been achieved through the incarnation, God is present in the decision as its "quasi-formal" cause; in other words, God's will is present in the decision as he bears human willing to himself. We can see that human decision making is inescapably dependent on the creative freedom of God and that, because this decision making is dependent on a *graced* transcendentality, it cannot escape the presence and will of God in every decision. This means that in every decision one is confirming one's fundamental option of a yes or no to the presence of God and to his will. This is true of human action, generally. In the case of prophetic perception and action, however, what we can recognize is that an individual, in solidarity with others, perceives the call to action for others as that call is recognized within the horizons of a free and loving self-surrender or free dependence on

---

[23]Rahner, *Grace in Freedom*, trans. Hilda Graef (New York: Herder & Herder, 1969), p. 229.

[24]Ibid.

God who is both the origin of that freedom and its means. For the prophet, this prophetic decision involves a decision for God; to refuse to proclaim the word would be to refuse God. We can only note the sense of constraint on the part of prophets, as if they can do no other than to speak, even at times as if their own salvation depended on it.

It is clear in the case of the prophet that the message or action of the prophet is integrally related to the being or identity of the prophet. We have been considering in general terms how a human decision can be a divine decision and how the free act of the prophet of necessity must be grounded in the freedom of God. At this point, however, we need to give further attention to the significance of human freedom as the self-actualization of a particular individual or group. As we have seen, freedom must be understood as self-disposal or self-determination. Freedom has to do with the coming to be of oneself and the expression of oneself. For the prophet or prophetic community, it means the coming to be of a prophetic self, a word of self which is a word of God, and therefore a prophetic word. Freedom as self-realization before God is the a priori condition for the possibility of a truly individual and unique word, the coming-to-be of the expression of a unique self, with a unique calling. With this in mind we will now consider more fully the ontological foundations, in Rahner, for an *individual* concrete knowledge.

Ontological Foundations of an Individual Concrete Knowledge

General Anthropological Observations

In Chapter II we recognized that, for Rahner, there are two basic aspects of conscience or practical reason, namely, a general and an individual moral knowledge. Corresponding to these aspects of practical reason are two aspects of human *being* which Rahner distinguishes, and which we can term 'common human nature' and 'individual human nature'; and also, correspondingly, human nature as immutable and mutable.

'Common human nature' is a reference to that which is essential to being human which all human beings participate in 'by nature'. For example, 'by nature' (as supernaturally elevated) all human beings participate in 'grace' (at least as offered); it is an ontological necessity in being human. Rahner uses the term "person" to point to the reality of the individual person's necessary, personal, existential (and therefore individual and unique) appropriation of that which the person is 'by nature'. 'Individual nature', therefore, refers to that dimension of being human which, for each individual person, constitutes his or her spiritual uniqueness. Correspondingly, it can be said that there is a universal and immutable aspect to human being which applies necessarily to all human reality and also a mutable aspect to human being which allows for the free decision and personal appropriation of each person's unique and individual nature. This latter aspect of human being has been largely ignored in natural law theory.

Traditionally, natural law theory has operated with the concept of the substantial form or the immutable essence of the human being (following the line of thought of Aristotle and Thomas Aquinas) which accounts for the possibility of an essential ethics. Rahner seeks to maintain this natural law position while expanding it with the notion of a "formal existential ethics." This expansion of natural law theory is based in the recognition of human subjectivity which has come to explicit attention in modern philosophical movements (since Descartes and Kant). The former traditional theory tended to be developed in a cosmocentric way; that is, natural law and human essence were conceived in a way analogous to 'things' which do not act on themselves and change themselves in a definitive way. Human self-actualization, as we have been noting in our discussion of freedom, is a realization and determination of one's own nature and not merely the accidental modification of a static substance. Rahner's anthropocentric approach takes seriously this subjective and personal reality of the human being and its significance for a theological ethics.[25]

The human being as transcendental subject and person determines his or her essence (although this self-determination always takes place in the midst of that which is already given and therefore out of human control). Human essence, therefore, in this respect, is not only malleable, determinable, subject to change, but *must* be determined and changed, for this self-determination is the expression of the essential reality of being human. But this means also that there is something about human essence which is not subject to change; for human transcendentality and self-determination (which is always historical, finding categorial expression) are essential to being human in a primary way and therefore are immutable. We cannot deliver ourselves from our transcendentality (and remain human) even when we deny explicitly this transcendental reality; nor can we remove through our self-determination the given predetermined material nature in which our transcendentality expresses itself. Consequently, Rahner can speak of an immutable or 'inner' essence as well as a mutable essence. We really do determine what we are to become and therefore determine our essence; and yet we cannot alter the necessity of this transcendentally grounded self-determination as irrevocably essential to our humanity or the necessity of its being historically expressed.

Furthermore, we might add, the question can be raised as to *what* human activity is appropriate to this immutable essence and therefore of concern to the development of an essential ethics, and what belongs to the truly malleable, mutable nature of the human being and cannot, therefore, be designated as *in principle* essential to human reality. Since this necessary, essential nature of the

---

[25]*SM*, v.s. "Person: 2. Man, c. Theological," by Karl Rahner. See also Rahner, *Spiritual Exercises,* trans. Kenneth Baker (New York: Herder & Herder, 1965), pp. 115-16 and "The Dignity and Freedom of Man, *TI* 2:233-63. Also, Peter Eicher, *Die anthropologische Wende: Karl Rahners philosophischer Weg vom Wesen Des Menschen zur personalen Existens* (Universitätsverlag Freiburg Schweiz, 1970), pp. 356-64.

human being is always expressed within categorial and provisional historical reality, it is not always entirely clear what is provisional and mutable, and what is necessary to the human being's transcendental nature and therefore immutable. Furthermore, Rahner does not assume that only the immutable essence of the human being provides us with what is normative. Rather, the nature of the individual, of the person, of the unique situation, of historical destiny is also the basis for what is 'normative' in human life or, in other words, there is an *individual* essential reality (and not only an essential reality that refers to the universal and general, to 'humankind').[26] Consequently, there is an "essential (and general) ethics" which corresponds to the immutable essence of the human being and to 'common human nature' and an "individual existential ethics" which corresponds to the uniqueness of the individual and human historical destiny.[27] We have recognized in Chapter II a "general moral faith-instinct" which corresponds to this immutable and universal essence, at least as it finds expression in each new historical moment as a result of a self-awareness of a common shared humanity encountering the new historical situation. The "individual concrete knowledge" dealt with in the same chapter does not strictly correspond to the "mutable essence" as described above; but rather, the mutable aspect of human nature allows for the unique nature of the individual. It is the nature of individuality which necessitates an individual concrete knowledge. It is to the nature of individuality that we now turn.

The Nature of Individuality

Rahner's ontological observations on this subject begin to be formulated very early in his writing career, and although they never achieve a detailed elaboration, nevertheless, they do give a philosophical foundation to his epistemology of individual concrete

---

[26]Rahner, "Genetic Manipulation," pp. 230-32.

[27]Rahner, "Formal Existential Ethics," pp. 215-34 and *Dynamic Element*, pp. 13-41.

knowledge. Already in 1946 in his essay "Der Einzelne in der Kirche," published in *Simmen der Zeit*, Rahner suggests some preliminary philosophical observations about individuality, although he believes he cannot elaborate more fully an ontology of the individual; for it would not, in any case (at least at the time), meet with general acceptance.[28] The point he does make is that the concept of the 'individual' is correlative to (and not the opposite of) 'common' or 'community'. It is only seen as opposite on the spiritual-personal level when it is assumed to be absolute and therefore opposed to 'community', except as community is allowed in the sense of an aggregate on the material level (in which case we have individualism). (To understand community only in terms of the material-biological sphere is collectivism.) Rahner points out that 'individuality' does not always mean the same thing; it is an analogical concept which varies in its meaning with the degree of being that is conceived. Being in its lowest degree is merely closed into itself, into its own singularity as distinct from other forms of being, and can only go outside of itself by being possessed and changed into that which is other than itself. The highest degree of being, on the other hand,

> is the greatest mystery of our Faith, the most perfect individuality who, in the fullest sense, exists for his own sake and is immutable, but nevertheless excludes nothing of the perfection of any other being, having all reality within himself; who gives himself totally and yet for this very reason possesses himself most completely; in whom perfect individuality and perfect community do not conflict but *are* each other.[29]

The human being is situated between these two ontological extremes. On the one hand, our 'individuality' is expressed in the

---

[28]Rahner, "Der Einzelne in der Kirche," *Stimmen der Zeit* 139 (1946). Later published in Rahner, *Gefahren Im Heutigen Katholizismus* (Einsiedeln: Johannes Verlag, 195), pp. 11-38. It can be found in translation in Rahner, *Nature and Grace: Dilemmas in the Modern Church* (New York: Sheed & Ward, 1964), pp. 9-38.

[29]Rahner, *Nature and Grace*, pp. 13-14.

delimitation of *matter* by which we are confined to *this* particular expression of the one common humanity. On the other hand, our individuality is an expression of *spirit*, of subjectivity, an expression of our infinite openness which as open to being in its totality is the basis for the possibility of being a partaker in the perfect individuality of God.[30]

In "On the Question of a Formal Existential Ethics" (first published as "Über die Frage einer formalen Existentialethik" in 1955), in which Rahner calls for the development of a formal existential-ethics (a logic of individual concrete knowledge), he again takes up the question of a theology and a positive ontology of the individual.[31]

> Man is destined to eternal life as an individual and someone in the concrete. His acts are, therefore, not merely of a spatio-temporal kind as is the case with material things; his acts have a meaning for eternity, not only morally but also *ontologically*. . . . Man with his mental and moral acts, therefore, cannot be merely the appearance of the universal and of what is–in this universality alone–'eternal' and ever-valid in the negative expansion of space and time. In him, the individual, there must rather be a given [sic] a positive reality; expressed differently: his spiritual individuality cannot be (at least not in his acts) merely the circumscription of an in itself universal nature through the negativity of the *materia prima*, understood as the mere repetition of the same thing at different points in space-time.[32]

Rahner believes this spiritual individuality is not unthomistic; the ontological basis for it can be found in Thomas's assertion that "God cannot even *de potentia absoluta* create a second Gabriel."[33] It is possible, that is, to conceive of the notion of the individual which is not merely subsumed under the universal as one of many repeated expressions of the ideal.

---

[30]Ibid., pp. 14-16.

[31]Rahner, "Über die Frage einer formalen Existentialethik," *ST* 2:227-46.

[32]Rahner, "Formal Existential Ethics," pp. 225-26.

[33]Ibid., p. 226.

Anyone, however, who can grasp this thomistic thought of something real which cannot be subsumed unequivocally under a universal idea or under a law, cannot reject the idea from the very start that something like this is conceivable–indeed, must be postulated–also in man as a spiritual person, as that existent who does not resolve himself completely into *forma-materiae-esse*. We may also say: if (and in so far as) man as a spiritual person participates by his acts in the permanency-in-itself in its ordination to matter as the principle of repeatability, then he must also participate in that spiritual individuality which is not merely the sameness of the repeated universal and not merely a case of the law.[34]

In Rahner's view, the notion of *forma-materiae-esse* applies to all created reality. That is, an existing reality is the material appearance or individuation of its formal (and universal) essence (and therefore its delimitation to *this* and not *that*, and to this *kind* of this) in its act of existing. Human reality can be conceived along these lines but must not be reduced to this ontological conceptuality, for human reality is not merely the repeatable material expression of a universal essence locked up in a material individuation. Rather, *human* being, by virtue of being not only matter, closed into itself, but spirit, infinitely open and therefore positively active in the definitive making of itself, is individually unique in a positive sense. Human being actualizes itself, *becomes* its unique self through knowledge and love, through its transcendental openness to the infinite God who gives it, its unique identity.

We have referred to the immutable and mutable nature of the human being. We can expand on this somewhat at this point. The individual human being shares in the universal nature of a common humanity which has an essential immutability and yet also has a mutable aspect which in the individual expression of this universal nature allows for the expression of the individual's unique nature. In this sense, we can speak of a unique substantial form or essence of the individual. The individual, therefore, is not merely the material expression of the universal but of an individual and unique essence which the universal nature allows. This indi-

---

[34]Ibid.

vidual nature does not express something opposed to and outside the bounds of the universal but something more specific which is, in fact, the individual's destiny and the direction of history.

Consequently, there is an essential (and general) ethics grounded in (or abstracted from) the universal nature which all human beings have in common and are subject to and an existential-ethics of the individual whose material content can only be discovered by the individual in his or her concrete activity and in response to his or her unique calling.

> . . . in so far as man belongs to the material world by his concrete activity, his activity is an instance and fulfilment of something universal which determines his actions as something different from the individual and [standing over against him] i.e. as *law* expressed in universal propositions. Insofar as the same man subsists in his own spirituality, his actions are also always more than mere applications of the universal law to the *casus* in space and time; they have a substantial positive property and uniqueness which can no longer be translated into a universal idea and norm expressible in propositions constructed of universal notions. At least in his actions, man is really also (not only) *individuum ineffabile*, whom God has called by his name, a name which is and can only be unique, so that it really is worthwhile for this unique being as such to exist for all eternity.[35]

Rahner recognizes that the human moral situation is not only governed by the 'law', by a universal ethics; but rather that within the individual situation there may be a variety of morally permissible actions which could be taken under the law and yet which, for the individual, are not all morally justifiable, for the individual may perceive that one among a number of actions is the one that must be taken in this situation, at this time, because of who he or she is as an individual in his or her own positive individuality.

By its very nature there can be no individual existential-ethics of a material nature, for the content of such an ethics is individual, corresponding to the uniqueness of the individual's destiny and the

---

[35]Ibid., pp. 226-27. The translation in *TI* ("opposed to it") does not accurately express the sense of the German, *ihm Gegenu berstehendes* ("Existentialethik," p. 238). The universal stands over against the human being as law.

historical moment.   Nevertheless, there can be an individual existential-ethics of a formal nature; that is, "the formal structures and the basic manner of perceiving such an existential-ethic reality" can be developed.[36]

Rahner, as we have seen, has given us a formal existential-ethic in his essay, "The Logic of Concrete Individual Knowledge in Ignatius Loyola." There he also reflects briefly on an ontology of the individual. He notes again that, while Thomism lacks such an ontology, the concept can be found in Thomas's idea of angels since, for Thomas, angels do not subsist in matter and therefore are not subject to this material principle of individuation but rather receive their individuality from the uniqueness of their substantial form which is unrepeatable.[37] As we saw above, Rahner believes that something of this angelic ontology must be developed in regard to the human being. The self-subsistent form of the human individual

> . . . must share the specific individuality of the angels, because it is not
> completely "immersed" in, communicated to, material space and time which
> is the principle of numerical multiplicability and repetition of what is
> identical, as opposed to the individual distinctiveness of a number of
> singular terms.[38]

Obviously, Thomistic angelic ontology cannot be brought as a whole into a consideration of an anthropological ontology which would include a great many nuances. What would have to be asserted, for Rahner, in an ontology of the human being, as we have noted, is that there is both an *in materia subsistere* and an *in se subsistere* and that these are "dialectically contrapuntal and only in their unity state the distinctive constitution of the human

---

[36]Ibid., p. 229.

[37]Rahner's own view of angel mythology is that it expresses a natural and, in a sense, a material reality. In fact, for Rahner, there is no created reality that is not subject to the principle of 'prime matter'. See Rahner, "On Angels," pp. 235-74.

[38]Rahner, *Dynamic Element*, p. 112.

spirit . . ."[39] Because human beings not only subsist in matter but subsist in themselves, their actions and the imperatives to act, which they experience, are not only the expression of the universal (as that subsists in matter) but also express the uniqueness of spiritual persons. But this also means, as we have seen, that there are imperatives which "cannot be known solely by methods of abstraction and sense experience, which is always an experience of a material particular, an individual instance."[40]

Individuality and Prophetic Experience

We have seen above that human transcendentality, on the one hand, grounds the possibility for self-determination and therefore excludes individual human reality from merely a material individuation; and, on the other hand, as *graced*, human transcendentality grounds the possibility of realizing individual reality as the unique call of God who establishes his creatures' identity. As such, this aspect of being human provides the ontological basis and necessity of the experience of coming to know the unique word of prophetic perception. In other words, the unique and timely word of a prophetic character is *necessary* if the human being is, in fact, spirit; that is, if human reality is constituted by a graced transcendentality which is essentially a receptivity for God's actual self-revelation in which the true individuality of the human being is known and experienced as coming from God who is absolutely incalculable and uncontrollable (rather than merely the result of the particularity given by 'matter'). Furthermore, this ontology of the individual provides the ontological grounds for the experience of individual calling and therefore of the prophet's experience of vocation as the bearer of the unique and timely message 'from the Lord'. The prophet is the person who, through the 'logic of individual concrete knowledge', comes to realize this unique message and mission (which are both integral to his or her

---

[39]Ibid., p. 113.

[40]Ibid., p. 114.

individual nature). Furthermore, the message and mission of the prophet, as we shall see, are integral to the individuals or people (and their unique nature) to which he or she is sent. Nations, societies, communities, and civilizations in each new historical moment come to be, not merely as the result of past configurations or as the material expression of universal human nature, but also as a response to new visions, decisions, initiatives of an individual, unique character, a response which may be understood as reaching out to the absolute future, that is, to the extent that those decisions are freely dependent (at least implicitly) on the creative freedom of God. Thus this individual aspect of human reality, of a spiritual nature, can be applied even to the human family and its history.

Clearly when Rahner speaks of an individual concrete knowledge he means a knowledge fitted for the individual concrete person, group, or society and not only knowledge of an individual for the individual. In relation to prophetic knowledge we are concerned with knowledge which comes to the individual for the sake of the other. The question we must now address is, What makes possible not only a 'private revelation' but a prophetic revelation, a word for the other? In seeking to address this question we must consider further the dimensions of human freedom. We must recognize that freedom comes to expression in the material of this world, a world of others, and that transcendental love is a condition for the knowledge of the other.

Transcendental Love and the Knowledge of the Other

Human Bodiliness and the Objectification of Freedom as a Condition of Intercommunication

Human transcendentality has a history. In human freedom subjects possess themselves, actualizing themselves by going outside themselves in the possession and determination of what is other than themselves, always at the same time expressing themselves in the other and becoming themselves (or refusing themselves) through the other. In their possessing and determining the other they also possess and determine themselves. In fact the other (which includes their bodiliness) can be understood, in a sense, as an extension of themselves. The material world is an extension of the selves of subjects and their actions and, as such, is a condition of creaturely freedom.

In his essay "The Body in the Order of Salvation," Rahner directs us to our experience of bodiliness. "Through bodiliness the whole world belongs to me from the start, in everything that happens." He points out that we cannot think in a simplistic way of our body as ending with our skin. Rather there is a sense in which (and from the vantage point of a modern physics) "we are all living in one and the same body—the world." Our bodiliness is the sphere of intercommunication with others. We live in the sphere of others. Furthermore, bodiliness is the means by which we 'appear' to each other. It is our utterance or expression of ourselves and this happens in the 'space' in which others express themselves. "In his bodily nature [the human being] enters into a sphere which does not belong to him alone." Rahner makes the point that the human being necessarily utters himself or herself; it is essential to human nature. Consequently, Rahner indicates that "there is no 'inwardness' which does not stand open, as it were, to what is without."[41] Freedom, which is grounded in human transcendence, is only realized in its objectification.

Human beings, in realizing their essential nature, necessarily utter themselves. This does not mean that their expression of themselves is unambiguous. Rather, since the bodily nature of human being involves a synthesis of the expression of the self-determination of the subject, on the one hand, and 'external' forces and influences, on the other, there is an ambiguity that can never be eliminated. There can be no clear, unambiguous differentiation made between that in human expression which is the result of self-determination and that which is received from 'without'. Never-

---

[41]Rahner, "The Body in the Order of Salvation," *TI* 17: 86-88.

theless, it is constitutive of human reality to express itself. (Consequently, Rahner can say that it was necessary that the Logos of God become flesh.) This means, in other words, that 'the other' always necessarily enters into the reality of the individual. There is no merely 'private' experience or knowledge. Nor is there any purely spiritual experience: "The loftiest spiritual thought, the most sublime moral decision, the most radical act of a responsible liberty is still a bodily perception or a bodily decision."[42] And therefore open, in a sense, to the other.

Therefore, it can also be said that the most 'spiritual', charismatic knowledge also involves knowledge of the other. It is never 'purely' spiritual but is mediated by and dependent on an a posteriori knowledge. Even a so-called 'private revelation' is not entirely private but comes to expression in the self-realization of the individual in community, at least implicitly, and in that sense also has a prophetic, outward-to-others dynamic. Rahner makes the point that "there are no spheres which can be clearly separated from one another in an existential cleavage."[43] My individual and 'private' reality is also always, at the same time, constituted by others, by human history, by the world. The realization of my individual nature is always a self-realization in solidarity with others as they also have informed the expression of my individual existence. The conclusion can be drawn for prophetic knowledge, in which a word is directed to others, that that word is already present in the prophetic individual as constitutive of a human reality which is always a social reality, always informed by the other and open to the other.

Saying that the word which has to do with others is inescapably present in the individual because of the nature of human reality, does not imply that the word will necessarily be an adequate one. If prophetic knowledge is not simply a matter of an unmediated revelation but is dependent on the a posteriori

---

[42]Ibid., pp. 85-89, 82.

[43]Ibid., p. 87.

knowledge of the world, the adequacy of the 'prophetic word' will, at least in part, depend on the adequacy of that knowledge of the world. This is a subject which we will be giving attention to in the next chapter where we consider the conditions in human being which make the prophetic word ambiguous.

Another aspect of the prophetic dynamic, however, which determines the adequacy of the word for others, has to do with the nature of a loving solidarity with others. Obviously, the expressiveness of human subjects, through the medium of 'matter', does not assure, in itself, the kind of knowledge of others that is necessitated by a prophetic word which seeks the fuller self-realization of the other. It does not, in and of itself, assure that the other will not remain hidden in its essential meaning. In *Hearers of the Word*, Rahner makes the point that the "innermost meaning of self-subsisting being," the being's originating intention 'behind' the performance which appears, can remain dark to others. "It can become luminous and understandable for another only when he co-posits (*mit voll zieht*) it himself as a free act, when he loves it."[44] That is, he must will what the other wills in order to know what the other knows in its origins. The implication is that for there to be a true knowledge of the other there must be a solidarity grounded in love. In the following discussion we seek to grasp Rahner's way of conceiving the nature of the love of neighbor as that is grounded in the love of God and related to the knowledge of the other.

Transcendental Love of Neighbor as a
Condition for the Knowledge of the Other

Freedom understood as love finds its fullest expression in the unity of the love of God and neighbor. We have noted that there are spheres of freedom; more broadly speaking the original act of

---

[44]McCool, ed., *A Rahner Reader*, p. 39. See also Rahner, *The Love of Jesus and the Love of Neighbor*, trans. Robert Barr (New York: Crossroad, 1983), pp. 99-100.

freedom and love is actualized in the concrete, material, historical reality of the world. Freedom and love have a world and a history. We have recognized that the transcendental openness of human beings opens up for human beings the world as their world, as the place of their knowing and willing. This transcendental openness is, in a sense, the 'space' in which objects of knowledge and freedom are apprehended. This world of objects is the environment of human beings. It is ordered by the knowledge and freedom of human beings for the expression and determination of themselves. Consequently, the world is a world of persons, and the things of the world are ordered to the reality of persons. The world is the medium through which human beings come to actualize themselves through their relationship, in freedom and love, to their neighbor. The knowing subject comes to himself or herself through the other, comes to know himself or herself as a personal self through the personal other.[45]

> ... the known personal thou is the mediation, the 'being-within-oneself' of the subject. This condition is even clearer and more radical in the case of freedom. The free self-disposal, when morally right and perfect, is precisely the loving communication with the human *Thou* as such. . . . Yet since knowledge (being in itself already an act) attains its proper and full nature only in the act of freedom and therefore must lose and yet keep itself in freedom in order to be completely itself, it has a fully human significance only once it is integrated into freedom, i.e. into the loving communication with the Thou. The act of personal love for another human being is therefore the all-embracing basic act of man which gives meaning, direction and measure to everything else.[46]

In other words, we realize our true nature and the coming to be of ourselves in the love of our neighbor. Furthermore, this a priori openness to our neighbor, to the personal *Thou*, which makes possible our knowledge and free loving of the other, is

---

[45]Rahner, "Reflections on the Unity of the Love of Neighbor and the Love of God," *TI* 6:231-52; "The Commandment of Love," pp. 341-55; and *Love of Jesus*, pp. 69-74.

[46]Rahner, "Unity of Love of Neighbor and God," pp. 240-41.

essentially that transcendental openness and orientation whose source and term is God. We have already described this as a "necessary willing" and as the love of God (which nevertheless can be refused). Consequently, the love of God grounds the possibility of love of neighbor, and alternatively the love of neighbor is the concrete occasion of our love for God. Furthermore, this love of neighbor (or refusal to love the neighbor), since human transcendence has been elevated by grace to the reception of God's self-communication, is at the same time a welcoming (or refusal) of God himself in his Logos, in his concrete expression of himself in our neighbor. When a person loves another person unconditionally, it is only because his or her loving is borne by the unconditional love of God, a love which is directed unthematically to the God-Man (and therefore to the single human race and all human beings) and as such is able to unconditionally love that which is concrete and individual. That is, the unconditional love of God goes out to the conditional, finite creature because God is there, having expressed himself there in his incarnate Logos.[47]

Again, in other words, the transcendental experience of the human being, in which God is experienced implicitly, is only realized through the experience of the world. Just as the transcendental dimension grounds the possibility of categorial knowledge, so also the categorial and historical dimension of human reality makes possible the experience of transcendence. Historical reality is primarily the reality of the human being and, consequently, it is in the human being as a 'Thou' that God is experienced as the transcendental horizon in which the Thou is presented. In the love of the neighbor, God also is present and loved as the condition, the ground and goal of that unconditional loving. The neighbor is "loved forth into God." And as human beings open themselves to their neighbor "they receive the possibility of going forth from themselves, coming out of them-

---

[47]Rahner, *Foundations*, pp. 295-96.

selves and loving God."[48] What we are recognizing here is that the
love of neighbor as grounded in the transcendental experience of
the human subject before God is, in fact, constitutive of human
reality. What we need to see further is how this loving is the
condition for knowledge of the neighbor.

What we are concerned with here is the importance of praxis
and the love of neighbor for prophetic knowledge. We have noted
already that freedom and knowledge mutually condition each
other, that volition is an inner element of knowledge and that
knowledge finds its fulfillment in loving. In knowledge, the other
is made present in order to be welcomed, to be loved. But also,
for one to know the other, one must go out to the other, already
be welcoming the other. In fact, if one would really know and
understand the actions of the other, one must love what the other
loves ("If any man's will is to do his [the Father's] will he shall
know. . . ."). "In final analysis, knowledge is but the luminous
radiance of love."[49] Consequently, the knowledge of our neighbor
and of the human situation that is critical for our times can only
be obtained through love.

Furthermore, this loving cannot be considered only as a
disposition but also in its activity. Rahner makes the point that
while a distinction can be made between disposition and act,
between 'inner' and 'outer' experience, nevertheless, a disposition
is fulfilled and therefore realized only in its act. Love must
appear, must express itself in the concrete in order to be love, in
order to be itself.[50] When we apply this understanding to our
relationship to our neighbor and the world of humanity, the
importance of the activity of loving for knowing, for seeing things
as they are becomes clear. The concern of liberation theology for
praxis and for solidarity with the poor as foundational for doing

---

[48]Rahner, *Love of Jesus*, p. 72.

[49]McCool, ed., *A Rahner Reader*, pp. 40. 39-41.

[50]Rahner, "Some Thoughts on 'A Good Intention,'" *TI* 3:105-28 and *Love of Jesus*, pp. 72-73.

theology proves to be extremely significant.

In other words, what we must recognize here is that love, not only as a disposition, but as objectified in the concrete, in solidarity with the neighbor, is a condition for the possibility of knowing the neighbor in more than a peripheral, theoretical manner and therefore the possibility of a word for the neighbor which actually speaks to the basic context and meaning of the other's existence. What we are, in fact, recognizing, to come at this in a slightly different direction, is that practical reason and prophetic perception cannot be reduced to a deduction from theoretical reason. Practical reason, as Rahner points out on many occasions, is not merely the outcome of the synthesis of, on the one hand, the analysis of the historical situation and, on the other, the rational deduction from basic principles of human nature. Practical reason stands in its own right as a basic aspect of human self-realization in which the human being decides about what is to be, about what he or she is to become (and not merely by analyzing what is). Consequently, practical reason (and prophetic perception) can never wait until the facts are in, in part, because the new fact has yet to be actualized. In relation to my neighbor, I do not know my neighbor merely by a theoretical reason by which I analyze my neighbor's situation and personal makeup but by the risk of relating, welcoming, affirming, creating a relationship in which I take up the concerns of my neighbor as my own. It is only in deciding for my neighbor, willing what my neighbor wills, that a true knowledge of my neighbor is possible. It can be said of prophetic knowledge, therefore, which is dependent on a knowledge of the other, that it is conditioned by, or grounded in, transcendental love and (recognizing that love is not merely a disposition but concrete action) in praxis, in the concrete practice of love toward the other.

This does not exclude the importance of the knowledge of theoretical reason for a prophetic knowledge. Rahner has emphasized the importance of the political, social, and historical sciences and the analysis of the present situation of the world and of the church. He has made the point that such an analysis must be rigorous, and that it is in fact *necessary* for a prophetic kind of knowing.[51]

Discerning the Prophetic Word for the Other

We have been making the point that prophetic knowledge is dependent upon an a posteriori knowledge as well as the a priori condition of transcendental freedom. The logic of concrete individual knowledge, by which an individual or the church recognizes the imperative of the moment, is an element in the individual's or church's perception of the present situation and of the particular concerns, amidst the abundance of data, which must be addressed for the further self-realization of human reality and community.[52] We can connect this to what we noted above concerning love of neighbor and God and the significance of *praxis*. If my neighbor is "loved forth into God," then in that transcendental openness to God who is the infinite horizon in which my neighbor is received, and in solidarity with my neighbor, there can be a perception of what is congruent with that basic transcendental openness in terms of the concrete will of God for my neighbor. This, at least, seems to me to be implied in Rahner's thought. This can be expanded, of course, to include the 'neighbor' or 'other' of a social group, a nation, the church, a civilization.

In other words, the essential dynamic involved in the individual's discovery of the timely and unique will of God for himself or herself is the same dynamic for the prophetic individual's coming to recognize the word of the Lord for others. The material content of that word can be present to the individual as a result of theoretical reason and loving solidarity with others, and yet its perception as the 'word of the Lord' is essentially conditioned by that transcendental love of the other which reaches out to God

---

[51]Rahner, "Theological Problems in 'Pastoral Constitution'," pp. 307-08 and *Handbuch der Pastoraltheologie* II/I, pp. 180-88.

[52]Rahner, *Handbuch*, pp. 185-86.

and, through a time of testing or a more 'direct revelation' (as described in Chapter II), is recognized as the word congruent with the experience of that fundamental openness to God. (We are leaving aside here, as a peripheral issue, the question of a knowledge not obtained through normal cognitive means; that is, for example, the question of clairvoyance. Whatever the nature of such parapsychological phenomena, they also are dependent on this basic prophetic dynamic if assumed to involve a prophetic word.)

Thus far we have been concentrating on human freedom or transcendental love as the a priori condition for the possibility of an individual concrete knowledge from God directed to others. In large part we have outlined the anthropological foundations for prophecy as they are present in the theology of Karl Rahner. There is, however, one additional and crucial step that must be taken. Transcendental love in its origins gives us the divine grounding of the prophetic word and the basis for its uniqueness and, furthermore, love in its objectification means solidarity with our neighbor in such a way as to insure a word for others. Nevertheless, in Rahner's theology, it is this transcendental dynamic understood as transcendental hope which grounds the possibility of continually reaching beyond the status quo including the present objectifications of love so that the ever new call of God might be realized. We now turn to Rahner's definition of hope and its significance for prophecy.

Hope as the Transcendental Condition for Prophetic Knowledge

Faith and Rationality

We can begin by recognizing that faith, hope, and love in their origins express the one transcendental reality of the human being. We have seen this in terms of the nature of love. The same, however, can be said for faith. In fact, Rahner defines faith in its ground as freedom (the same definition he gives to love). Faith is that transcendental openness of the human being which is an openness for God's offer of himself in his self-communication, an openness which in relation to this self-communication (and borne by this self-communication of God) means receptivity, self-surrender, faith (as *fides qua*). Furthermore, faith in its transcendental ground is also rationality understood as the openness of the human being which makes rational expression possible.

Faith is the ultimate event of freedom and rationality. It is freedom as the self-surrender and commitment of the human being to God. And it is rationality as that is grounded in the mystery of God (which is the infinite 'space' in which the world is understood and known). Rationality can be understood in its origins as mystery opening up the world in categorial and conceptual expression. In freedom human beings come to themselves in the actualization of themselves and the acceptance of the mystery of God which upholds their existence. In rationality human beings grasp the reality of this mystery as the foundation of rationality and in freedom accept it. Rahner makes the point that "the history of revelation is the history of rationality" understood in this radical sense of rationality coming to recognize and accept the mystery which is its ground and which is come near in history.[53]

This faith which is open, accepting of the mystery of God, and which seeks to understand, to grasp this reality in history, finds expression in words and concepts (as *fides quae*). That there are religions expressing this reality of mystery is, at least in part, an illustration of this. But, furthermore, for the Christian the absoluteness of faith, of acceptance of the historical revelation of God in Jesus of Nazareth (which cannot in itself as historical and conditional provide this unconditional commitment) is grounded in faith as freedom and rationality.

In other words, faith, in its transcendental ground as the acceptance of mystery and as the openness given in mystery for understanding and categorial knowledge, expresses itself in commit-

---

[53]Rahner, "Faith between Rationality and Emotion," *TI* 16:60-78, and *SM*, s.v. "Faith: 1. Way to Faith."

ment and rational perception. Just as love as self-surrender in its origins expresses itself categorially in the giving over of self in love to the neighbor, so faith, which is the same self-surrender in its origins, expresses itself in rationality in coming to see the world from the vantage point in mystery. Faith as freedom and rationality, when it encounters the witness to Jesus as the 'absolute saviour', receives what it already knows in its origins. It finds its true expression, that which reveals categorially and historically what is already 'known' in its origins and foundation.[54]

By focusing on the nature of faith in its transcendental ground and categorial expression Rahner is able to relate faith and love in their existential ontological unity as well as develop the intrinsic relationship between faith as *fides qua* and *fides quae*, between faith as *fiducia* and *assensus* and faith as *notitia*. Faith (the same can be said for love) has a particular view of things. Faith provides the horizons in which the world is seen. When we concern ourselves with prophetic knowledge we are concerned with the knowledge of faith (which can also be called the knowledge of love and hope).

Hope as the Unity of Faith and Love

We now turn to Rahner's essay "On the Theology of Hope," for what it says about hope in its origins and as related to faith and love. Rahner points out, as we have already noted, that there are two basic modes to the human being's one act of self-realization, namely, knowledge and freedom (which corresponds to faith and love). Rahner relates this human duality to the divine duality of

---

[54]Rahner, *Foundations*, pp. 228-64. Rahner notes the "inevitable incongruence between relative historical certainty and absolute commitment" (p. 234). "Freedom always decides absolutely," which does not mean it cannot decide in regard to Jesus with all the historical ambiguity involved (p. 235). Rather the essential transcendental orientation of the human being, which is open for the self-communication of God and therefore "searches" for the "absolute saviour" in history, when it encounters the objective reality of Jesus of Nazareth and the witness to him can respond with an absolute "yes," which is of the nature of transcendentality.

two 'processesions' in the trinitarian conception of God in which God is conceived as the incomprehensible mystery (the Father) who "utters himself and possesses himself in love."[55] Since, as we have seen, human nature constitutes receptivity for God's self-communication, it can be assumed that this nature corresponds to the divine self-expression and self-giving; these 'processions' of the one God form the a priori conditions for human knowing and willing and in view of the incarnation sustain human self-realization in faith and love. In other words, just as the incomprehensible mystery (the Father) expresses himself in his *Logos* (the Son) and welcomes and loves the expression of himself (the *Pneuma* constituting this loving) and does so into his creation, so in the human being's one act of self-realization in which he or she responds to this self-bestowal of God himself there are also two modalities: faith, by which this self-expression of God is known; and love, by which this self-giving God is welcomed.[56]

This being the case, Rahner raises the question of where the other 'theological virtue' of hope belongs. He notes that the problem is reinforced by the apparent historically anterior position of the dual combination of faith and love in the biblical sources. Nevertheless, he takes seriously St. Paul's reference to the trilogy of faith, hope, and love, and their abiding nature. The notion of hope as abiding eternally creates a problem for a traditional conception of hope as provisional and as ending in the final consummation.[57] With these thoughts in mind we can formulate Rahner's definition of hope and his answer to the questions he has raised.

Rahner points out that the notion of hope as provisional, as based in our everyday experience of hoping for something until it is achieved (at which time hope ceases), is inadequate "in the

---

[55]Rahner, "On the Theology of Hope," *TI* 10:245.

[56]Ibid., pp. 245-46.

[57]Ibid., pp. 246-47.

extreme" when referring to theological hope, for hope as directed to God (and sustained by God) goes out to that absolute and incomprehensible mystery which does not cease to be mystery when it is attained in the "final consummation."

> The event in which this takes place [the final consummation], inasmuch as it is made possible by the divine self-bestowal, is not the act in which the absolute mystery which is God is finally overcome and solved, but rather the act in which this truly unfathomable mystery in all its finality and its overpowering acuteness is no longer able to be suppressed, but must be sustained and endured as it is in itself without any possibility of escape into that which can be comprehended and so controlled and subordinated to the subject and his own nature as it exists prior to any elevation by grace.[58]

This 'possession' of God is the "radical transcendence of self and surrender of self" which is "the act of reaching out for truth into the unfathomable mystery," and the act of loving surrender which is grounded in and sustained by the unconditional love of God. This " 'letting of one's self go'," in faith and love which is sustained by God's self-bestowal (by 'grace'), this "one unifying 'outwards from the self' attitude into God as the absolutely uncontrollable," can be termed 'hope'. As such, hope

> is a process of constantly eliminating the provisional in order to make room for the radical and pure uncontrollability of God. It is the continuous process of destroying that which appears, in order that the absolute and ultimate truth may be intelligible as comprehended, and love may be that which is brought about by our love.[59]

In other words, hope is that element in human experience which always presses beyond the provisional expressions and objectifications of faith and love for the uncontrollable and incalculable, the absolute mystery which is God. In hope

> we dare to commit ourselves to that which is radically beyond all human control in both of man's basic dimensions, that, therefore, which is attained

---

[58]Ibid., p. 249.

[59]Ibid., pp. 249-50.

precisely at that point at which the controllable is definitively transcended, i.e., in the ultimate consummation of eternal life.[60]

Hope is that attitude of pressing on beyond all provisional realities to the reality of eternal life. The graced transcendental receptiveness to God which, as we have seen is faith and love in their origin, can also be recognized as hope, as that transcendental orientation which is never satisfied with the provisional expressions of faith and love but must ever surpass them in its reaching " 'outwards from self' into the uncontrollability of God." Hope is, thus, "the basic modality of the very *attitude to the eternal* which precisely as such sets the true advance towards eternity 'in train'."[61]

Furthermore, this hope which is the 'outward from self' movement toward incomprehensible mystery, actualized in the concrete in knowledge and freedom, is also the movement toward the incalculable God as salvation. In other words, hope as the commitment to the incalculable, sustained by God's gracious self-bestowal ('elevated by grace'), is, at the same time, the surrender to the incomprehensible God as the God not of anger, but of grace: "For he who commits himself to the absolutely incalculable and uncontrollable is committing himself to the blessed one and to salvation."[62]

This graced reality of hope is an existential in human existence precisely because of Christ. He is the "hope of the world," because through him this graced hope or theological hope "definitively establishes itself in the world." In Christ the *crucified*, surrender "to the disposing hand of God" is historically realized in the most radical way. Through this radical act of the crucified Christ, God has made himself humanity's absolute future, so that the one act of self-realization (for all human beings) "in theory and practice, in knowledge and in free love" is oriented to the blessed

---

[60]Ibid., p. 250.

[61]Ibid., pp. 250-51.

[62]Ibid., p. 255.

incalculable God. Thus "the act of hope stands revealed as the acceptance of this orientation towards the incalculability and un-controllability of God." This act, however, must be differentiated into faith and love for it to be objectified. Thus hope is the unifying factor in the interplay of faith and love.[63]

Transcendental Hope as the Foundation for Prophetic Knowledge

We have seen above that hope is the acceptance of the basic transcendental orientation to the incalculability of God which realizes itself in knowledge and love. As such it is grounded in God's self-bestowal in Christ, and therefore in Christ's surrender in hope to the incalculability of God. What we need to see in addition to this is that hope is the basis in the Christian and in human being for the venture into the new and unforeseen. As oriented to the absolute future of God, it criticizes every pro-visional plan and program and commits itself to the incalculable in risking ever new provisional objectifications in knowledge and freedom of the incomprehensible and incalculable mystery. As such, this dynamic of hope can be seen as a transcendental condition of prophetic knowledge which is precisely concerned with the 'new' word or call to action. This is implied in Rahner's last section of his essay "On the Theology of Hope," for there he relates hope to practical reason.[64] He notes that "praxis" is not related to theory as merely the bringing into practical action of that which has already been planned as assumed in theory, but rather praxis results from the commitment to the unplanned.

---

[63]Ibid., pp. 255-56. Rahner has made the point that "Christian theology is always a theology of the Cross" ("Church as Critic of Society," *TI* 12:241). He can say this because the one act of God's self-revelation (God's Logos) in Jesus Christ is the act of self-surrender, of self-dying into the hands of God the Father. The historical death on the cross is the radical culmination and symbol of this act. See Rahner, *On the Theology of Death*, trans. Charles H. Henkey (New York: Herder & Herder, 1961).

[64]Rahner, "Theology of Hope," pp. 256-59.

Man himself, in the very process of breaking down the factor of the incalculable already present *beforehand* in his life, actually builds up those incalculable factors which are produced by *himself*. Now the effect of these two elements is that in the very act of venturing upon the [this-worldly] future which is unforeseen and incalculable . . . in his practical life as understood here, man realizes, and necessarily must realize his eschatological hope that is to say 'outwards from self' to the absolute incalculable future.[65]

In other words, the human being inescapably and necessarily, as essential to being human, actualizes his or her eschatological hope (or orientation to the *absolute* incalculable future which is God), as he or she ventures into the proximate, incalculable future. In so doing,

> every structure of [mundane] life, whether present or *still to come* in the future, is called into question by hope as that in which we grasp at the incalculable and uncontrollable, and in this process of being called in question the act of hope is made real in historical terms.[66]

Rahner is pointing here to two aspects of this dynamic of hope. First, there is a socio-critical and prophetic character to this hope which cannot simply maintain what is. In reaching out to the uncontrollable God of the absolute future, it continually criticizes all provisional this-worldly structures of our existence. Second, hope gives expression in new forms to the incalculable absolute future. In this second aspect, the dynamic of hope is the precondition for the new imperative, for the unique word or call to action of the moment. Rahner sees that this transcendental hope makes possible the concrete imperative which cannot simply be deduced from the theoretical side of faith.

---

[65]Ibid., pp. 257-58 and "Zur Theologie Der Hoffnung," *ST* 8:576-77. I have tried to bring some clarity to the translation in *TI* 10. See Rahner, "Hoffnung," p. 577: "Aus diesen beiden Momenten aber ergebt sich, dass im so verstandenen praktischen Wagnis der inner weltlich unvorhergesehenen und unverfügbaren Zukunft der Mensch seine eschatologische Hoffnung als 'Von-sich-weg' auf das absolute Unverfügbare realisiert und realisieren muss."

[66]Rahner, "Theology of Hope," p. 258.

> Precisely *in what* this hope is to [take place] in the concrete . . ., precisely *what* the Christian is to hold firm to . . . this is something which 'theoretic' faith cannot answer as a simple deduction from its own tenets. This concrete imperative is not merely the result of applying the theory of faith in practice. . . . But this hope summons the Christian and Christianity to venture upon this imperative, underivable in each case, in which they have constantly to decide anew between whether they are to defend the present which they already possess, or to embark upon the exodus into the unforeseeable future. This is something which hope can do, for hope itself has in fact already all along achieved something which is even greater. In it man has surrendered himself to that which is absolutely and eternally uncontrollable and incalculable by any powers of his. In the power of this greater hope he also possesses the lesser hope, namely the courage to transform the ['structures of mundane life'], as the Council puts it, and the converse too is not less true. In this lesser hope the greater one is made real.[67]

We can recognize that this dynamic of hope, in which that transcendental openness to the absolute future is accepted, is the same dynamic we attended to in the last chapter when we considered the 'logic' by which a concrete imperative was discovered. There we saw that a concrete individual knowledge was obtained through the experience of congruence with that graced transcendental openness to God which *as accepted* is what is meant by faith, love, and hope in their *origins*. Nevertheless, hope can be viewed as the acceptance of that fundamental openness to God, as that entails an essential openness to the absolute future which calls into question and seeks to surpass all provisional objectifications of faith and love. What we are recognizing is that the concrete imperatives for the unique historical moment, that is, the unique and timely word, are made possible by the transcendental dynamic of this 'graced' hope in human life. In other words, the human being's experience of transforming the present structures into new forms, which bear within themselves the incalculable (and which are not merely the rearranging of the old), is grounded in the transcendental dynamic of a 'graced' hope, which is itself oriented to the absolute future of God. Human transcendentality, which

---

[67]Ibid., p. 259; "Hoffnung," p. 578.

makes calculation and planning possible, also makes possible the new and previously unforeseen initiative, as this transcendentality is understood as surpassing all present and proximate future programs in its orientation to the absolute future; in this sense, transcendentality can be grasped by the word 'hope'. Since hope originates in, and is borne by, the absolute future which is God; and since it is the precondition for the possibility of the new, concrete, and timely initiative, it can be seen as the basis for a prophetic knowledge. This conception of hope provides at least another way of recognizing that the unique word of prophetic knowledge originates in God. It also places emphasis on the timeliness of the prophetic word.

It is, in fact, this transcendental hope which gives history an eschatological thrust, or better; it is in hope that we can grasp the eschatological direction of history. History is one-way directed; it moves toward an absolute future. This became a recurring theme for Rahner as he came into dialogue with theologies of hope. Among those essays explicitly concerned with the significance of the future I mention the following: "Marxist Utopia and the Christian Future of Man" (*TI* 6), "The Theological Problems Entailed in the Idea of 'The New Earth' " (*TI* 10), "Immanent and Transcendent Consummation of the World" (*TI* 10), "A Fragmentary Aspect of a Theological Evaluation of the Concept of the Future" (*TI* 10), "The Question of the Future" (*TI* 12). These reflections of Rahner's are further elaborations of what it means that the human being is the subject of a graced transcendental hope. It is to the significance of the future for the timeliness of the prophetic word that we now turn.

Transcendental Hope and the
Timeliness of the Prophetic Word

When we speak in the following pages of the orientation to the absolute future we are referring to the same reality which

Rahner refers to by the term *Vorgriff* and when we consider how this orientation to the absolute future governs human becoming, we are referring to the same reality as that expressed in Rahner's discussions of the relationship of spirit and matter in the act of becoming and evolution; and we will see that this orientation to the future is also constituted by a transcendental and eschatological hope.

The One-Way Character of History

First of all, the one-way character of history can be seen in the irreversibility of human freedom and action. As we have already recognized, human freedom has a context in which its decisions are expressed, a prior condition for the objectification of those decisions which is itself, at least partially, the result of previous decisions. Consequently, this context or sphere in which decisions are made, limits, in part, the possibilities available to freedom. The previous decisions, which have excluded some possibilities in favor of others, now determine the kinds of decisions that can in this moment be made. There is, in this sense, no going back; history is irreversible.[68]

Secondly, this one-way character of history can also be seen in terms of freedom in its origins, that is, in its transcendental grounds. Human transcendentality, which we have considered to be an infinite openness to the incomprehensible God and, as such, the precondition for human knowledge and freedom, can also be understood as the infinite reaching out to the absolute future. As such, human self-transcendence and becoming can also be understood in the light of the absolute future as always arriving. It is to this notion of the future orientation of human being and history that we now turn. We will give particular attention to Rahner's essay, "The Question of the Future" (*TI* 12).

---

[68]Rahner, "Experiment with Man," pp. 218-19.

Human Reality as Future-Oriented

Rahner notes, first of all, that the question of the future constitutes *the* question which the human being is. Human self-actualization in knowledge and freedom is grounded in a transcendentality which can be understood as an orientation to the absolute future. Furthermore, the orientation to the future, in some respects, is more apparent for the modern human being. For modern humanity history does not constitute merely the neutral place and time that must be endured and in which one must make one's individual passage, but rather it is itself viewed as planned and shaped by the human being:

> . . . man is, at least in the first instance, the one who has made something of himself, one who at the individual and collective levels alike, makes plans and projects for himself—in a certain sense takes control of himself, not merely drawing out what is already there, but creatively discovering that which is not there, that which belongs to Utopia. And it is in this way that man shapes the present in the light of the future.[69]

Human planning, therefore, is done precisely with an eye to the future. It is in this sense that the future influences the present.

In order to clarify the kind of power the future has over the present, Rahner makes a distinction between the "absolute future" and the "this-worldly" or proximate future. The *"absolute future* is God himself or the act of his absolute self-bestowal which has to be posited by him alone." The *'this-worldly' future* signifies that which is conceived as yet to be achieved but which will be brought about in space and time.[70] We are concerned with what Rahner has to say in this essay about the nature of these two futures and how they mutually condition each other. By attending to the relationship of the absolute and proximate futures we will be elaborating the nature of human being as the question of the

---

[69]Rahner, "The Question of the Future," *TI* 12:183. See also Rahner, "Marxist Utopia and the Christian Future of Man," *TI* 6:60.

[70]Rahner, "Question of the Future," pp. 185, 184-86.

future and therefore will be pointing again to the precondition in being human for a timely word of a prophetic kind.

Rahner recognizes two aspects of the proximate future. The first can be conceived in evolutionary terms, by the element of causal factors, in which the content of the future is "the sheer outcome of present and past." Futurology essentially operates by the analysis and calculation of past and present configurations as they are seen as the seeds of the future. The other aspect of this proximate future is the new and creative, the element of human freedom which takes the material of the present and past and shapes and plans a new reality. Thus history can also be conceived as involving genuine self-transcendence. These two elements are not to be conceived as two separate realities but rather as elements "which mutually demand, and dialectically condition one another."[71] Nevertheless, it is this second element which causes us to consider the relationship of the proximate future to the absolute future, for even this creative, free element must be conceived as having a 'cause' and not merely as issuing from the void which cannot produce anything.[72]

Rahner gives us three theses in this essay. The first thesis is that "Christianity in its true essence is the state of radical openness to the question of the mystery of the absolute future which is God." The incarnation of the Logos of God can be conceived as God's entrance into the world as its absolute future. This self-bestowal of God means that the absolute future toward which human history is directed has been "definitively promised" in Jesus Christ, and therefore Christianity consists in this "abiding openness" to the absolute future which is always arriving and whose arrival has been promised. The second thesis is that "the 'this worldly' future of man always constitutes an open, and abidingly open, question." Rahner makes three points about this thesis. One, the 'this-worldly' future as an always open question

---

[71]Ibid., pp. 186-87, 187.

[72]Ibid., p. 187.

can be seen in the fact that the prior conditions of nature and environment which the human being alters, and the time necessary for changes to take place, can never be known comprehensively. Therefore a question mark is placed before all human planning. Two, in the contemporary situation the number of possibilities for decision making is increasing, and the choice of one possibility eliminates other choices; and yet the possibilities opened by one decision and the choices that will be taken in the future cannot be determined; thus the openness of the 'this-worldly' future. Three, the nature of freedom in its origins (as we have seen) has a transcendental basis and is not merely the outcome of a finite series of causes (although in retrospect causal explanations can be given). Consequently, the proximate or 'this-worldly' future must be seen as an always open question.[73]

The third thesis has to do with the theologian's role as "the guardian of this *docta ignorantia futuri*." In the context of this thesis of the Christian's defense of the unknowability of the future, Rahner raises the question of the mutually conditioning relationship of the 'this-worldly' future and the absolute future, a question of particular significance for our concerns.

Rahner observes that "the utopian is the expression of the mutuality of this conditioning relationship." That is, the 'this-worldly' future, when it is the medium of the absolute future, can be understood as a utopian expression which critiques the present situation and calls it forth into a new reality. We have already observed this dimension of futurity in the nature of Christian hope, which in going beyond the provisional expressions of faith and love impels us to new concrete expressions of the absolute future. "This means that the utopian factor in history belongs essentially to the achievement of the fullness of Christian life as realized in man's assent to the absolute future and to absolute hope." This utopian element itself must always be seen in its provisionality, as the medium of the absolute future, and therefore as replaceable by

---

[73]Ibid., pp. 189, 190, 190-98.

another 'this-worldly' future which is also always open. Rahner believes the theologian must maintain this *docta ignorantia futuri* particularly before those who in a rationalistic manner require the "revolutionaries" of each age to have the future program, which will replace the present order being critiqued, all planned out. Rahner notes that this is impossible, for "the will to achieve a future also involves a commitment to the unknown." His point finally is that all strivings after a 'this-worldly' future are grounded in and critiqued by the transcendental hope oriented to the absolute future, and that the strivings for the 'this-worldly' future constitute "the medium in which hope for the absolute future is maintained."[74] In other words, human planning and self-transcendence, and therefore the new and timely word, the word of the 'this-worldly' future, are made possible by the transcendental openness of the human being for the absolute future which bestows itself in history and is mediated by (and yet, at the same time, critiques) utopian 'this-worldly' futures.

What we have been recognizing in the foregoing discussion is that human history is not merely the cause and effect outcome of past configurations of events but is also the result of a reaching out into the future, a reaching out which is itself grounded in a graced transcendental openness to the *absolute* future. This openness to the absolute future, which is the incomprehensible God who bestows himself upon history, is the condition for the historical self-determination of the human being which at the same time means the possibility for the new historical realization as an outcome not of the past but of the future. The "proximate future," the goals, plans, and imperatives of a utopian nature, which impinge upon the present, mediate the absolute future as that is affirmed in this transcendental openness. It is in the nature of being human that becoming is not merely the reformulation of the past but response to the future. Therefore, the utopian expression or timely word is necessary to and inescapable for a truly human

---

[74]Ibid., pp. 198-201.

reality. To be human is to be *the* question of the future. When this human reality as questioning openness to the absolute future finds expression, it does so in the plans, imperatives, 'new' messages of a 'this-worldly' future; and insofar as these new messages are borne by the implicit affirmation of the absolute future's arrival (the incomprehensible God's self-bestowal), then these utopian expressions are also the timely word of a prophetic character.

Primary and Secondary Revelation

Throughout this chapter the anthropological foundations of prophecy have been elaborated with Rahner's theology of revelation in the background. In the manner of a summary, this theology of revelation is viewed more explicitly in relation to prophecy.

For Rahner, human transcendentality is, as we have noted, the precondition for two basic aspects of human self-realization, namely, knowledge and freedom; and this transcendentality, which is constituted by God as its infinite horizon can be understood as that infinite openness for the revelation of God himself. (If God did not constitute the receptivity of the human subject toward God then there could only be a human word about God, and not the Word of God itself.) This transcendentality, furthermore, can be understood as a 'graced' transcendentality, and as such, makes intelligible the Christian experience of faith, hope, and love and the forgiving nearness of God. This *graced* transcendentality, which has been established as an existential for all human beings by God's self-communication in Jesus Christ, must also be conceived as the condition for all acts of knowledge and freedom. Consequently, in every act of knowledge and freedom, God is present, not only as the infinite horizon which makes these acts possible, but as the abiding presence who is known and willed implicitly in each act—either in affirmation and acceptance or refusal. The Ignatian spirituality of finding God in all things, so present in Rahner's thought, can be seen here. This graced transcendentality or 'supernatural existential' is the basis for the possibility of a divine origination of a human word and, therefore, at least one of the factors in being human which makes the prophetic word possible.

Furthermore, this transcendentality must necessarily have a history. It must appear; it must find categorial and historical expression. Without God's actual, positive giving himself (in his Word) to his creation, that transcendentality could only be experienced as a holy yet distant mystery; it would not be experienced as a *graced* transcendentality. With the event of the Word of God's incarnation in Jesus Christ, human transcendentality has achieved the goal toward which it is directed and has found definitive and final historical and categorial expression. Consequently, the only transcendentality human beings know is a graced transcendentality. Rahner makes the point that both the graced transcendentality or supernatural existential and the categorial and historical word in Jesus Christ constitute the Word of God. In other words, both the hearing in faith and the word that is heard can be understood as God's Word. Word and Spirit form a unity; God's categorial self-communication and its reception (in the Spirit) constitute the one event of God's self-revelation.

> Both (the categorial Word and the event in time and space of salvation) only continue to be the Word-act of God by being experienced and understood in the same transcendental sphere of the Spirit, created by God in his communication of himself in the Spirit. This "transcendental" sphere is, however, only experienced and made fully explicit when it is oriented towards its categorial, historical objectivization in the event and Word of salvation. Insofar as God's forgiving and deifying communication of himself as a free, personal self-disclosure of the God, who is in himself inaccessible to man in his innermost being and in his free activity, has the character of a word, the whole experience of this God who reveals himself can quite correctly be called the Word of God.[75]

The notion that this graced transcendentality or sphere of the

---

[75]*ET*, s.v. "Word of God and Theology," by Karl Rahner.

Spirit is itself God's Word is the basis for Rahner's conception of "anonymous Christians" and for the recognition of a genuine prophetism outside of Christianity and 'official' salvation history. The definitive and final event of salvation in Jesus Christ and the history that leads up to him and bears witness to him can be said to be the 'official' history of salvation, while the universality of the 'supernatural existential' means, also, that there is a universal history of revelation and salvation.[76]

In addition to the definitive and final event of God's self-revelation in Jesus Christ, which Rahner has referred to as primary revelation, there is also, as we have seen, a secondary kind of revelation. This at least is a way of conceiving prophecy if we are to understand it is a revelatory kind of knowledge (as God's word). In order to see more specifically how prophecy is grounded in this primary revelation, we turn to some observations Rahner has made in a recent essay.

In his essay "On Angels," Rahner raises the epistemological (and theological) question as to "what can fall in principle and a priori in any way into the sphere of an actual supernatural revelation. . . ." He makes the point that "in a supernatural revelation . . . properly and primarily only God himself (in his self-communication) can reveal himself."[77] The fundamental mysteries of the faith (Trinity, incarnation, and the sending of the Spirit) can be understood as following on this basic conception of revelation as well as other related realities such as the mystery of the church. Rahner considers, however, other realities that are accessible to reason but which have been understood traditionally as objects of revelation. The question is raised as to how finite created reality, truths accessible to natural reason, can be objects of revelation. This is particularly a question related to prophetic revelation and,

---

[76]Rahner, *Foundations*, pp. 153-75.

[77]Rahner, "On Angels," *TI* 19:240, 242. Rahner's approach to the question of angels, essentially involves answering the question as to what about natural human experience brings to expression an angel mythology (pp. 235-74).

in fact, Rahner briefly takes up the problem of prophecy in this essay as an example of this secondary kind of revelation. The example is given of an Old Testament prophet who proclaims a political directive within a particular historical situation as a word of revelation. Rahner sees the need for modern fundamental theology to attend "to the concrete happening in the prophet's consciousness, to the claim made that his word, which is primarily the datum of his own consciousness, is God's word."[78] In what sense is the self-revelation of God involved in a political assertion for which appeals can be made to natural (critical) reason? Rahner provides us with the following brief answer:

> . . . we assume that revelation can always be approached only in faith and that such a faith always and at all times, even though completely un-thematically and without verbal objectivation, must be sustained by God's self-communication (by what we are accustomed to call 'uncreated grace') and that (even though implicitly and unthematically) it always affirms the actual self-communication and self-revelation of God in the sense of our basic axiom which is that revelation has primarily to do with God's revela-tion of himself. On this assumption, it can certainly be said that a finite reality and the proposition related to it can be affirmed as revealed when and insofar as their being sustained by faith properly so-called as immediacy to the absolute God and their [a finite reality and the proposition related to it] synthesis [with it (faith)] are [immediately and compellingly] experi-enced. When (to put it somewhat boldly) the mysticism of the transcend-ental experience of grace is encountered in an indissoluble synthesis (not distorting the openness of this mysticism) with a categorial experience, this, too, may be understood as willed by God, as the will and sign of God, as revealed.[79]

An examination of this passage will provide one further

---

[78]Ibid., p. 245.

[79]Ibid., pp. 245-46 with corrections. See Rahner, "Über Engel," *ST* 13:393-94: "Unter dieser Voraussetzung Kann man wohl sagen: Eine endliche Wirklich-keit und der auf sie bezogene satz können dann als geoffenbart bejaht werden, wenn und insofern ihre Getragenheit durch den eigentlichen Glauben also Unmittelbarkeit zum absoluten Gott und ihre Synthese damit unmittelbar und zwingend erfahren werden." *Damit* should be translated as "with it" rather than "thus" for the synthesis Rahner is referring to is certainly the synthesis of a finite reality (and proposition related to it) with actual faith.

elaboration of the grounding of prophetic perception in a *graced* transcendentality. We have seen that faith and love, in their origins, are a receptive openness or self-surrender to God's self-communication. This receptivity can itself be understood as God's Word, insofar as it is made possible by God's receptive welcome of his own Logos as expressed in human being. Faith by its nature always affirms God's self-revelation (which is understood here as 'primary revelation'). However, faith can also express itself in propositions related to finite realities, so that such propositions themselves can be understood as sustained by God's self-communication and therefore as having a 'revelatory' character. The above passage indicates the element that must be present for such a "secondary revelation." First of all, such prophetic propositions, sustained by faith, must be experienced as having an indissoluble synthesis with faith. That is, the affirmation of the propositions must be experienced as an openness to (rather than a distortion of) "immediacy to the absolute God." We have already, in fact, noted this in the previous chapter in our discussion of individual concrete knowledge. Secondly, this experience of the synthesis of prophetic propositions with transcendental faith must be immediate and compelling. We have seen this also; that is, we have seen that the synthesis experienced is not that of discursive reasoning in which the experience of faith is objectified and deduced as logically congruent with a particular proposition but rather is a preconceptual, immediate reality. Furthermore, this experience has a compelling feature to it, an inner certainty which belongs to faith as that affirming receptivity to Being Itself, which of necessity must, as pure receptivity, affirm being; and therefore as *graced* receptivity affirms that which is congruent with the *immediacy* of absolute being which is God.

What we are again recognizing is that the possibility for a prophetic kind of knowledge, for a human word being divine, is present in the essential makeup of the human being as a transcendental subject, and that, as this transcendentality is conditioned by God's self-communication, this prophetic knowledge can be viewed as grounded in transcendental faith (and hope and love). Whether or not we can recognize, through self-reflection, the dynamic of prophetic knowing as described above, nevertheless, the possibility of such a dynamic of faith can at least be affirmed when we reflect on our own experience of transcendentality. In any case, the above description of prophetic knowledge means, essentially, that such knowledge is the knowledge of faith (the transcendental side of God's self-communication) as it finds categorial expression.

Rahner has put this very forcefully in *Foundations*, where he notes that the

> "light of faith" which is offered to every person, and the light by which the "prophets" grasp and proclaim the divine message from the center of human existence is the same light. . . . Looked at theologically and correctly, the prophet is none other than the believer who can express his transcendental experience of God correctly.[80]

While Rahner is concerned in this passage with the bearers of revelation, of the 'official' history of revelation, which concerns God's self-interpretation in history as integral to his self-communication and as governed by God's salvific will and providence; nevertheless, his definition of prophetic perception can be applied generally wherever "a self-interpretation which really succeeds and finds a living form takes place among men in such a way that particular people, their experiences and their self-interpretation become a productive model, an animating power and a form for others."[81] Not all are prophets, but wherever a person with the light of faith (which "is nothing else but the divinized subjectivity of man which is constituted by God's self-communication") expresses that transcendental faith in word and deed, more or less accurately, there is a prophetic message. Consequently, there is "something of a fluid boundary between believing prophets

---

[80]Rahner, *Foundations*, p. 159.

[81]Ibid., pp. 159-60.

and 'mere' believers."[82]   The point is that prophetic knowledge must be seen, not as a kind of "supernatural add-on," but as an expression of a *graced* transcendental reality which is an existential for all human beings and governs all acts of knowledge and freedom.

---

[82]Ibid., p. 160. That prophetic reality which forms part of the 'official' history of revelation can be distinguished by its sign of legitimacy in the continuity it has with other events which form a configuration with God's definition and absolute self-communication in history (pp. 160-61).

Chapter IV

The Prophetic Dynamic and the Criteria for Discerning Genuine Prophecy

We have assumed from the outset that the question of prophecy in the church is not a question the church is indifferent to. Rather, the church has its origins in a prophetic movement and has a history of prophetism. Nevertheless, we have recognized that the church lives in an age (and is part of that age) which questions the grounds of revelation and prophecy. It is not at all assumed in our age that a human word can at the same time be a divine word or that a 'unique' and 'timely' word can be anything more than the result of material and historical configurations. What I have attempted to demonstrate in the foregoing discussion is that there is a way to show that a prophetic kind of knowing is both intelligible and inescapable for human being. In Rahner we find an anthropological method which is capable of demonstrating that to be human is to be prophetic. He has shown us the anthropological grounds for prophecy.

In the first chapter I summarized the principle aspects of a phenomenology of prophecy as that has been addressed by biblical scholars. This seemed an important starting point since the discussion of prophecy in the church today must somehow connect with its origins. What we saw from that discussion was that the prophetic message can be characterized as a unique and timely word directed to others and originating from God. Whatever the particular historical and categorial expressions of this reality, they could be included by this definition. In the second chapter we sought, from Rahner, a description of the kind of perception in human experience which involved the knowledge of such a unique and timely word originating from God. What we recognized is that there is an aspect of human knowledge that involves a 'charismatic' or 'prophetic' element. In Chapter III I attempted to demonstrate the way in which Rahner has conceived the anthropological foundations for this prophetic kind of knowing. What we have seen is that this prophetic element is inherent to human reality and community. The charismatic or prophetic element is an inescapable and necessary aspect of being human. In this chapter I will give a brief overview of the nature of this charismatic and prophetic dynamic as that has been developed in the foregoing discussion. Then we will seek the implication of this for the problem of criteria for identifying true prophecy. We will see how Rahner addresses the question of the discernment of true from false prophecy. This will involve not only attention to the dynamic of prophecy but also to the implications of human finitude and sin for the ambiguity of the word, and especially to what Rahner considers additionally ambiguous in today's situation. We will see that the question of discernment has to be addressed on several fronts. Finally, I will raise the issue of the relationship of the prophetic dynamic to paranormal phenomena and the significance of 'miracle' as sign for the activity of discernment.

The Dynamic of Prophecy

We have seen that prophetic perception is grounded in a graced transcendentality. That is, the possibility of a unique and timely word from God is based in the infinite openness of the human being. This openness to the totality of being, and therefore to God, is not only the precondition for all acts of knowledge and freedom, but is the ground for the possibility of knowing God and God's will, at least insofar as God reveals herself. Rahner's position is that, since God revealed herself in human reality, since she has come near, God is always present in mediated immediacy as an existential of human being. In all human knowing and acting God is present, at least as offered (or accepted or rejected), in the act of knowledge and decision making. This unthematic 'knowledge' of God can find categorial expression. Examples of the expression of this graced transcendentality (as accepted) include elements of the world's religions, the individual's trusting acceptance of death, the love of neighbor, the hope that reaches out to the incalculable future and criticizes every utopian 'this-worldly' future. Also, as we have seen, this graced transcendentality is expressed in the individual's perception of the decision fitting for the particular historical moment.

   We have recognized that there is a graced practical reason. While we realize that, for the Christian, Christian instruction, the content of faith, and rational analysis will play a part in this graced practical reason, nevertheless, we have seen that its essential dynamic character can be recognized in what Rahner has called a "general moral faith-instinct" and "concrete individual knowledge." For both aspects, the 'light of faith' (or the graced transcendental openness of the human being) is the essential dynamic which makes these modes of knowing possible. In the case of a general moral faith-instinct there is a perception, a general sense of things that perceives the universal and essential norms (grounded in our common humanity) as they apply to the specific situation, a perception which is grounded in the self-awareness of our common, shared humanity and therefore not merely a matter of a rational deduction from preconceived theological principles. In the case of a concrete individual knowledge, there is the coming to know the particular imperative or word for the historically unique and individual situation, a knowledge which, because of its unique and individual character, cannot be simply deduced from general principles or from the theoretical knowledge of the gospel.

We have seen that this individual concrete knowledge at times is arrived at by a time of testing to see if it is in harmony with the foundational experience of openness to God. At other times this individual concrete knowledge comes in a more direct manner. There is the perception that this is the word that must be proclaimed in this moment and the content of this word and its fittingness for this situation are recognized in their unity. This graced practical reason or prophetic perception may involve a 'sense of things' which one seeks to put into words; it may also involve images, thoughts, words that are formed in conscious awareness. Regardless of the mode of this perception there is always the experience of a synthesis of the subject's transcendental openness to God and the particular categorial expression; that is, the categorial object of practical insight does not hinder this transcendental openness in the experience of the subject but rather appears in harmony with it, as expressive of it and therefore confirming the word (and mission) of the subject or prophet. This individual concrete knowledge can be understood as the prophetic dynamic in its origins. As an individual perceives the imperative of the moment by the light of faith, that is, as an individual grasps a concrete call to action within the infinite expanse of this openness to God and this call to action is experienced as congruent with and maintaining and not hindering that openness and therefore experienced as God's will, there we can recognize a dynamic which has a prophetic element. Such a dynamic can be termed prophetic (in the full sense in which we have understood the term) when what is known and willed involves a word for the other, for the community. What we are recognizing is that a particular dynamic of human knowledge and decision making, which is *necessary* to certain kinds of human knowledge (choices regarding vocation, marriage, individual direction) is the necessary dynamic of *prophetic* knowing as that involves also solidarity with the other. Thus the prophetic dynamic, in its origins, is an element of human freedom and knowledge as that is experienced in the life of the ordinary believer. This dynamic is operative in the life of a believer as he or she seeks to understand and act in the 'light of faith'. This same dynamic becomes prophetic when what is perceived and acted on involves not merely the individual believer's pilgrimage in faith but the larger community's pilgrimage and is an imperative for action, therefore, 'for others'.

Since this prophetic dynamic is an element in the lives of believers as they seek to respond to a word of the Lord by the 'light of faith', this dynamic is also the basis for prophetic discernment. We will see that the same fundamental dynamic by which the prophet perceives a word of the Lord is essentially the same dynamic by which the hearer of the word discerns the word as a message from God. Before taking up the question of discernment, however, it will be helpful to remind ourselves of that which makes for the ambiguity of the prophetic word and makes the question of criteria for discerning true from false prophecy especially critical. This will mean reviewing what Rahner has said concerning the configurations of human finitude and sin. We will give particular attention to what Rahner considers to be the ambiguities inherent in today's situation. This will set the stage for the crucial question of this chapter, namely, that of discerning true prophecy.

The Ambiguity of the 'Prophetic' Word

We are considering the basis for the ambiguity of the word as that appears in the whole question of a true and false prophetism. As we saw in Chapter I, there have been various criteria developed in the history of prophetism in ancient Israel and the early church for discerning true prophecy. In early Christianity criteria involved primarily Christian teaching and behavior. And yet we recognized that such objective criteria were insufficient for discerning between two mutually exclusive concrete imperatives or messages which in themselves were neither explicitly heretical nor morally impermissible. We are not raising the question at this point as to the possibility of discernment in such a case. Rather, we are seeking to recognize the dimensions in human experience which produce the kind of ambiguity associated with the prophetic word, a word which is unique and timely, originating from God. We are not concerned here, in other words, with messages of an overtly heretical nature which the church can 'easily' dismiss as a teaching foreign to the gospel (although we are concerned in part with what Rahner has described as latent heresy). What we are asking is, What is there about the human condition which makes it difficult to recognize whether a particular message is or is not the particular word of the moment 'from the Lord'? We are concerned here with human finitude and sin and with the situation of the world today as that contributes to the ambiguity involved in perceiving God's word for these times.

Original and Objectified Freedom and Its Significance for Understanding Sin

We have seen how Rahner distinguishes between freedom in its origins and freedom in its objectification. This, of course, has significance for the situation of human guilt. As we saw, for Rahner, freedom is understood as self-actualization involving the whole of human existence.

> Although it exists in time and in history, freedom has a single, unique act, namely, the self-actualization of the single subject himself. The subject's individual acts must always and everywhere be mediated objectively in the world and in history, but he intends one thing and he actualizes one thing: the single subject in the unique totality of his history.[1]

This one act of self-realization, which is mediated objectively in space and time, is a definitive and final act; for it is the act of a subject whose term and source of transcendence is God. Since God is the source and term of transcendence, the horizon in which the categorial object is known and willed, God is affirmed or denied unthematically in every free act. The finite object of

---

[1]Rahner, *Foundations*, p. 95.

human freedom is the medium through which freedom as transcendentally oriented to God is realized. As we have seen,
freedom is freedom in relation to God always and everywhere.
The *Vorgriff auf Esse*, this transcendental reaching out to God,
which grounds human willing of finite objects, can be understood
as God's summons of her creatures to herself. The goal of this
summons, which is the knowledge of God in mediated immediacy,
has been achieved through the incarnation and is an existential for
all human beings. This means that human being is actualized in
the unthematic response to the transcendental summons of God as
that is mediated through the categorial world, and that in this
actualization God is known (at least implicitly) not merely as
asymptotic goal but as the achieved goal of human being, as
present in mediated immediacy.

What we are continuing to maintain is that human freedom
ultimately has to do with God (not only as asymptotic goal but in
God's appearing) and therefore means the possibility of a "yes" or
"no" to God as present.

> If the subject is borne by his transcendental immediacy to God, then really
> subjective freedom which disposes of the subject as a whole and in a final
> and definitive way can occur only in a "yes" or "no" to God because it is
> only in this way that the subject as such and as a whole can be affected.[2]

Only by a 'yes' or 'no' to the transcendental ground of his or her
being does the subject decide about himself or herself as a whole.
We indicated this earlier by the notion of a "fundamental option"
as the basic act of the human being. As we have seen, this 'yes' or
'no' means the possibility of receiving or refusing God in her self-
communication as that is present and mediated in categorial
objects and particularly in the neighbor. This does not mean,
however, that this 'yes' or 'no' is constituted by the sum total of
good and bad acts.

---

[2]Ibid., p. 100.

Such a "no" to God is not originally merely the moral sum which we calculate from individual good or evil deeds, whether we treat all of these acts as having equal value, or whether we believe that in this sum what matters is the temporally last individual act in our lives, as though this were of absolute importance merely because it is temporally last, and not insofar as it recapitulates in itself the act of freedom of a whole life in its single totality.[3]

The fundamental option for or against God (of transcendental faith or disbelief) has to do with the single whole of one's life and is the transcendental precondition for the various finite acts which give expression to it.

This radical 'yes' or 'no' of one's fundamental stance remains hidden, however, since it is not one finite objective datum among others, but rather originates in the transcendental subject. It is mediated by the material spheres in which it operates and therefore a "yes" can be hidden by the evil material taken up in its objectification. Conversely, a radical 'no' can hide behind a seeming righteousness, material it participates in (the objective material of 'God's law', moral norms, learned forms of ethical behavior) and, as such, its objectification does not express its true nature. ". . . behind the facade of bourgeois respectability there can be hidden a final, embittered and despairing 'no' to God, and one that is really subjectively done and not just passively endured."[4]

Rahner makes the further point that this 'yes' and 'no' to God are not parallel realities. Rather, the 'no' to God is sustained by the necessary 'yes' to God of our transcendental orientation. The 'necessary willing' of transcendentality as we have referred to it earlier grounds the possibility of a 'no' to God, but, consequently, such a "no" to God affirms the reality of God implicitly by its transcendental grounding.

---

[3]Ibid., p. 101.

[4]Ibid., p. 102.

We have been recognizing the possibility of a radical 'no' to God, that is, a personal and original refusal of God.[5] We have seen that this 'no' to God remains hidden in its origins and by its objectification. This means, for Rahner, that

> A person never knows with absolute certainty whether the objectively guilty character of his actions, which he can perhaps establish unambiguously, is the objectification of a real and original decision of freedom saying "no" to God, or whether it is more in the nature of a manipulation which has been imposed upon him and which he endures, and which has about it the character of necessity.[6]

In other words, for Rahner, one cannot by empirical observation, on the basis of the character of one's actions, know with certainty one's own fundamental stance; one cannot know whether or not one has decided for or against God and therefore whether one lives by faith or not. We are always faced with the possibility that our lives can be grounded, not in faith, but in the refusal of God's grace. Furthermore, since freedom in its origins has to do with the whole of one's life "it is not finally and definitively actualized until it has actively passed through the deed of life and into the absolute powerlessness of death. . . . " Consequently, the possibility of sin as a radical "no" to God (a stance in unbelief) "is an existential which belongs to the whole of a person's earthly life and cannot be eradicated."[7]

In Chapter III we distinguished between freedom in its origins and freedom in its spheres or objectifications. What we have seen is that freedom as the self-actualization of a subject takes place in the world and in history. It has a context or sphere in which it operates which is prior to its operation and not of its

---

[5] By the use of the term "personal," Rahner is signifying an act which has to do with the whole of the person as person, an act of that kind of being which is distinguished by subjectivity or personality. Such an act of refusal or acceptance is transcendental, having to do with the very origins of personal being.

[6] Rahner, *Foundations*, p. 104.

[7] Ibid., p. 104.

own making. The freedom of the subject is actualized in the medium of a world which has already been determined by the actions and history of other persons. The material of this world, including prepersonal necessities, is appropriated by the free subject and is made an intrinsic and constitutive element in the actualization of freedom. This also means that the guilt which marks human history, the objectifications of sin are "a permanent factor in the situation and realm of the individual's freedom . . ."[8] The subjective, original decision, which is necessarily objectified, expresses, not only the subjective decision, but something of the material which is prior to the decision, material which is marked by the guilt of others. Sin, therefore, as the objectification of the refusal of God by others is a permanent factor in human life which codetermines the objectification of a free, personal decision and as such also threatens that decision, acting as a tempting and seducing influence. The notion of 'concupiscence' in its narrowest sense can be understood as involuntary and spontaneous desire, as prepersonal influences oriented to finite goods which, because of the human situation in sin, can act as a seductive resistance to human free decision in its openness to God.[9] Since even human activity, grounded as it is in transcendental faith (in a radical "yes" to God), is objectified in the material of the world and a history which is co-determined by sin (and thus participates in the objectification of guilt), this activity is always ambiguous. "It always remains burdened with consequences which could not really be intended because they lead to tragic impasses, and which disguise the good that was intended by one's own freedom."[10] We can

---

[8]Ibid., p. 107.

[9]Rahner, "The Theological Concept of Concupiscentia," *TI* 1:347-82 and "Theological Reflections on the Problem of Secularisation," *TI* 10:341-48.

[10]Rahner, *Foundations*, p. 109. This objectification of guilt in the material of the world is how Rahner understands 'original sin'. "Personal sin" which is the personal and transcendental act of the human subject cannot be associated with 'original sin' for it cannot be passed on but is the original act of the individual. The sin or guilt which is passed on is the objectification or consequence of

apply this conception of the ambiguous situation of human reality to the question of prophetic knowledge and its ambiguity.

Prophecy and the Codetermination of Guilt

We have understood prophetic perception as a kind of perception which recognizes the imperative for the moment as a summons from God. We have seen that such a prophetic summons must be grounded in God's self-communication as an existential of human reality. Rahner has made the point that there is a "fluid boundary between believing prophets and 'mere' believers."[11] Human transcendentality, which is the condition in human being which makes faith in its receptivity to the divine self-communication possible, is also the condition, as elevated by grace, for knowing individual concrete knowledge or the timely imperative. Prophetic knowledge, as we have seen, can be understood as the knowledge of transcendental faith. Prophetic knowledge in its objectification necessarily participates in the material of the world and history which is marked by sin. Consequently, the ambiguity which is present in all objectifications of transcendental faith (or the 'fundamental option' of a radical 'yes' to God) is also present in the objective word of prophetic knowledge. Even when the 'prophetic word' is not the expression of a foundational and idolatrous 'no' to God but is grounded in faith, it nevertheless can only come to expression in the material of a guilt-laden world, including the material makeup of the prophetic individual with all of his or her distortions, blind spots, inadequacies. In this sense, the prophetic word is always codetermined by sin. This codetermination, when considered in its material nature today, can further demonstrate the ambiguity involved in prophetic knowledge, especially as it appears in the present situation.

In summary, we can identify, in Rahner, four basic possibilities for prophetic expression as the categorial actualization of a

---

personal sin.

[11]Rahner, *Foundations*, p. 160.

graced transcendence:

    1. The 'prophetic word' may be a categorially adequate expression of a fundamental 'yes' to God, of faith.

    2. The 'prophetic word' may be categorially inadequate (to the historical situation), distorted, or an objectively wrong expression of a subjective fundamental 'yes' to God which, although originating in 'good faith', nevertheless because of the codetermination of guilt or because of the limits of knowledge, language, world view, is misdirected in its objectification.

    3. The 'prophetic word' may be an objectively and seemingly moral and 'orthodox' expression of what is nevertheless a radical "no" to God in unbelief.

    4. The 'prophetic word' may categorially be expressing what, in its transcendental reality, is a radical 'no' to God.

    What we are recognizing is the ambiguity that is involved in the objectification of human transcendentality. The transcendental reality of faith, hope, and love must necessarily be actualized in the concrete, but, as we can see, its objectification, because of human finitude and sin, does not necessarily mean an unambiguous expression of this reality. When today's situation is brought into the picture, some further nuances to this ambiguity are seen.

The Ambiguity Inherent in Today's Situation

    Rahner believes that today's situation, in which faith must realize itself, is qualitatively different from previous situations; it is different *in kind*. We have entered a new epoch in which, in a quite concrete and explicit way, history has become world-history.[12] There was a time when the Christian faith was realized in a

---

[12]There are many places Rahner has taken up this subject of today's situation and what it means for theology, the individual Christian, and the church and its mission. Here are a few: Rahner, "Reflections on Dialogue within a Pluralistic Society," *TI* 6:31-42, "What Is Heresy?" *TI* 5:468-512, "Heresies in the Church Today?" *TI* 12:116-41, "On the Situation of Faith, *TI* 20:13-34, and *The Christian Commitment*, pp. 3-37. See also the references in the introduction, n. 16.

relatively homogeneous society where, at least within an isolated space, people could discuss, argue, and plan within basically the same world view. This is no longer the case. We are in the beginnings today, as Rahner has pointed out, of a world history in which the homogeneity of viewpoints and social structures has been lost. The pluralism of the former time was *external* to the history and social structures and philosophy of a relatively isolated society and civilization. Today our world is increasingly and concretely one, and pluralism is an *internal* aspect of its reality. This is true, not only in regard to the intercommunication of diverse cultures and societies, but is true of the situation within western civilization. Contrasting world views, diverse methodologies and philosophies face each other within a common society and culture, and dialogue between individuals and groups involves struggling with linguistic and hermeneutical differences and varied epistemological starting points which are not simply assumed from the outset.

To this can be added, as Rahner has, the seemingly exponential growth of knowledge which has contributed to a pervasive relativism. The Christian as well as the theologian today must operate with an awareness that the extent of actual knowledge far exceeds anything either assimilable or manageable. In contrast to a previous period when a Christian thinker could know at least basically all there was to know, today a person can only know a very small portion of that which is actually known. As Rahner has pointed out, the prophetic element in the church is dependent, at least in part, on knowledge of the world today, knowledge that is to be found, for example, in the social, historical, and human sciences. This means, therefore, because of the abundance of knowledge today, a new kind of burden for prophetic knowing.

We can see, then, that the pluralism of today's world, the changing horizons of meaning, the fundamentally diverse philosophical and epistemological approaches as the context and the material in which the prophetic dynamic must realize itself, presents an added ambiguity to prophetic perception and reality.

Rahner has addressed this ambiguity as it faces the individual Christian, the church, and the theologian. What he has said in these contexts has implications for prophecy. Concerning the individual today, he points out that the individual

> does not normally express his knowledge in the form of a firm statement, meant to be permanently certain and more or less absolute, but as provisional, open to question, hypothetical, valid for the time being; if further knowledge is acquired, this is seen only as superseding a hitherto accepted hypothesis.[13]

This can be readily applied to prophetic reality as it is realized in today's situation. A person today, while convinced of the necessity of proclaiming a concrete, timely imperative within the life of the church and while experiencing it to be congruent with the summons of God in his or her life, nevertheless, may be quite reticent about proclaiming such an imperative as a "Thus says the Lord" which would give it an 'absolute' character. Many would be much more comfortable with the kind of phrase we find in Acts: "For it has seemed good to the Holy Spirit and to us . . ." and the emphasis would be on "has seemed."[14]

With regard to true and false prophecy we are not likely to view things as being so sharply a black and white issue as was the case in an earlier age when contrasting positions could be set out in opposition to each other and both positions be understood by opponents and simply rejected or accepted on the basis of the principle of noncontradiction. Today we may not always be so certain we understand what the other is saying even though we have some understanding of the words used and are able to bring what is being said, to some degree, within our frame of reference. Rahner has written of a kind of "intellectual concupiscence" which prevails in today's situation in which the relativity of viewpoints, the pluralism, and accumulation of knowledge in a situation co-

---

[13]Rahner, "Situation of Faith," p. 16.

[14]Acts 15:28.

determined by guilt adds an additional burden to our knowing and deciding and therefore also to our proclaiming and hearing the word of the Lord for today.[15] One may in good faith reject a message or call to action as 'false prophecy' simply because within one's own horizons of meaning it appears either to make no real sense or seems simply wrong (if not in an objectively moral way, then as wrong for this time). It can also be the case that we embrace that which is actually giving expression to 'heretical' underlying beliefs which are not readily discernible because of this situation of pluralism and "intellectual concupiscence." Rahner has referred to a kind of "cryptogamic heresy," which is characteristic of today's situation, in which one's attitudes and beliefs are formed within a pluralistic society.[16] The point he makes again is that we do not live in a society with a homogeneous 'Christian' structure and world view which "protects" the individual's thinking and actions. Rather the "existential environment" of today's individual is

> co-formed by attitudes, doctrines, tendencies which must be qualified as heretical and as contradicting the teaching of the gospel. All these heretical elements which thus co-determine the existential environment of each individual do not necessarily need to objectify themselves in theoretical propositions. . . . Actual behaviour, concrete measures etc., can be determined by a heretical attitude, without this attitude formulating itself reflexly in abstract doctrinal propositions. It is sufficient if it realizes itself in the concrete material of life.[17]

Rahner makes the point that such a cryptogamic heresy is inescapable; it is part of the human condition particularly as characterized by today's situation. Everyone is "infected" by it.[18] Furthermore, it is not something that can be addressed by the

---

[15]Rahner, "The Foundations of Belief Today," *TI* 16:5-7.

[16]Rahner, "What Is Heresy?" pp. 492-512.

[17]Ibid., p. 499.

[18]Ibid., p. 500.

church's magisterium; rather the fight against such heresy falls largely to the conscience of the individual.[19] For our concerns, the element of this cryptogamic heresy is particularly significant because the categorial expression of it (whether the expression of a subjectively heretical stance–the radical "no" to God–or of a participation in objective heretical tendencies), this expression can be that of a concrete imperative and therefore have a seeming prophetic character. Hiding behind a 'prophetic' message for our time may be simply the 'heretical' tendencies and emphases of our time. What we are noting here is that the nature of today's situation has compounded the ambiguity involved in prophetic expression.

What we are recognizing is that, for Rahner, human reality is codetermined by grace and guilt (although not equally). This codetermination affects the expression of the prophetic dynamic in human reality and as such is an aspect of the ambiguity of the prophetic message. Because human transcendentality can never become an object of reflection as an object among other objects since it is the precondition for knowing and willing finite objects and not itself such a finite object, therefore the transcendental grounding of a categorial prophetic expression always has a hidden character to it. One can never know with *empirical* certainty that what lies behind such a prophetic expression is transcendental faith or unbelief. Furthermore, since human transcendentality always comes to expression in an already given categorial reality, the material codetermined by guilt which is taken up by transcendental faith and love can distort the categorial expression of that graced transcendentality. Add to these elements of the human condition the situation of today, which includes the pluralism internal to human society and a knowledge (that the prophetic dynamic is dependent on) which inescapably far outstrips the individual's own limited knowledge, there is a compounding of the ambiguity already inherent to prophetism.

---

[19]Ibid., p. 509.

Criteria for Discerning True Prophecy

With these factors in mind we take up the question of criteria, a particularly important question in the entire history of prophetism. The question can be put this way: How does the community of faith, the church, know the genuineness of a prophetic message? After all, the community lives by its response to the word of the Lord and must take seriously God's call, and yet it must not be led astray; therefore, in spite of the many difficulties and ambiguities it *must* 'test the spirits'. We have recognized the problem with identifying any absolute objective criteria for discerning genuine prophecy. Since the individual concrete knowledge of prophecy is not merely the rational deduction from a universal principle but rather the unique call of God for the particular historical situation, the knowledge of whether a prophetic word is from God or not cannot be merely a matter of its conformity to an essential ethics or the general principles of the gospel. It is possible to have two mutually exclusive prophetic imperatives, both of which conform to evangelical principles. Discernment, in such a case, cannot involve some objective universally recognizable criterion. However, the same kind of testing as to the congruence of a particular decision with the transcendental openness as this is experienced within the prophet can also be the kind of testing that a community undergoes. It is not itself an 'absolute', objective, and universally recognizable criterion, for this transcendental openness, as we have seen, cannot be objectified (except in an analogical way); it is the ground of the decision and cannot itself be made an object.

Consequently, it cannot be shown with objective certainty that this transcendental dynamic involves a fundamental 'yes' or 'no' to God. Furthermore, the kinds of ambiguities suggested in the preceding discussion cannot simply be dismissed. The act of discernment must take into account these ambiguities and in fact must recognize its own participation in them. This does not, however, exclude the community's 'testing of the spirits' by considering a particular imperative laid upon the community as to its congruence with the community's experience in the 'light of faith'. The church, in order to fulfill its mission, must risk deciding in regard to those charismatic summons that are made available to it.

This issue of criteria is taken up directly by Rahner in *Visions and Prophecies* where he considers possible criteria for visions. Very briefly, he excludes such criteria as the visionary's piety, personal honesty, mental health, clarity, stability, objectivity, impression of real sensory perception (in a vision), and extraordinariness of the prophetic experience. The paranormality of a 'prophetic' experience is no criterion. Its paranormality does not mean its cause is either pathological or transcendent. Rather, Rahner makes the point that such experiences, while extraordinary, can be quite natural and nonpathological. Since parapsychological phenomena have played a significant role in the history of prophetism and at times have been seen as a criterion of a prophecy's genuineness, we will consider briefly their relationship to the prophetic dynamic before pursuing further the question of criteria.

As we have seen, while parapsychological phenomena are associated with the history of prophetism, such phenomena are by no means essential to prophetic perception. They can simply operate as the stereotypical behavior by which others have recognized a prophet. We have seen that prophetic utterances assume a whole range of psychological and sociological forms. The primary identification of an utterance as 'prophetic' has been the claim that this concrete word for others originates from God. In the age in which we live the prophetic word may be expressed in much more 'ordinary' and 'rational' ways and its divine origination may only be implied or remain hidden because of the reticence typical of our age on the part of the prophetic individual to claim such authority. Nevertheless, because of the association of parapsychological phenomena with prophetism and because of the presence of such phenomena in modern pentecostal movements it may be helpful to consider the way Rahner has conceived the relationship of this prophetic dynamic to such phenomena.

Prophecy and Paranormal Phenomena

Rahner has taken up the related question of the relationship between such phenomena in mysticism and its significance for mystical theology. What he has said in "Mystical Experience and Mystical Theology" is applicable to our concerns here.[20] As he has indicated in this essay, whatever difference there may be between normal and paranormal experiences, it is a 'natural' one. That is, the difference does not lie in some special supernatural intervention such that the one undergoing such an extraordinary experience has somehow reached a higher spiritual level than that of the reality of grace. From a theological standpoint there can be no intermediate or special state between that of grace and the glorified state. Consequently, parapsychological or paranormal experiences, as is the case with ordinary experiences when they become prophetic expressions, arise from a person's fundamental stance in faith.

> *Psychologically* mystical experiences differ from normal everyday processes in the mind, only in the natural sphere; and insofar as they are fundamentally learnable. Like every other act of man's–for example a conscious act, a free act or an act of reflection–these really natural spiritual processes can also be 'elevated' through God's self-communication, habitually or at any given moment. That is to say, they can acquire radical form, in the direction of the immediacy of the self-communication God. This normally takes place in the normal 'supernatural' acts of faith, hope, and love, which constitute the Christian life as such.[21]

From what we have indicated above concerning the dynamic nature of prophecy, we can recognize that the form of prophetic expression is not the crucial element but rather the central element is its grounding in a graced transcendental reality. There is no greater spiritual, moral, or ontological significance to a prophetic

---

[20]Rahner, "Mystical Experience and Mystical Theology," *TI* 17:90-99.

[21]Ibid., pp. 95-96.

expression being of an extraordinary rather than ordinary character. As we have seen, the paranormal character of a prophetic
expression may be due more to certain psychological propensities
in a given prophet as well as sociological influences, than to the
spiritual dynamic involved or the content of the prophecy. In
regard to a 'private revelation' Rahner recognizes that "It may
appear today in a very different way, less spectacular and visionary,
which may indeed be a criterion of its genuineness."[22] We cannot,
in principle, rule out parapsychological expressions from a
'Christian' prophetism. At times certain extraordinary expressions
may, in fact, express an intensity of experience in faith. Nevertheless, the extraordinariness of the form of prophetic expression can
never be a sign of its genuineness.

Perhaps Rahner's attitude toward extraordinary or paranormal experiences within a Christian prophetism can best be
summed up by his words in *Visions and Prophecies*:

> Though God speaks to us in divers ways, it is not clear *a priori* that his
> most important instructions will be given in visions. Rather they are
> contained in the Gospel and are proclaimed by the Church in her
> "ordinary" preaching. God's Spirit stirs—sometimes at least—even in the
> Church's theologians and various "movements", even if they cannot appeal
> to visions. Lovers of revelations and apparitions should not forget either
> (as often happens) that Christ appears to us most surely in the poor and
> suffering. In the Sacrament and in the grace of the Holy Ghost, offered to
> every Christian, we have God's most real presence. The Cross is true
> mercy, and charity the highest of all gifts. If we do not recognize the hand
> that chastises us as God's merciful and healing hand, we shall not find him
> in "revelations" either.[23]

What we have been recognizing is that, for Rahner, there can
be no absolute objective criterion by which to determine the
genuineness of a prophetic message. At least beyond the general
boundaries of the gospel and Christian teaching there is no such
criterion. Certainly Christian teaching provides a criterion and, as

---

[22]*ET*, s.v. "Revelation: 4. Private Revelation," by Karl Rahner, p. 1472.

[23]Rahner, *Visions and Prophecies*, p. 85.

Rahner sees it, the magisterium of the church is responsible for providing guidance to the faithful in regard to the message and content of various prophetic movements as to their faithfulness to the gospel. It can be clear, for example, in St. Paul's words, "that no one speaking by the Spirit of God ever says 'Jesus be cursed!'. . ." (1 Cor 12:3). But even in regard to that which can be judged by the criterion of the gospel, it is not always clear when we are dealing with heresy as was indicated in the preceding discussion by what Rahner calls "cryptogamic heresy." In any case, the prophetic message, as we have indicated, by its very nature excludes the possibility of a criterion, at least when it is within the boundaries of the gospel. For one thing it may be an imperative for action that has no particular reference to the gospel and an object of knowledge quite apart from what we have called primary revelation. Also, such an imperative in its definiteness can exclude other possibilities for action which objectively are also in conformity with evangelical principles. If, for Rahner, there can be no objective criterion for discerning true from false prophecy, this does not mean there is no possibility for discernment on the part of the community of faith and that the community is simply left to either a casuistic ethics or to the many whims of the moment on the part of its members. Essentially, in the same manner by which the prophet knows the individual concrete imperative, the community can receive and know that imperative as a divine summons. The community at least can and does test the prophetic imperative in the light of faith by a "logic of individual concrete knowledge" as described in Chapter II.

This understanding of discernment can also be seen as consistent with the traditional notion of a miracle as the legitimizing sign that a revelation is from God. In the teaching of Vatican I and in Roman Catholic apologetics (as well as in the theology of the New Testament) miracles confirm the divine authorization of a prophet and, in particular, confirm the primary revelation of God in Jesus Christ, the eschatological prophet. (This is true in a unique sense of the resurrection as confirming the salvific action of God in Christ.)[24] While 'miracles', in relation to the secondary revelation of charismatic prophecy in the church, may not have the same significance as they hold for the 'official' and particular history of revelation of the Old and New Testaments; nevertheless, Rahner does give some place to miracles in regard to prophetic visions in the life of the church, as does traditional Roman Catholic mystical theology. Rahner assumes that, for a prophetic vision to have a binding force upon the community, it must be, in a sense, validated by a miracle. In *Visions and Prophecies*, Rahner sees the 'miracle' as the only criterion which can give a prophetic vision validity.[25] In this sense, Rahner does affirm a criterion for genuine prophecy at least as regards 'visions'. However, as we shall see, his understanding of miracle bears out what has been said in the foregoing as to the absence of an absolute objective criterion.   In *Visions and Prophecies*, Rahner provides little development to the notion of miracle and is relatively content with the traditional definition. In *Foundations*, however, he shows much more care in his treatment of the notion of miracle, and considers miracle to be criterion in its function as 'call'.

Miracle as Criterion

In *Foundations* Rahner takes up the question of miracle in the context of God's self-revelation in Jesus Christ and therefore is particularly concerned with miracle as a manifestation of God's self-communication. I will consider Rahner's discussion of miracle and then suggest some implications of his notion of miracle as a criterion or legitimizing sign of prophecy and what this may mean for the exercise of charismatic prophecy in the church. What I will attempt to show is how Rahner's concept of miracle has significance not only for the traditional notion of legitimizing sign in

---

[24]René Latourelle, *Theology of Revelation*, including a commentary on the constitution "dei verbum" of Vatican 2 (Staten Island, NY: Alba House, St. Paul Publications, 1966), pp. 391-405.

[25]Rahner, *Visions and Prophecies*, pp. 82, 103.

relation to the 'official' bearers of revelation, but also in relation to charismatic prophecy in the church, thus showing its continuity with the experience of prophecy today.

Rahner's approach to the question of miracles is similar to many recent theologians (perhaps most notably Paul Tillich). He takes up the New Testament notion of a miracle as a sign, a *semeion*. It is an expression or objectification of God's nearness, her salvation and revelation.

> The "sign" is an intrinsic element in the salvific act itself and belongs to this salvific act of God. It is its manifestation in historical tangibility, the outermost layer as it were in which the revelatory and salvific act of God reaches into the dimension of our corporeal experience.[26]

This means, furthermore, that miracles "are not *facts bruta* but an address to a knowing subject in a quite definite historical situation."[27] A miracle is, in this sense, a concrete expression of God's grace which calls for a response from the recipient of the miracle. (There are no miracles without a recipient.) Rahner clarifies further this notion of miracle by showing how, in a modern interpretation of the world, the notion of miracle as the suspension of the laws of nature can be dispensed with. He points to an understanding of the world in which

> every stream, every dimension, of reality is constructed from the lower to the higher, that is, from the empty and indetermined to the more complex and full, and it is open for the higher dimension. The higher dimension implies in its own reality the lower dimension as an element in itself, and subsumes it into itself in the Hegelian sense, both preserving it and surpassing it. It does not therefore violate the laws of the lower dimension, no more than the higher can be understood only as the more complex instance of the lower and be explained by it.[28]

Rahner points to the "multivalent" nature of what is material and

---

[26]Rahner, *Foundations*, p. 258.

[27]Ibid.

[28]Ibid., p. 259.

biological (the lower sphere of human reality) which is its openness to being formed by freedom (and therefore, as such, need not be conceived as changing in its essential structure).

> Therefore the world of the material and the biological, as an intrinsic element of historical spirit, can become the manifestation of it. By its own intrinsic nature, and because of its indetermination and further determinability, the lower material and biological world can be integrated into the higher order without losing its own laws and structure because of this integration.[29]

This means that the higher appears in the lower, both higher and lower appearing together without "being able to be completely separated from each other."[30] When the higher reality referred to is that of a spiritual, personal reality, then the personal decision in freedom must be able to appear in the interpersonal experience of history and as such be a call to the individuals who make up that history.

For Rahner, God's creation of the world must be seen as a moment in the process of God's self-communication to the other of her creation. The structures and laws of the created order are conditioned and presupposed by God's supernatural self-communication such that they are capable of receiving her Logos, are the precondition for the Logos. "The law of nature and also of history must be regarded from this vantage point as an element within grace, that is, within God's self-communication, and hence also as an element within the history of revelation and salvation."[31] As such, the laws of nature and history do not have to be abolished in order for God's Logos to appear, since they are understood as the precondition for the appearance of the Logos. Consequently, any expression or sign of God's self-communication or any salvific act can be understood as an expression of this one process of

---

[29]Ibid.

[30]Ibid., p. 260.

[31]Ibid., p. 261.

God's self-communication as it is realized in its own historical precondition.[32]

> In view of these reflections perhaps we may say: a miracle takes place in the theological sense, and precisely not in the sense of a preternatural marvel, when for the eyes of a spiritual person who is open to the mystery of God the concrete configuration of events is such that there participates immediately in this configuration the divine self-communication which he already experiences "instinctively" in his transcendental experience of grace, and which on the other hand comes to appearance precisely in the "miraculous", and in this way gives witness of its presence.[33]

Rahner is making the point that God's self-revelation (as an existential in all human existence, because of the definitive and final self-revelation in Jesus Christ) expresses itself in our lives, in the material-biological and historical dimension of the created order (which is precisely by its nature receptive to this 'supernatural' existential). These expressions of God's grace can be understood as 'miracles', and can take on an indefinite variety of forms. As an expression or sign of God's grace, however, a miracle or wonder is a call to individuals which awaits personal response, so that "it performs the function of a call in such a way that this person in this situation is morally obliged to obey this sign." Where a person perceives in the concrete configurations of his or her existence a meaning which serves as a sign of God's presence and call, there is what is meant theologically by 'miracle'. This, of course, means that an individual is open to the ultimate meaning of his or her existence.[34]

> When we regard miracles in this way as an event, which can be encountered within the range of our human experience, we are presupposing with regard to the nature of a miracle as sign that a person is inwardly open to the fact that his existence is ultimately not at his own disposal, and that he

---

[32]Ibid., pp. 260-61.

[33]Ibid., p. 261.

[34]Ibid., pp. 261-62, 262.

has the capacity to perceive the concrete meaning of his existence.[35]

The possibility of a miracle presupposes that one is open to God's call in the concrete expressions of one's existence. The individual must keep alive

> that humble and receptive wonder in which he accepts the events of the world of his experience in its concreteness. If he scrutinizes them responsibly, they offer themselves as a call, and he knows that he is empowered and obligated by them to an historical dialogue with God. Holy Scripture is also familiar with this fundamental willingness in man to believe as a presupposition for the experience of a miracle for Jesus always says: "Your faith has made you whole."[36]

From this viewpoint the prophetic word itself can be understood as a miracle, in its divine origination and in its experience as such by the hearers of the message. It is not necessary to look for some supernatural intervention of the universal laws of nature in order to establish the genuineness of a prophetic vision. Rahner implies this already in *Visions and Prophecies*.[37] And this is certainly the implication of his discussion in *Foundations*. The 'miracle' aspect of prophecy is its grounding in God's self-communication as an existential in being human. A prophetic word can be experienced as a 'wonder' and as a sign of God's presence and call for the person who has 'ears to hear'. We have already described the dynamic of this 'hearing', the logic of this kind of concrete knowledge. In other words, the traditional notion of 'miracle', as a legitimizing sign of a prophetic vision or utterance, does not have to be understood as an accompanying event in which the laws of nature are suspended in order to prove the divine origination of a prophecy (as if such a suspension of 'universal laws' could itself be proved). Rather, for the one who has 'ears to hear', the events and configurations of history themselves are laden with 'signs for

---

[35]Ibid., p. 262.

[36]Ibid., p. 263.

[37]Rahner, *Visions and Prophecies*, p. 46.

the times', expressions of God's ever 'new' call to her people. The bearer of this summons of God and the hearer of this message know it as a 'word of the Lord' by that spiritual discernment whose logic we have described as a logic of individual concrete knowledge. Other than this, there is no absolute 'objective' criterion. What we are recognizing is that the traditional notion of miracle as an objective criterion cannot be held without qualification, for a miracle is not, in and of itself, objective as if it were in a neutral manner available to anyone and did not need the receptivity of faith.

For Rahner, the criteria for discerning a prophetic word or imperative as genuine certainly include its conformity to the gospel and to reason. It must remain within the boundaries of Christian teaching and morality. Furthermore, it is to be expected that prophetic figures and movements will bear signs of God's presence. These do not need to be 'extraordinary', but rather they will express the wonder of God's grace most clearly in the 'ordinary' acts of faith, hope, and love. (Is not the life style of a St. Francis of Assisi, for example, itself a sign of God's presence and love as well as a prophetic call consistent with his prophetic message?) These 'objective' signs or criteria for the genuineness of a prophetic word cannot, however, provide absolute certainty as to the divine origination of a word in its concrete uniqueness and timeliness. In the case of Christian teaching and morality, such universal criteria cannot establish the genuineness of one particular imperative over that of another imperative, both of which conform to Christian teaching and yet mutually exclude each other. The concrete signs of life style or of message on the part of a 'bearer of revelation' cannot, in themselves, indicate the genuineness of a message, given the hidden character of the transcendental grounding of life style and message. For the hearer of the message, the discernment involved must be of the same nature as the discernment on the part of the proclaimer of the message. And as we have seen, that discernment involves the logic of concrete individual knowledge in which a particular message or imperative is tested as to its congruence with the transcendental experience of the love of God as that is mediated by the concrete, historical reality.

Furthermore, since discernment is laden by the ambiguities inherent in the human condition and today's world, discernment necessarily must take place in the midst of a multitude of voices. The truth of the prophetic word is recognized within the parameters of a world codetermined (along with grace) by guilt and in a world which has become increasingly complex and pluralistic in its knowledge and frames of reference.   Given such a situation, we can expect a plurality of discernments in the life of the church and a need for a holy tolerance of opposing viewpoints and decisions. Much latitude needs to be given for the existence, especially within the global community of faith, for actions that are experienced as a call from God, or the call of faith, and which nevertheless may be in seeming opposition to each other. Much care must be given to contexts. Many prophetic messages will only be able to be discerned within the situation of a particular community and within a local context. It is simply impossible in many cases (maybe most) for a magisterium to address the question of true or false prophecy and is, in fact, unnecessary given the responsibility of local and regional communities. There certainly may be many situations in which a group sharing the same context with another but having different horizons of understanding may see the biases the other fails to recognize.

The variables of context and viewpoint as well as ideological and attitudinal biases, do not exclude the possibility of discernment but rather increase the necessity of discernment, a discernment with humility which allows for a diversity of messages and actions in varying situations. When communal discernment takes place it is always within particular, proximate horizons which are themselves in need of continual testing. If anything, the ambiguity inherent in today's situation demands a greater dependence on a truly prophetic and spiritual dynamic of discernment.

Chapter V

Prophecy and the Community of the Eschatological Prophet

We have seen that the prophetic element, when understood as a dynamic aspect of practical reason and as grounded in human reality as graced, is a necessary element of human freedom and decision making; it is necessary to human history which is one-directional and future-oriented. It is a necessary aspect of being human, and being human is not only a matter of being individual but also means being social. Essential to human reality is the interrelationship of human subjects as individuals related to individuals and as individuals related to society, to social structures and institutions, to a political order, even of global proportions. Community, in its many dimensions, is essential to human reality, and prophecy is inherent to community and the social fabric.

What we are concerned with in this chapter is the significance of prophecy for the *Christian* community. We will seek to recognize both the necessity of ecclesial Christianity and the necessity of the prophetic element in the church's expression of its nature. We will begin, first of all, with the question of how ecclesial reality in its formal and dynamic aspect is inherent to human reality. Secondly, we will treat briefly the question of the church as 'founded' by the eschatological prophet, Jesus. This will lead us to a discussion of the material content of an explicit

169

ecclesial Christianity and the relationship between prophecy and the memory of Jesus. Thirdly, we will seek to demonstrate more specifically how, for Rahner, the prophetic dynamic is necessary to the self-realization of an ecclesial Christianity. And fourthly, we will seek the implications of this for the relationship of the church and the world in the socio-critical task of the Christian community.

Foundations of Ecclesiality

As we have seen, Rahner consistently seeks the ontological and anthropological preconditions for the many aspects of human existentiell reality. He seeks to show what there is about being human which is sufficient to explain our multifaceted experience, including the complex experience of Christianity. This is his approach also when he takes up the question of the ecclesial nature of Christianity as can be seen in his treatment of the question in *Foundations*. He is, first of all, concerned with the question of why an *ecclesial* Christianity is necessary. What about being human and Christian necessitates an ecclesial realization of Christianity? Certainly the Christian movement as originating in Jesus Christ, with the particular historical and material content involved, is crucial for answering this question, and Rahner does take up this aspect of the question. And yet, in order to respond to the conception of a bourgeois and individualistic approach to religion, which essentially sees Christianity expressed in a quite individual manner, and in order to see that ecclesiality is grounded in the nature of being human, Rahner points to the interpersonal and social dimension of being human.

Church as Social Realization of Christianity

Community is essential to the realization of human nature and therefore to the salvation of humanity, as that salvation concerns the whole of human reality. This is the point Rahner makes in *Foundations*:

> If man is a being of interpersonal communication not just on the periphery, but rather if this characteristic co-determines the whole breadth and depth of his existence, and if salvation touches the whole person and places him

as a whole and with all of the dimensions of his existence in relationship to God, and hence if religion does not just concern some particular sector of human existence, but concerns the whole of human existence in its relationship to the all-encompassing God by whom all things are borne and towards whom all things are directed, then this implies that the reality of interpersonal relationship belongs to the religion of Christianity.[1]

Rahner's point is that to be human is to live in relationship. Human existence would be unintelligible without the recognition of the existential necessity of intercommunication and sociality. Since the self-communication of God is the essential ground of human being (and in fact, as we have seen, is the foundation of human interrelatedness), then it also follows that this self-communication of God must find social and therefore ecclesial form:

By the very nature of Christianity, church must be understood in such a way that it springs from the very essence of Christianity as the supernatural self-communication of God to mankind which has become manifest in history and has found its final and definitive historical climax in Jesus Christ. Church is a part of Christianity as the very event of salvation. We cannot exclude communal and social intercommunication from man's essence even when he is considered as the religious subject of a relationship to God. If basically God is not a particular reality alongside all other possibilities, but rather is the origin and the absolute goal of the single and total person, then the whole person including his social and interpersonal dimension is related to this God. By the very nature of man and by the very nature of God, and by the very nature of the relationship between man and God when God is understood correctly, the social dimension cannot be excluded from the essence of religion. It belongs to it because man in all of his dimensions is related to the one God who saves the whole person. Otherwise religion would become merely a private affair of men and would cease to be religion.[2]

Community, therefore, is constitutive of human being and ecclesial community is constitutive of human being as related to God. This ecclesial community, of course, has a history. As the history of the community of God in Jesus Christ it mediates salvation.

---

[1] Rahner, *Foundations*, p. 323.

[2] Ibid., p. 343.

Church as the Necessary Historical
Mediation of Salvation

As we have seen, 'revelation' (or salvation) is not merely based in human transcendentality in its infinite openness to the absolute mystery which is God, but rather human transcendentality is the empty openness for receiving God's self-communication which, in order to be received, must come to be in history. That God's self-communication has come to be in history, in Jesus, means the self-communication of God has an objectivity to it which escapes the narrowness of the expressions of an individual's religious feelings and confronts the individual from the 'outside' as having an authority over his or her life. The church, as the community of Jesus Christ and as the bearer of this objective revelation, carries with it the authority of this objectivity as the norm for our subjectivity. (It is not necessary for us to deal more specifically with Rahner's conception of the nature of this ecclesial authority—something which has ecumenical significance.[3])

> ... if salvation depends on the concrete event of [Jesus'] cross, death and resurrection, then this salvation cannot only be found in and based upon a subjective interiority. The concreteness of Jesus Christ as something which challenges me must confront me in what we call the church.[4]

Since salvation (and revelation) is not merely a matter of individual subjective interiority but rather of an objective historical and social nature, then the church, as the social and historical realization of this salvific event in history, is necessarily also, in its "categorial concreteness," the mediation of salvation and grace. The church belongs to the history of revelation and continues to bring to expression the self-communication of God in the world. As we shall see, the prophetic dynamic is necessary to the church's continued making present of the Logos of God in ever new

---

[3]Ibid., pp. 343-44.

[4]Ibid., p. 344.

historical situations.[5]

In order to recognize more clearly the significance of this 'objective revelation' and material content of the church's faith for prophecy in the church, we turn to a consideration of the Christian community as originating with Jesus, the eschatological prophet. We take up the importance of the memory of Jesus for ecclesial prophecy before further elaboration of the dynamic nature of prophecy in the church.

The Community of the Eschatological Prophet

Up to this point we have largely been concerned with the transcendental preconditions in the human being for the possibility of the dynamic of prophecy. We have seen that these preconditions involve a transcendental openness to infinite mystery which has not remained merely an asymptotic reaching out to a goal that could never be realized but the achievement of the goal of this transcendence in the union of God and humankind in Jesus Christ. We have seen, therefore, that the possibility of prophecy is based in the event of God's self-communication, as that grounds what Rahner has called the "supernatural existential." Consequently, our christological assertions have not gone much beyond the significance of God's self-revelation for the dynamic of prophecy as rising out of a graced transcendentality. We have recognized that this graced transcendentality or experience of the Spirit can itself be understood as the Word of God, as it is in fact the self-expression of God in humanity. This, of course, as we have seen,

---

[5]Ibid., p. 345. For Rahner the church is the primal sacrament. While the whole created order is sacrament and symbol of God as 'supernaturally' elevated by grace, the church is primal sacrament because it gives explicit expression to God's self-communication in human, social reality. The church is "the proclaiming bearer of the revealing word of God as his utterance of salvation to the world . . ." (Rahner, "What Is a Sacrament?" *TI* 14:143). In other words, the church is the sacrament of salvation to the world in its pointing the world to the grace that has entered the world.

does not exclude objective revelation. Rather there is no transcendentality without its categorial and historical expression. For Rahner, Jesus Christ, his life, death, and resurrection, is the definitive and final historical objectification of this graced transcendentality, and as such is the ground of this graced transcendentality for all human being.

What we want to see at this point is the significance of the *content* of this objective revelation for prophecy in the church. In other words, we need to see how the objective knowledge of Jesus Christ, of the apostolic message is important for the prophetic element in the church.

The Central Importance of the Historical Jesus for the Church

What we are recognizing is that the gospel of Jesus Christ has two aspects to it. On the one hand, it involves narrative, message, objective word, concrete event; on the other hand, it must be received and appropriated to be known as the gospel it is. The second aspect, namely receptivity, graced transcendentality, spirit, has been our predominant concern. This does not mean that the objective message about Jesus Christ is unimportant for prophecy, rather, the question of the dynamic nature of prophecy causes us to focus on this transcendental aspect. At this point, however, we take up the question of the importance of the historical Jesus and the message about him for the prophetic life of the Christian community. We are concerned with the question of how this gospel and its historical grounding provide for the Christian community's self-understanding, as that is expressed in the dynamic of prophecy. We will seek Rahner's answer to this question by first of all recognizing the kind of significance the historical Jesus has in Rahner's thought through focusing on the importance of Jesus as eschatological prophet or absolute saviour. Then we will consider how this objective knowledge of Jesus functions to inform the church of its prophetic nature and, further, how the material content of this knowledge serves prophetic proclamations.

New Testament scholars have pursued the question of the self-understanding and claims of Jesus. One particularly significant avenue in recent years has revolved around the notion of Jesus as 'eschatological prophet'.[6] It is certainly beyond the scope of this work to go into the exegetical and critical work on this subject. We will have to content ourselves with some of the conclusions of this work and with certain theological observations. The image of Jesus as eschatological prophet is formed by, among other factors, the recognition that Jesus both proclaimed the nearness of God's reign and assumed that God's reign was arriving through his message and deeds, that, in fact, the reign of God was breaking in upon the world as a result of his mission which included his death (however Jesus may have interpreted his death).

Rahner himself, in *Foundations*, takes up this conclusion of a number of New Testament scholars that Jesus saw himself as the 'eschatological prophet', although Rahner's choice of terms is

---

[6]The four gospels have retained for us in varying degrees the popular view among Jesus' contemporaries that he was a prophet. For the evangelists themselves the title 'prophet' does not hold a major position in their portrayal of Jesus. For Mark and Matthew it has no significant christological importance. For Luke 'prophet' is important as a way of portraying Jesus' mission which ends in suffering and death. For John, it seems, the *notion* of Jesus as the 'eschatological prophet' occupies a significant place. Generally, however, the Gospels and other New Testament writings indicate that for the early church, the title 'prophet' was inadequate for designating the reality of who Jesus was.

As far as Jesus' self-understanding is concerned there is no indication that he ever explicitly referred to himself as a prophet. There are indications, however, of an indirect nature, that he viewed his mission as prophetic and, in fact, as the one who is the eschatological prophet, the one who announces and, through his deeds, brings in the reign of God. Some of those indirect indications as Aune has outlined them include Jesus' sense of divine calling, symbolic actions, certain characteristics of his speech, and his eschatological thrust. Also, there are a number of predictive sayings and actions which his contemporaries perceived as miracles and thus associated him with the prophets of the Old Testament. See Aune, *Prophecy in Early Christianity*, pp. 153-88 and also Reginald H. Fuller, *The Foundations of New Testament Christology* (New York: Charles Scribner's Sons, 1965), for his arguments concerning Jesus as the eschatological prophet.

generally the "absolute saviour."[7] We can hardly elaborate in detail Rahner's conception of Jesus as absolute saviour and how that fits with what we have already indicated about his Christology. Briefly, however, we note that Rahner believes there are two theses which must be shown to be historically credible in order to show, at least in a minimal way, the grounds for the whole of an orthodox (Chalcedonian) Christology. The first thesis is that Jesus presented himself as the *eschatological* prophet, as the one through whom the reign of God (and therefore God) was being made present in a final way. The second thesis is that Jesus rose from the dead, revealing the victorious arrival of God's reign. Without reflecting further on Rahner's elaboration of these theses, it is clear that, for Rahner, the historical grounding of Christianity is crucial. The meaning of Jesus of Nazareth is not simply determined by the subjective transcendental experience of human beings. Although this transcendental experience forms a "searching Christology" (an implicit search for the absolute saviour), it cannot simply make up its own saviour (as if what was made up was in reality saviour). Rather, human transcendentality, in its implicit search for the self-expression of God in history, comes upon this Jesus of Nazareth as the answer to its search, and although history, in itself, in its empirical nature, can never offer more than the provisional–and historical science, more than probability–nevertheless, this search for the absolute saviour, when it ends in faith, means an unconditional commitment to a historical (and therefore conditional) reality, for it recognizes the coming to be present of unconditional mystery, the absolute and final objectification of a graced transcendentality (or, in other words, the breaking in of God's reign), so that history with all its provisionality is recognized as directed to the nearness of God (as the expression of a graced transcendentality).[8]

---

[7]Rahner, *Foundations*, p. 246.

[8]Ibid., pp. 228-305. Rahner notes the circular character of faith knowledge which involves the synthesis of the "objective ground of faith" and the "subjective

The particular point for our discussion is that, for Rahner, the work of historical-critical scholarship and the development of a Christology from below is not superfluous but rather crucial to the task of theology and to the proclamation of the gospel today, for it is the historical Jesus who is the ground of the church's faith. But this also means that the historical witness to Jesus, the memory of his life, suffering, and death are crucial for a Christian prophetism. This is clear in two respects. First, the apostolic witness to Jesus and the gospel presupposes prophetic activity, and secondly, the gospel provides material content for the prophetic message.

The Gospel Presupposes Prophetic Activity

That the gospel presupposes prophetic activity is something we have already seen. Our discussion of the anthropological presuppositions for the prophetic element lead us to the point where we could take up a christological viewpoint in which the implications of the gospel could be seen in terms of the nature of human reality. We saw that there is, in the experience of being human, a graced transcendentality that is made intelligible by the gospel of Jesus Christ which says that God, the absolute mystery, has become the ultimate goal of human being and not as distant and out of reach, but as near and fulfilled. We have seen the gospel, therefore, as an ontological reality in the nature of being human which is realized in each individual's existentiell self-realization and in expressions of human community.

In his essay "The Function of the Church as a Critic of Society," Rahner takes up the gospel origins of the view of the church as prophetic. Among the aspects of the gospel which he believes points to the prophetic nature of the church (aspects we have already recognized), there is the "proclamation of the absolute hope in the absolute future which is God himself" which provides a viewpoint "from which to criticize and estimate the relative value of all the individual goals which can be planned and

---

willingness to believe" (pp. 230-35).

set up on the part of historical man," not merely rendering them insignificant but giving them their radical seriousness as they are viewed before the absolute future, to be expressions of the future; also, the unity of love of God and love of neighbor and its implications in the social and political dimension and the recognition that the gospel is the gospel of the cross–"Christian theology is always a theology of the cross." As a call to follow the Crucified, the gospel means the acceptance of failure and death and therefore the courage to be committed to tasks without assurance of success. What we are recognizing is that the gospel is the basis for the Christian community's understanding of its prophetic calling.[9]

Prophecy and the Memory of Jesus

The explicit, material content of the gospel, the memory of Jesus and his suffering and death, becomes crucial for a Christian prophetism. The importance of this for the 'practical reasoning' of the Christian community is given much more attention by a former student and friend of Rahner's, namely, Johannes Baptist Metz who believes the lack of attention to this aspect in Rahner's theology is its primary weakness.[10] While the memory of Jesus and

---

[9]Rahner, "Church as Critic," pp. 253-41, 239, 241.

[10]Johann Baptist Metz, *Faith in History and Society: Toward a Practical Fundamental Theology*, trans. David Smith (New York: Seabury Press, 1980), pp. 32-48, 154-68. Metz has criticized Rahner's transcendental approach as tending to be divorced from history and concrete human reality in such a way that Rahner's human subject does not receive the critique of practical reason formed by an attention to the concrete historical situation and praxis of the subject. The resulting formulation of the human being as subject tends to adopt uncritically the middle-class subject of today's post-Enlightenment world. Metz believes Rahner's theology has been determined too much by the questions of the Enlightenment rather than allowing the critique of a practical reason formed by the memory of suffering to raise the questions and give direction to his theology.

While I believe Metz is pointing to a certain weakness in Rahner's theology, nevertheless, I believe he has overstated the case; and, at least theoretically, Rahner has been careful to maintain a transcendental-historical approach in which the concrete historical subject is of major importance. Rahner has recognized the need for a balance between theoretical and practical reason and has, in fact, welcomed Metz's practical fundamental theology for its bringing a balance to

his suffering in narrative and story do not have a predominant place in Rahner's theological formulations, nevertheless, the content of the gospel certainly remains crucial for his understanding of a Christian prophetism. In his essay, "Prophetism," Rahner refers to those prophets who follow Jesus Christ, *the* prophet: "Jesus Christ is *the* great prophet, the absolute bringer of salvation. This does not mean that prophecy has simply ceased. . . . But the only prophets are those who strive to uphold his message in its purity, who attest that message and make it relevant to their day."[11]

Jesus Christ is the "eschatologically final prophet" who is revealed as such by God's raising him from the dead. As eschatological prophet he brings to a close the open-ended prophetism of his Old Testament predecessors. Rahner makes the point, in *Visions and Prophecies*, about the unsettled nature in the dialogue between God and humanity before Christ:

> Before Christ it was still possible for something unprecedented to happen in history (without terminating history) that could change man's whole relationship to God. . . . Man had to be ever ready for a new revelation, which might radically alter the course of his salvation; though in retrospect, once these revelations were promulgated, man could see that they were part of the hidden plan of God, and that God's later acts were based in fact upon his earlier ones.[12]

The situation has changed with the coming of Christ, at least for Christians; the open-ended possibilities for God's revelation

---

theology which, in its present state, is weighted to the theoretical. See Rahner, "Reflections on Methodology in Theology," *TI* 11:89:

"Nor does our interpretation of transcendental philosophy involve any denial of the fact that in the concrete situation of a particular epoch or a particular individual it may be necessary, in coming to a decision of the practical reason, in concrete practice to be 'one-sided' and in a certain sense to forget the prudent balancing of one factor against another in the dialectic of a transcendental philosophy because otherwise it would deprive the legitimate one-sidedness of the concrete decision of its force."

[11]*ET*, s.v., "Prophetism," by Karl Rahner.

[12]Rahner, *Visions and Prophecies*, pp. 23-24.

have been replaced by the "definitive and final phase" of God's self-revelation, such that the "expectation of the revelation of God in history has been superseded by expectation of the revelation of God which will end history." There can no longer be any "revelations" which "substantially alter the conditions of our salvation." This, of course, does not mean there cannot be "revelations," but that they cannot be, as Rahner puts it, "new assertions" but rather, they are "new commands" or imperatives. Even if we recognize that many prophetic utterances even of a Christian prophetism (as noted in phenomenological studies) are not *explicitly* 'imperatives', nevertheless, the point is that the Word of God in Christ is the definitive and final word, such that it cannot be superseded but rather applied in ever new and varying situations.[13]

This means, then, that the objective content of the gospel of Jesus Christ, the explicit witness of the Christian community to the eschatological prophet as it maintains its memory of him, is the basis for a Christian prophetism which seeks to bring the eschatological word of Jesus (and the event of the eschatological Word which Jesus *is*) to bear on the new situations in which it finds itself. This is essentially the first point which Rahner makes when considering the prophetic nature of *Gaudium et Spes* (the *Pastoral Constitution on the Church in the Modern World*). In his essay "on the Theological Problems Entailed in a 'Pastoral Constitution'," he notes that the instructions of this pastoral constitution, which are of a prophetic nature, have, in principle, a doctrinal basis. "For what could be the starting point for such instructions, from which they could derive their standards and the authority which they do ultimately claim to have, if not the message of the gospel, the doctrine of the faith which the Church upholds and proclaims in

---

[13]Ibid., pp. 24-25. As we have already noted, there can be words of comfort, judgment, assurance, warning, which are not strictly speaking 'imperatives' but which are the words necessary in particular situations for the further self-realization of the community of faith. Such messages are not "new assertions."

virtue of her teaching authority?"[14]

It is clear that, for Rahner, there can be no new revelations which could add anything to the message of the gospel. Rather, a Christian prophetism always proceeds from the gospel of Jesus Christ and applies that gospel to new situations. The gospel message and the memory of Jesus inform and inspire the prophetic word and yet, as we shall see (and as implied in our earlier discussions), this prophetic word can be expressed without explicit reference to the gospel message and treat of situations in a way that is possible for a quite 'natural' and secular knowledge. (We have already seen that this prophetic dynamic is a 'natural' expression of being human.) We will see this point more clearly as we take up the question of what about being the church necessitates a prophetic element in its life and mission. We will approach an answer to this question by an examination of Rahner's essay "On the Pastoral Constitution" which in large part is concerned with this question or at least with showing that charismatic or prophetic instruction is necessary for the church to be church.

The Necessity of the Prophetic Dynamic for an Ecclesial Christianity

Theological Instructions

In this essay Rahner raises the question of the nature of a "pastoral constitution," reflecting on the peculiar nature of the Vatican II document, *Pastoral Constitution on the Church in the Modern World*, which in large part is an analysis of the modern situation and the role of the church in the modern world.[15]

---

[14]Rahner, "Theological Problems in 'Pastoral Constitution'," p. 295. For the Vatican II document, *Gaudium et Spes* (1965), see Austin Flannery, ed., *Vatican Council II; The Conciliar and Post-Conciliar Documents* (Northport, NY: Costello, 1975), pp. 903-1014.

[15]For several analyses of this Vatican II document and Vatican II generally, see Bonaventure Kloppenburg, *The Ecclesiology of Vatican II*, trans. Matthew J. O'Connell (Chicago: Franciscan Herald, 1974); Warren A. Quanbeck, ed.,

Rahner's concern with this document revolves around the question of how a "pastoral instruction" of this nature (which seeks to analyze and to apply doctrinal principles to the modern situation) is possible. As we have recognized, Rahner notes that this Constitution is not without doctrinal basis and yet wonders why "directives" or "instructions" (*Weisung*) are derived from doctrinal principles rather than "norms" which could "be presented as belonging integrally to the official teaching of the Church."[16] In other words, the question is raised as to the nature of these 'instructions', such that they do not have the same doctrinally binding force as 'norms'. Thus, "what sort of awareness of the situation does the Church have, that it leads her to try to respond to it with an instruction precisely of this kind . . .?"[17] The question being raised concerns a prophetic perception which gives rise to a prophetic instruction.

Rahner makes his starting point for responding to the above question with a thesis of an ontological character:

> While recognizing to the full the validity of the universal, we must say that any free decision, as a concrete individual act, and therefore as an act of the person endowed with spiritual faculties in the concrete, is never merely one instance among many sharing a common nature. And for this reason it can never, in the last analysis, be fully deduced from universal principles.[18]

We have already seen the basis for this thesis in our discussions of the concrete knowledge and ontology of the individual. We have seen that there is a kind of knowledge of an individual, concrete nature which cannot be totally reduced to the universal as if it were merely one among many objectifications of the

---

Challenge and Response (Minneapolis: Augsburg, 1966); and Edmund Schlink, *After the Council*, trans. Herbert J. A. Bouman (Philadelphia: Fortress Press, 1986).

[16]Rahner, "Theological Problems in 'Pastoral Constitution'," p. 296 and "Zur Theologischen Problematik einer 'Pastoral Konstitution'," *ST*

[17]Rahner, "Theological Problems in 'Pastoral Constitution'," p. 297.

[18]Ibid.

universal. Nevertheless, it remains under the universal, and the "abstract intelligence," as it reflects on and objectifies this knowledge, must refer to the universal. In other words, this individual concrete knowledge has a rational element to it in that, in order for it to be objectified, communicated, and given a rationale, it must refer to the universal aspect of common human nature.

With this recognition of a concrete individual knowledge, Rahner believes he can provide a definition of the kind of instruction or directive involved in a pastoral constitution.

> Instruction [*Weisung*] is the counsel to take a concrete decision which, while it is intended to give reality to a universal nature and to a universal principle in a specific situation . . . is nevertheless incapable of being derived from this universal in any full or compelling sense, either in respect of its content or in respect of its binding force, but remains, both in its uniqueness and its factuality, that which belongs to history, and something which, in the last analysis, can be understood only in its actual realisation.[19]

Rahner notes that instruction understood as defined above is by its very nature also a decision and in fact corresponds to what we have already recognized as the expression of a graced practical reason. Rahner makes the point that

> every analysis of a situation on the part of a concrete individual subject must be something more than merely material for the speculative intellect to theorise about in an absolutely neutral manner. In all cases and inevitably it must also be the spontaneous act of the practical intellect. In other words it must *ipso facto* itself be a decision.[20]

What again is being seen is that this dynamic (and prophetic) element is inescapably and necessarily the act of a concrete individual subject who faces situations which hold more than one morally permissible option when considered in the light of univer-

---

[19]Ibid., p. 298 and "Zur Theologischen Problematik einer 'Pastoral Konstitution'," *ST* 8:618.

[20]Rahner, "Theological Problems in 'Pastoral Constitution'," p. 299.

sal norms, and yet who must make a decision of an individual nature, a decision which constitutes the action that ought to be taken for *this* situation and moment. Furthermore, this individual decision which instruction is (the prophetic word comes through individuals), is a decision for others, for convincing others, "using the intercommunication which exists between one human subject and another in order to make that other choose one specific decision among several possible ones. . . ."[21]

The question Rahner raises next has to do with what kind of binding force such instructions have; after all, this instruction, being an individual decision, cannot simply be rationally deduced from a universal norm. "From the theological point of view this binding force is, to the extent that it is a genuinely moral element that is in question here, to be interpreted on the basis of the *summons uttered* by God in the concrete to the individual, and directing him to take a specific decision."[22] This kind of instruction has a binding force; however, it is not the "binding force of universal norms considered as divine commandments." It does not have the binding force of a command applicable to all people in all situations at all times. Rather, since it is an instruction (and summons from God) which arises out of the unique concrete situation, it speaks to those specific individuals or groups of individuals who discern for themselves that it is a call upon their lives. The discernment and testing involved in such a decision has already been indicated, and this concrete individual knowledge, this mode of knowing is true, both for the instructor and those who receive instruction. The hearers of this *theological* instruction (as Rahner terms it since it is a summons from God) must test and discover for themselves within the concrete situation whether this instruction is, in fact, an instruction from God directed to them. Whether or not it is *explicitly* recognized as 'from God' is not necessary, but rather that it is perceived as bearing a moral obligation.

---

[21]Ibid.

[22]Ibid., p. 300.

Charismatic Instructions as Essential
to the Life and Mission of the Church

The next step in Rahner's reflections on a 'pastoral constitution' is to apply the above observations on 'theological instructions' to the action of the church. This leads us to our primary concern in this section which has to do with the necessity of the prophetic element as grounded in the essential nature of the church.

Rahner makes the point that the "Church is not merely an upholder and interpreter of the truth of revelation," but as a subject (constituted as a society) must make decisions in the concrete and, in its 'official' and representative ministry, offer guidance to its members who must take up actions in the concrete and unique situations of their time. The church has a power to guide which goes beyond the nature of divine commandments of a universal nature. This is the case because the church must realize itself in the concrete and in the ever new historical situation. The ontology of the individual, as we have seen, can also be applied to a society in the uniqueness of its historical self-realization. This is certainly true for the church. Furthermore, since the church (as any society) is made up of individuals, the concrete realization of its nature happens through the individual actions of its members.

> The realisation of her own fulness is something that is necessary and a duty for the Church, something, more over, in which there is an element of contingency, since it belongs to the dimension of concrete history, and since *de facto* it can be achieved only through the free decision and the free act of individual Christians.[23]

What we are recognizing, therefore, is that there belongs to the essential nature of the church a power to guide or a kind of 'instruction' which is of a different nature from that of universal divine commands, and that this instruction is necessary to the realization of the church in history.

As we have seen already concerning this 'individual concrete

---

[23]Ibid., pp. 301-02.

knowledge', it is recognized not simply on the basis of moral principles (although it cannot go beyond the bounds of such principles) but as a divine summons in the concrete, as the thing that ought to be done here and now, although other morally permissible possibilities may be present.

> . . . in her practice the Church must act in this way, just as an individual man also, in a concrete situation, follows the 'dictates of his conscience' in selecting one of various possibilities even when his theoretic intelligence is incapable of recognizing any one of these possibilities as absolutely and certainly the only one which can be entertained.[24]

Rahner recognizes, however, that it is not enough to say that the church, like an individual, acts according to the "highest dictates of conscience," but rather, the power to guide must be seen in the light of the church as guided by the Holy Spirit. The church is maintained in faith, hope, and love through the assistance of the Holy Spirit who makes it possible for the church to express its life in ever new ways. The "Spirit extends precisely to the whole range of those decisions, acts, omissions and mutual influences in all their variations, in which the abiding of the Church in Christ is realised in the concrete." Thus this concrete decision of the church in regard to its specific historical situations can be termed a "charismatic decision" and this instruction, a "charismatic instruction." Rahner recognizes that the whole church is given the Spirit; but this means, then, that the Spirit can even speak through the church's official representatives, even though we may "wish that this power of the Spirit could be manifested more clearly and in ways which transcend all merely institutional levels."[25]

While recognizing this charismatic influence of the Spirit, Rahner, at the same time, wants us to see that this recognition of the decision and instruction appropriate to the specific situation is nevertheless a "*human* recognition, with all the necessary prior

---

[24]Ibid., p. 304.

[25]Ibid., pp. 305, 306.

conditions, developments and systems of thought which belong to a human process of recognition, and above all to the recognition of a particular individual factor in history." Furthermore, since the church is involved in concrete action in history, it is dependent upon a knowledge of the historical situation (and consequently does not "draw her life *solely* from the revelation of God"). The church of necessity, in order to realize itself in history and as a condition of its essential nature, must make use of a knowledge "which does not belong to the *depositum fidei*."[26]

Rahner points out that this factor (namely, the knowledge of the situation) in the church's recognition of the concrete action needed within a particular situation is something quite amazing considering that this means struggling with the complexity and plurality of human knowledge, the dependence of the church on the "experts" in various fields and on methods of retrieving knowledge outside the church's control. That the church risks such an undertaking at all is because it is necessary to its own life and mission. In considering the situation of its times and the actions necessary, the church must make use of all those scientific methods involved in the analysis of the situation. Nevertheless, such decisions for action can only be arrived at and express the church's own essential reality, as the community of the eschatological prophet (and therefore of the Spirit), through the charismatic assistance of the Holy Spirit. This assistance does not "exclude the fact that the Church may fall short in her analysis of the situation through human limitations and human failures, or even through culpable obstinacy and narrow-mindedness, the refusal to recognize her own faults, a lack of charity in recognising the value of those outside her etc." But such obstructions in the church's decision making do not dismiss the reality of the Spirit's assistance.

---

[26]Ibid., pp. 307, 308. See also Rahner and N. Greinacher, *Handbuch der Pastoraltheologie II/1*, pp. 178-76, 180-88; and Rahner, *The Christian Commitment*, pp. 3-37.

On the contrary, this influence of the Spirit is manifested primarily in the following two facts: first that the Church actually does venture upon an analysis of this sort, not attempting to suppress the factors adverse to herself which she may under certain circumstances have to recognise in doing so, but rather facing up to them in all openness and humility; second, that the Church is able to select from the incalculable number of individual facts and findings to which such an analysis gives rise those in particular to which the charismatic summons of the Spirit directs her when it is mediated to her in the process of arriving at her decisions and instructions.[27]

These observations provide Rahner with the position from which to define a 'pastoral constitution', that is to define a set of instructions issued by the official ministry of the church, instructions which are not merely the rational deduction of principles from the essential message of the gospel. The definition he gives is as follows:

The essence of a Pastoral Constitution consists in instructions issued by the Church primarily for her own members, and to some extent over and above this for all men who are ready to pay attention to the Church. These instructions are issued in view of the contemporary situation as evaluated under the charismatic influence of the Spirit and in response to the charismatic summons of God.[28]

While Rahner is particularly interested here with the instructions of the official ministry of the church (and, in fact, goes on to raise the question as to whether the "Pastoral Constitution on the Church in the World Today" is, in fact, a 'pastoral constitution' as he has defined it), we have been interested in the broader question of the possibility of such 'charismatic instructions', whether 'official' or 'unofficial'. (In fact, in this essay and elsewhere Rahner makes it clear that such prophetic instructions and ministry are more likely to be expressed at the grassroots level.[29] Our particular con-

---

[27]Rahner, "Theological Problems in 'Pastoral Constitution'," p. 311.

[28]Ibid., pp. 311-12.

[29]Ibid., pp. 312-13. Rahner speaks of charismatic individuals in the history of the church but believes we cannot exclude the possibility of the 'official'

cern with this essay by Rahner has been with the necessity of prophetic instruction for the self-realization of the church.

We have seen in this essay that Rahner applies the a priori conditions for human being and knowing to the concrete life of the church. This has meant seeing the church in its transcendental and historical aspects and recognizing that the church as a society of individuals can itself be understood as a subject.

The church as transcendental subject necessarily actualizes itself in history, and as with the individual person who must make decisions of a concrete, historical nature, the church also must make such decisions, coming to them through the operations of an individual concrete knowledge which we have already described. Such knowledge comes through individuals in the church and is also received by individuals who test and discern the instructions given in the same essential mode that such knowledge is discerned by the 'instructors'.

This historical realization of the church's essential nature also, necessarily, by virtue of its historical nature, means the church is dependent on a knowledge of the historical situation and therefore on a knowledge that is not derived simply from the *depositum fidei*. And yet, in the midst of all the rigorous analysis of the historical situation, using whatever scientific methods available, the church can come to recognize the elements that need to be focused on and the actions taken as the result, not simply of social analysis, but of the charismatic summons of the Spirit. Rahner, as we have seen, recognizes that neither the individual nor a society can wait until all the evidence is in (how much more true in the face of an overwhelming growth of knowledge), but as important as the analysis is, must nevertheless bring it to an end in the making of a decision. As we have already seen, that coming to a decision, involving a concrete knowledge of an individual kind, is grounded in the graced transcendental openness of the subject or, in other words, in the Spirit-borne openness to the absolute mystery, God.

---

church also giving such instructions!

We recognize again that we are dealing with a "secondary revelation"; not the revelation of something unattainable by 'natural' reason, but of a perception of historical reality available to natural modes of knowing under the influence of the Spirit.

While charismatic instruction has generally come from the grassroots level, through lay individuals and movements, it can also come from the official and representative ministry of the hierarchical church, from the teaching office of the church, for the Spirit who maintains the church in the gospel also gives direction in the realization of the church's life and mission in history, and does so through the institutional aspect of the church which is also Spirit given.

It can further be noted as implied by the above assertions that where the church (which is always also the church of sinners) fails to give adequate attention to the historical situation or respond to the charismatic summons of the Spirit but instead merely seeks to repristinate the past or treats its plans for action as if they could simply be rationally deduced from the theological principles of the gospel, then the church also fails to express its essential nature in the new historical moment, which is to say the church fails to be (to that extent) the community of the eschatological prophet. Furthermore, this means the church fails in its mission in the world. In the following section we take up the question of the significance of the prophetic element for the church's relationship to the world.

The Church as Critic of Society

We are taking up the question of the church's prophetic stance in society. We begin, however, with the broader question of the relationship of church and world in Rahner's thought. In this way we will see the significance of the prophetic element in the context of Rahner's general conception of the church and the world.

The Relationship of the Church and the World

Rahner has on many occasions taken up the question of the relationship of church and world, particularly as that has concerned the church in the modern world. The most succinct and yet content-filled outline of the church-world relationship can be found in his article entitled "Church and World" in *Sacramentum Mundi*.[30] I will lift up some of the main points of this essay in order to give the broad framework in which the socio-critical role of the church must be conceived.

First of all, after Rahner briefly considers the history of the question he gives three meanings of 'world'. The term 'world' expresses (1) the "whole of creation as unity," (2) the place of sin (therefore, the Christian is to come out of the world, in this sense), and (3) the place where one finds eschatological salvation. These three meanings of the term 'world', in fact, express three basic aspects of the world as the history of the human being, for the world is the history of transcendence in which transcendence has achieved its goal in the nearness of God through the gracious self-revelation of God in history. As we have seen, this self-revelation of God in history means that God is not only the world's efficient cause (and the world therefore understood as 'creation'), but God has become the world's quasi-formal cause, so that in God the world realizes its true nature (and therefore can be considered as 'redeemed'). That it is the history of the human being and of personal decision has come to mean it is a world of sin and redemption. "It is a unity in difference of saving action and guilt."[31]

Secondly, Rahner reflects briefly on the term 'church', designating the church as essentially the fundamental sacrament of the world. This is a significant concept for Rahner (as well as for Roman Catholic theology generally; it is a notion made use of in the Vatican II document, *Lumen Gentium*). For Rahner, the

---

[30]*ET*, s.v. "Church and World," by Rahner. (Also in *SM* under the same title.)

[31]Ibid., pp. 237-39, 239.

church as sacrament means that the church expresses before the world, the world's own *inner entelechia* which is the eschatological arrival of the Logos of God. It continues the explicit expression of God's victorious self-revelation. As he notes in "Church and the World," the church and the reign of God are not identical; rather, the reign of God has come to the world as a whole and is expressed in the life of the world. The church as fundamental sacrament of the world is "the eschatological and efficacious manifestation (sign) in redemptive history that in the unity, activity, fraternity, etc. of the *world*, the kingdom of God is at hand." The church, in other words, is the explicit sign and symbol of what God's intentions are for the world and in fact, of what God is doing in the world.[32]

Thirdly, Rahner notes that the church-world relationship has a history which, in part, involves a process of change in perceptions from a Greek "cosmocentrism" to an "anthropocentrism," a change from a world conceived as numinous to a world viewed as available for human manipulation. This change Rahner believes is based in the spirit of Christianity although the church has not always explicitly realized this and has, in fact, in the past reacted negatively to the world's secularization.

This history of the church and its relation to the world is an ongoing *history* and therefore incalculable and, as we have seen, means ever new expressions of concrete decisions under the charismatic summons of the Spirit. Because it is incalculable "it is difficult to reduce it to a formula." Nevertheless, with reservations, Rahner observes the following:

> Yet we might perhaps say that it is the history of the Church's growing self-discovery and of the increasing emancipation of the world into its own secular nature by the Church. The Church comes to know itself more and more as "not of this world" and at the same time as the sacrament of the absolute future of the world, which is not produced by the world by its own power but is given to it by God, as a supra-mundane grace, thus relativizing

---

[32]Ibid., pp. 239-40, 240.

in theory and practice any conception which the world forms of itself, in other words, opens it out to the absolute future.[33]

We will see more fully later on what this emancipation of the world means for the church's realization of its "diaspora" character.

Fourthly, Rahner mentions two basic misconceptions of the church-world relationship which he calls "integrism" and "esotericism." In the first case, the world is regarded "as mere material for the action and self-manifestation of the Church, and wants to integrate the world into the Church." In the case of the second, the world, rather than being affirmed, is fled as having nothing really to do with what counts which is the eschatological salvation of God.

Particularly significant are the fundamental reasons Rahner gives for the error of these conceptions. Integrism is false because it is impossible. It is impossible because one cannot "derive from the principles of natural law and gospel the human action which ought to be done *here and now*, although of course all action must respect those principles." Consequently, there can be no governments, political and social structures, economic systems, which are *the* Christian way, resulting from Christian principles. Furthermore, the actions "in the world" still concern salvation; they "can even be the subject of charismatic inspiration from on high, and, while remaining secular, a factor in the coming of the kingdom of God." Also, integrism ignores the plurality of knowledge and the situation of "concupiscence" which makes it impossible to integrate everything into a unified Christian system. Esotericism, on the other hand, is based on the false assumption that everything about the world is sinful and therefore fleeing sin and fleeing the world are the same thing. In other words, its view is that there is nothing about the world which is important for salvation.[34]

---

[33]Ibid., pp. 240-41.

[34]Ibid., pp. 241, 242, 241-43.

Fifthly, Rahner believes the true relation between church and world is reflected in a mean between these two extremes, which "lies above the two extremes as a unity, combining on its own basis both the unity and the difference of what is explicitly Christian and ecclesiastical on the one hand and the world and secular action on the other." This mean between extremes is expressed in two different ways, through the 'official' ministry of the church (magisterium and pastoral office) or through Christians (primarily laity) in the world. The difference which Rahner sees in the way the official and unofficial church expresses itself, it seems to me, is not a matter of an essential difference, but rather what can be expected in today's situation. Rahner may be providing us with his own 'prophetic instruction' with this word for the official church:

> at the present time it will be decisive to renounce all integrism even merely in practice.

> In its whole attitude it must make it quite clear that the Church is and wills to be nothing but the socially constituted community of those who freely believe in Christ, joined with him and with one another in their love of him; that it is not the religious institution of a State or of a secular society as such.

> . . . It is no longer possible for the Church to give directly concrete pre-scriptions regarding detailed economic organization, the actual direction of culture, the allocation of revenue for underdeveloped countries, space travel, regulation of the population, armaments or disarmament, etc., even if it were in principle able to do so. The Church will proclaim the general principles of the dignity of man, freedom, justice and love . . . The Church can certainly have the courage in certain circumstances like John XXIII, or Paul VI before the United Nations, to come forward as representative spokesmen of a Christian feeling for history or a Christian decision, even when the latter is "charismatic" rather than purely and simply a deduction from Christian principles, provided the distinction between the two is not obscured. But the Church must also really make clear the difference between Christian principles and the concrete decision which cannot be deduced from them alone, so that the limits of the possibilities open to the official Church (free of integrist claims) are plain.[35]

---

[35]Ibid., p. 245.

Certain things stand out in this extended quote above concerning the church's position at this point in history. Rahner, first of all, is not assuming that the official church cannot give 'prescriptions' in the sense of 'prophetic instructions', but it must make clear that it is giving such instruction; in other words, is giving its sense of direction for the moment and not *the* plan of action derived from Christian principles. Rahner's concern is that the church (given its history) steer clear of all integrist claims. In fact, we can see that if the church keeps clear of acting as if it were deducing from its Christian principles a Christian politics, form of government, economy, then it frees itself for prophetic expression. Even here Rahner makes the point that the 'official' church primarily speaks to its own members and whoever else will listen.

As Rahner sees it, Christians who take up their specific tasks in the world have a somewhat different relationship to the world than the official church. Here with the people of God the mean between the two extremes must be continually discovered anew, and its expression will vary with individual Christians. Some Christians will "flee the world" in an ascetic life style as a sign that the world and its final goal are not the same. Other Christians will express their vocation in quite secular tasks in the world as a sign that the world belongs to God; it is the world into which God has expressed himself. Rahner makes the point that "closeness to God and the world's own intrinsic reality are not inversely but directly proportionate." God's self-communication to the world has meant the acceptance of the world by God. Secularization and the world's autonomy are not simply signs of sin but the expression of God's own affirmation of the world and "emancipation of the world into its own growing independence." Because this secularization is also the expression of sin, there is always an ambiguity about the activity of the world. Therefore, for the Christian, the world has, on the one hand, "its own peculiar dimension of depth, inserted into it by the grace of God, and its ultimate dynamism must be experienced and accepted, for it is in these that it is open towards a direct relation to God." On the other hand, the Christian is "far from the thinking that the world is only Christian." The Christian can both enter into the secular tasks of the world, affirming them, submitting himself or herself to God in the world and, as well, take up his or her cross, accepting "the frustration of the world, and death, obediently and with hope against hope."[36]

In the final section of his article on "Church and World," Rahner takes up particular problems regarding the relation between church and world today, especially the diaspora character of the church. This is a notion he has developed in a number of places. We will refer, in particular, to his treatment of the notion in *The Christian Commitment*.[37] It is a notion that is especially significant for our discussion of the prophetic role of the church in the world.

The Church of the Diaspora

In *The Christian Commitment*, Rahner describes the present situation of the church. Rahner contrasts the situation of the church of the middle ages and the church of the modern era. He rejects the notion of a 'Christian Middle Ages' if that is understood as anything more than the influence of a Christian world view on an age which was relatively restricted in its possibilities. That there was such an influence was "not because of Christian principles but because of geographical, technical, economic and other factors . . ."; it was because of the narrow range of possibilities available for the expression of its life. In contrast, the modern era provides a "wide possibility of choice, carrying with it both the pain and the noble potentialities of freedom . . ." While there never has been a Christian era or Christian government or Christian economics, in the modern period this reality has become clear. It

---

[36]Ibid., pp. 245, 246, 247.

[37]Ibid., pp. 248-49. Also Rahner, *Christian Commitment*, pp. 3-37 and "On the Presence of Christ in the Diaspora Community According to the Teaching of the Second Vatican Council," *TI* 10:84-102.

has become clear to the world through its secularization and increasingly clear to the church as it faces the ambiguity of the myriad possibilities in all spheres of human and political life (an ambiguity that is compounded by sin). The church cannot offer a Christian political program that is in principle Christian; there never has been such a thing. (This is ontologically the case for in the human sphere there are *"only* limiting instances of the universal . . .") Christianity can never be stamped upon any age and the church has always been in a diaspora situation; it is only easier to recognize that now.[38]

What the Christian and the church can offer is a rejection of "certain conditions, tendencies, endeavors and actions as contradicting the Christian law of faith and morality."[39] The church can be a "sign of contradiction" in the world. The diaspora church is a church surrounded by nonbelievers in a world where political, economic, historical-cultural decisions are made, not by Christians, but by those who have no relationship to the church. Such a diaspora situation is not merely to be lamented but to be embraced as the will of God. It is God's will in terms of a "must" not an "ought." Rahner makes the threefold distinction among (1) a priori musts (as expressed in the ten commandments), (2) things which simply are though they *ought* not be (sin), and (3) realities that ought not be (ideally) but are not in themselves against divine law and may in fact be God's will, having a significance for salvation (the supreme example being the cross of Christ). The reality of the diaspora belongs to this third sphere.

> But to Christianity and the Church her Founder promised not only that she would endure until the end of time but, just as clearly, that his work would always be a sign of contradiction and persecution, of dire and (in secular terms) desperate combat; that love would grow cold; that he, in his disciples, would be persecuted in the name of God; that the struggle would narrow down to an ever more critical point; that the victory of Christianity

---

[38]Rahner, *Christian Commitment*, pp. 8-9.

[39]Ibid., p. 7.

would not be the fruit of immanent development and widening and a steady, progressive leavening of the world but would come as the act of God coming in judgment to gather up world history into its wholly unpredictable and unexpected end. This permanent state of contradiction, foretold to the Church and the Christian as a "must", is something that we must not water down.[40]

The church in the diaspora situation will be a church that grows from commitment, that does not find in the culture in which it lives, with its many forms of expression, anything uniquely Christian (and yet culture "will not be all disintegration and decay"), and it will be, sociologically speaking, a "sect" (though not theologically). And, there will be less confrontation between *the* church and *the* state since the church will form a minority with little direct political power. Such a diaspora church is in the position to be a sign everywhere, to be the sacrament of salvation to the world. As a diaspora church it has a "little flock" reality but can never have a ghetto mentality but rather must be open toward the world, existing for the sake of the world.

The Socio-critical Role of the Church

The diaspora church is the church which is a "sign of contradiction" in society; its very life and mission are a critique of the existing political structures. Rahner takes up this socio-critical role of the church and the significance of "prophetic instruction" for such a role in "The Function of the Church as a Critic of Society."

He recognizes, first of all, that in order for the church to be a critic of society, the church must be a critic of itself as a sociological and political reality. This self-criticism is, in fact, inherent in the church's own self-understanding. Rahner makes the point that only a confessional church, a church with a basic conception of its own nature, can criticize itself.

We can only transform an institution by criticizing it precisely if we can appeal in this criticism of ours to its own understanding of its nature, if we

---

[40]Ibid., pp. 18-19.

can demonstrate to it that the actual concrete form it has come to assume is, at least in part, in contradiction to that which it recognizes as its own true nature, as the law governing its initial emergence, and which it itself seeks to approximate to ever anew, albeit as an asymptotic ideal.[41]

Thus it is in the nature of the church to criticize itself and to do so in its own name.

Rahner also makes the distinction between social criticism and political action. We have already seen that he views the notion of the official church's engagement in politics as an integrist misconception of the church's relation to the world. The church cannot take away from society its own decision-making process including the concrete imperatives that must be discovered in the concrete historical situation. The church can bear witness to the moral boundaries it perceives, but the church must not seek to manipulate the political process for its ends. Rahner's initial definition of the socio-critical role of the church makes clear that what he has in mind does not involve political engagement of this kind.

It consists in opening up ever anew a perspective which transcends the concrete social reality such that within this perspective the social reality concerned appears in its relative value, and so as capable of alteration. To the recognition of this relative value and alterability of the social reality as it *de facto* exists it adds a further factor. For it provides the opportunity and the power to introduce practical changes into this reality even though it does not supply with this any concrete formula or any absolute imperative for a quite specific new social reality to be introduced by the use of creative forces in history.[42]

What the church brings to the historical situation is an open-ended perspective which breaks up the assumed absoluteness (and therefore idolatry) of ideologies. It therefore gives to the situation a perspective in which possible concrete alternatives can be recognized.[43]

---

[41]Rahner, "Church as Critic," p. 232.

[42]Ibid., p. 235.

[43]Ibid., pp. 233-35.

We have already seen how it is the gospel which provides the perspective to open up the historical situation to ever new opportunities for action. In this essay on the "Function of the Church as Critic of Society," Rahner lifts up again the diaspora character of the church, the gospel as addressing not only individuals but humankind as a whole in its history and, as noted earlier, the absolute hope of the gospel which is directed to the absolute future, the unity of love of God and neighbor, and the theology of the cross. These aspects of the gospel, as we have already seen, point to the prophetic and socio-critical nature of the church.

The next question Rahner takes up in this essay which is particularly significant for our concerns is the question of the "upholders" of this role of social criticism. He first of all notes that in regard to the official and hierarchical aspect of the church little attention, theologically, has been given to the question of its socio-critical role. It cannot be subsumed under the categories of the teaching and priestly functions of the church's officially appointed authorities. The teaching office is concerned "to preach the gospel in its abiding and permanent validity." Since the practical imperatives of a socio-critical nature cannot be sufficiently produced from the gospel by a kind of rational deduction of critical reason, what we are concerned with here is not the function of teaching as it is usually practiced. The same can be said for the general function of the pastoral office, at least as it has traditionally operated; its concerns have been directed to "guiding and instructing the faithful in the specifically religious sphere," and the socio-critical task has not been generally included in its role. That the socio-critical function of the official church has not found any significant theological definition is largely due to the fact that the awareness of this function could only develop where social change is occurring rapidly and humankind has reached a point where it is consciously planning its social structure on a wider social and global scale. That the question is now being raised is due to the historical development of the modern period in which increasingly humankind seeks to plan the course of its development on a large social scale in a rapidly changing world.[44]

Since this socio-critical function of the official church has not fitted easily into the traditional teaching and priestly offices as they have operated in practice, it has not been clear to theology as to the position and definition of this socio-critical role. For Rahner, however, it can be characterized as "prophetic instruction in social criticism." He makes two points about this instruction: (1) It differs from theoretical teaching which depends upon critical reason and the application of theological principles to the social sphere through a process of rational deduction. (2) It is an address to Christians (and others who will listen) which constitutes a call to historical decision making. It appeals to the freedom of Christians to respond in creative and responsible ways. It may even involve a concrete course of action, but when it does so, as we have seen, it must make clear that what is being called for is "prescribed and demanded by the circumstances of that particular moment in history, something which cannot ultimately be determined on any theoretical basis" (and therefore cannot be offered as *the* Christian mode of action in any absolute sense). Since it is addressed to the freedom of Christians it must be experienced by them as an imperative of the historical moment in order for it to have for them a binding character.[45]

Rahner calls this function of social criticism "prophetic instruction." It is "instruction" or "directive" (*Weisung*) because "it is not simply a conclusion deduced from general Christian norms." It is prophetic "to the extent that it is the outcome of a conviction that it is sustained not merely by those 'this worldly' forces from which the future can be held to derive, but by the Spirit of Christ."[46]

---

[44]Ibid., p. 243.

[45]Ibid., pp. 243-44.

[46]Ibid., p. 244 and "Die Gesellshaftskritische Funktion der Kirche," *ST* 9:584.

This prophetic instruction is to be found in both the official representatives of the church and Christians in general, although the primary upholders of this prophetic role are the latter. Again the point is made that when it is the case of 'official' prophetic instruction, such instruction must be distinguished from doctrinal pronouncements in the kind of binding character they have for Christians; "of their very nature they are (whether explicitly or implicitly) subject to criticism on the part of the faithful and the world." In any case, the "main promoters" of this socio-critical function are Christians in general.

> . . . Christians themselves are something more than mere recipients of directives from the official bodies. They have to develop an autonomous initiative of their own from which they alone are responsible. They can do this even when they are not specifically commissioned or particularly encouraged to do so by the official bodies in the Church. . . . Under certain circumstances they can and must do this in the name of the gospel and their own Christian moral responsibility even when on the one hand other Christians or Christian groups oppose them in it, while on the other an autonomous initiative of this kind, together with the antagonisms within the Church which it entails, must still preserve mutual love and the unity of the Church.[47]

Because individual Christians and Christian groups can seek to carry through a particular social program, their socio-critical activity goes beyond that of the official church.[48]

----

[47]Rahner, "Church as Critic," p. 245.

[48]Ibid., p. 246. Rahner goes on in this essay to take up the problem of a theology of revolution, which he also takes up more substantially in his essay "On the Theology of Revolution," *TI* 14:314-30. While the question of the Christian's participation in revolutionary forces in a society is a significant one relating to the socio-critical aspect of Christian existence, we will not pursue it here since it is somewhat peripheral to our basic concerns. It simply can be noted that Rahner does see the place for revolutionary change (and, in fact, believes the global situation between the developed and developing nations calls for 'revolutionary' change), and Christians should be encouraged by the church to take part in particular forms of revolution according to the dictates of an informed conscience. (Rahner, "Theology of Revolution," pp. 323-34, 324-30.)

Summary

In this chapter we have recognized the transcendental necessity of an ecclesial Christianity. For Rahner, God's revelation and salvation and the arrival of God's reign must be mediated historically by a community which is the concrete realization and sign of this salvation. This ecclesial objectification of a graced transcendence is furthermore grounded in the final and definitive expression of this grace in Jesus Christ. This ecclesial Christianity must of necessity be prophetic. The prophetic nature of the church is presupposed by the gospel and by its being the concrete expression of the eschatological prophet, Jesus. Furthermore, as we have seen, this prophetic element is necessary to human reality and community and therefore is a transcendentally necessary dimension of the ecclesial community. Just as a dynamic element is necessary for the individual subject, so also is it crucial for the social subject in its concrete and historical realization of itself. It cannot escape the necessity of an individual concrete knowledge of a prophetic nature. What is true generally for human community is especially true for the church which is the creation of the eschatological Spirit and is to be the salvific sign of the eschatological reign of God. For it to realize its true nature in history, it must be able to objectify the truth of the gospel and the reality of God's salvific action in Jesus Christ in ever new ways. This objectification implies a kind of knowledge and action which goes beyond a rational deduction from general evangelical principles; it implies, rather, the prophetic dynamic we have been describing. We have also seen that this prophetic dynamic, because it means the concrete realization of the gospel in the world, also implies that the church will be a "sign which contradicts," a critical force within the world. The church cannot escape a socio-critical role in the world if it is true to its own nature and objectifies in ever new historical ways the reign of God which is always arriving.

Chapter VI

Implications

There are clearly ecclesial and theological implications for today's situation raised by the foregoing discussion. Paramount among them is the pronounced recognition within church and theology that the prophetic dynamic, this fundamental openness to the absolute future, is integral to individual and communal becoming. There is no communal or ecclesial becoming without prophecy. Such an affirmation is foundational to a community which finds its reason for being in the one who is the eschatological prophet. We have seen that the community of the eschatological prophet is to be a sign of that future of God's making into which the human community is called. In this chapter we will explore further some of the dimensions we would expect of a communal reality that finds its grounding in the prophetic. We will make some observations concerning the prophetic dynamic within ecclesial life and mission, within movements toward the unity of the churches, and we will also ask about the possibility of a prophetic element in theology itself.

Implications for Ecclesial Life and Mission

A Community Oriented to the Future

Both church and world cry out for a word that is relevant. The cry comes from a felt necessity. The actual, concrete, and

relevant message when given may not necessarily be welcomed–
we can run from that which we fundamentally need–but within
human experience there is a felt need for timely direction, unique
to *this* moment, for the message or decision which opens up the
new reality of the community in its coming-to-be. There is a
yearning for a word or decision that responds not necessarily to the
foremost questions being asked or the actions being called for, but
rather gives answer to those fundamental questions of praxis that
ought to be asked.

The church must go beyond answering merely the questions
the world asks. Indeed, the church is called into continuity with
the prophetic traditions of the Old Testament in which prophets
announced what God was about to do and what the people therefore must do in order to get ready for the coming new reality. As
the community of the eschatological prophet, the church is con-
firmed in its prophetic calling by being a sign of the reign of God
that has broken in upon the world in Jesus Christ. The church, to
the extent that it is true to its calling, is oriented to the future, the
future of God's reign. The church knows this from its own traditions. We have also been recognizing in the preceding pages that
the necessity of this future orientation is present within human
and communal experience generally; it is basic to humanity. There
is a prophetic element in human being which pushes beyond present questions to the future of our becoming. Consequently, this
prophetic element is not restricted to the church. Nevertheless, it
is the church which knows itself as the bearer of an eschatological
message and which therefore must attend to this prophetic element
with utmost seriousness.

When asking, therefore, about the implications of the foregoing chapters for the church's life and mission, the predominant
factor to be recognized is that the church is oriented to the future.
The church is under call to address the world from the future. It
cannot merely address the questions the world puts to it, but must
critique those questions from the vantage point of the new reality
of God's future.

To say that the church is future oriented means that it is not only the bearer of a message from the past, captured in documents needing reinterpretation within each age, but is called to speak from the future, *must* speak from the future if it is to remain a bearer of the eschatological message in continuity with its past. It is, in fact, this transcendental, future orientation we have been discussing which makes possible the unique and timely word that can truly address the present reality with its future becoming. If we understand past ecclesial documents, including scripture, as at least in part a realization of this prophetic dynamic, then we ought to understand part of the reason for their loss of power. They speak most powerfully to a particular moment or period within a history, and within particular cultures, societies, and groups, and thus in time become opaque or nonapplicable to another culture, society, or age unless made applicable by a prophetic "reinterpretation."

Therefore, for example, the confessional documents of the Reformation and the encyclicals of a previous age can lose their power not because they no longer speak truth but because their truth, at least in part, is an existential truth formed by and within a particular time, able to be truly understood within the particular conditions of that former time. They cannot continue to speak in the same manner for every age, nor can they, in themselves, determine the word for the present age. Each age must find its own word, is dependent upon the Spirit for it. For Rahner, the relationship of a future oriented graced transcendentality to its categorial expression implies that human culture and expression have the possibility of carrying within them a divine call and word which opens up human community to its future, and every age and people cannot escape the responsibility for that word. Where that word happens there is power for the truly new and the coming to be of real community. Consequently, the church must embrace its calling as a community oriented to the eschatological future. The church in its official and institutional structures must give room for the prophetic, open up to the prophetic.

Rahner's concern with the individual in the church is a concern for giving space to those charisms of the spirit and those unique gifts and vocations of individuals which address the present concrete situation of the world. His theological reflections on the dynamic element in the church serve as a radical call to the church to ensure room for that prophetic witness. Whether that which restricts prophecy is an 'orthodoxy' maintained and protected from above (Roman) or a bureaucratic and programmatic institutionalizing of the faith (Protestant) makes little difference. The need exists for an extensive reorientation by which the church increasingly recognizes and finds its direction from individuals, groups, and movements exhibiting prophetic charisms.

Prophetic witness may come to expression within the 'official' structures of the church, but is not primarily to be expected there. As important as they are, pastoral letters and ecclesial social statements are unlikely to provide the most discerning prophetic call or necessary word. Consequently, the church in its official structures must give room and freedom of expression to individual charisms, must expect them and even be guided by them. Furthermore, prophetic individuals, groups, and movements in the church must take their callings seriously. They cannot be intimidated by unyielding structures, but must find their reason for expression in their call and in the timeliness of the word given to them.

Addressing Questions Raised by the Future within the Present Situation

The questions which God's future addresses arise and are answered within the particular configurations of the present situation. The point has been made that the church cannot merely address the questions raised by the world, especially when that means addressing the questions of the economic and political "powers that be," the predominant questions before the public. The searching questions the church is called to address are formed within the same present reality as the predominant questions in the public arena, but as seen from God's future. As such the present situation is viewed not from the vantage point of the maintenance of a status quo by existing "powers," nor by ideologies critiquing each other, but by the coming power and presence of God which calls into question all present configurations and which ultimately comes to make all things right.

That the church must go beyond addressing the questions the world asks while speaking to present realities is a truism, and yet on this point, Rahner himself has been critiqued. Rahner has been faulted for letting his theology be determined inordinately by the questions of the Enlightenment.[1] There is no question that his "turn to the subject," when taken in isolation and thereby idealized, presents a dangerous undermining of theology as a discipline that is formed within and must speak to a particular context. While Rahner's weakness (or at least potential weakness) can be noted, it can also be recognized that he neither worked in isolation nor intended an idealized subject untouched by the demands of history, which indeed is a history of suffering. We may wish that his theology addressed more forcefully those questions raised by the "underside of history," where God's future forces us to look; nevertheless, the theological method he articulated continues to hold much promise for opening up a way to understand how the church does address those future oriented questions.[2]

---

[1]Metz, *Faith in History and Society*, pp. 158-66; Matthew L. Lamb, *Solidarity with Victims: Toward a Theology of Social Transformation* (New York: Crossroad, 1982), pp. 117-26. Lamb views Metz's criticisms of Rahner as a dialectical response to the dangers of a transcendental method disconnected from concrete, historical reality. Metz's "political hermeneutics of suspicion" may be "more directed at us, the readers in front of the text, than at the performance of Rahner behind the text" (p. 119).

[2]What must also be kept in mind is that Rahner's is a speculative theology; the questions he addresses, for the most part, are speculative questions and indeed the speculative questions of the Enlightenment. He understood this. He is, in fact, quite clear in his theology that a distinction must be maintained between a speculative and a practical theology. They are different disciplines with differing methods. While Rahner attended to the methodological foundations of a practical theology, he did little practical theology himself as he understood it. Furthermore, he would not claim that the speculative questions (as speculative) which he took

In many respects, Rahner's theology has similarities to the existentialist analysis which Paul Tillich viewed as a "protest against the spirit of industrial society" and a rejection of both supranaturalism and idealism.[3] There is no question that such an existentialist approach, as many have pointed out, must be deepened by a contextual movement from the underside of history, from the vantage point of the victim; God's future requires it. Nevertheless, that existentialist movement from Kierkegaard through Heidegger and connecting with the existentialist element in Thomas Aquinas surrounding the concept of *esse* as that comes to expression in Rahner, has continued power for addressing today's situation in which the idolatry of technology and consumerism continues to hold sway. The focus on the existential reality of the individual cannot remain a fixation on the meaning of the individual as individual but must be broadened to a focus on human existence within the context of a global village; as such it will be forced to attend not only to meaning but to justice.

Indeed, a requirement of the prophetic word is that it be contextual, and yet it can only be truly contextual when it is grounded in a fundamental solidarity with the other. The implications of this solidarity with the other must not be underestimated, nor the dimensions and the depth of this solidarity ignored.

Everything Rahner has written concerning the significance of matter and the conversion to the phantasm in *Spirit in the World*

---

up were necessarily the most important questions. They were nevertheless questions which needed answers for the church to speak *intelligibly* in the modern world. (Despite the fact that Rahner wrote volumes, he did leave many questions unanswered.) His works are filled with calls to others to take up those questions that moved beyond the deeply methodological concerns which were his. He often did little more than point in a direction, and he was acutely aware that there were other theological disciplines which could more adequately address questions that he raised as well as address other questions which needed to be raised. As for prophecy, Rahner gives us ontological foundations; he writes as a speculative theologian, not as a prophet.

[3]Paul Tillich, *Theology of Culture*, ed. Robert C. Kimball (London: Oxford University Press, 1959), p. 48.

is applicable here. Our bodies may provide for our individuation, but our *selves* do not end with our bodies; they come to expression in a world and in relationship to other selves. There is no individuality except in community, and there is no community other than the intersubjectivity of individuals. The possibility of the prophetic word is grounded, at least in part, in the fact that we are not only in the world but the world, which is a world of others, is also in us. The prophetic word therefore gives expression to that which is a part of the identity of the prophet, as the prophet exists *in community*.

Furthermore, Rahner makes it clear that the possibility of being-in-community is grounded in a knowledge and love that has its source in the Triune God. It is the communal being of God that ultimately provides the basis for community and solidarity. Consequently, the church, when it is true to its nature as community grounded in the communal being of God, is graced by a solidarity with the world which makes a clearsighted knowledge of the world possible, a knowing which makes a perceptive word possible.

In order to clarify further the dimensions and significance of this solidarity with the other for speaking a word to the other within the context of the other, it may prove helpful to enter into the discussion of recent years concerning the relationship between *theory* and *praxis*.[4] We can only touch on the discussion at this point; however, certain aspects of this discussion clearly have bearing on the contextuality and other-directedness of the prophetic word as that must come to be within the life of the church and its theology.

It is clear that, for Rahner, the relationship of theory and praxis involves a unity in difference, and to understand the

---

[4]David Tracy and Matthew Lamb have provided us with some categorizing of the various theological options present. See David Tracy, *The Analogical Imagination: Christian Theology and the Culture of Pluralism* (New York: Crossroad, 1981), pp. 69-79 and Lamb, *Solidarity with Victims*, pp. 65-88.

dimensions of this, one must attend to the source of theory and praxis in the human subject. As was pointed out in Chapter III, knowledge and freedom are those basic modes of uniquely human expression which, when grounded in a graced transcendentality, are rooted in faith and love. And for Rahner, as with St. Paul, the greatest of these transcendental gifts is love. On that basis alone we could assume that for Rahner there is a primacy of praxis over theory, although as we have seen, Rahner's way of conceiving their relationship is quite nuanced.

Without retreading a lot of ground already covered, we can simply state that for Rahner freedom and love provide both the stimulus to knowing as well as the welcome of what is known. Love reaches out in hope not only to what is but to what might and ought to be; love looks not only to the present but also to the future. Of course, love "looks," perceives, understands, knows by means of the entire dynamic of human knowing. (Rahner writes of the immersion in matter of sensibility, the conversion to the phantasm, the apprehension of the universal concept, the affirmative synthesis oriented to the 'in-itself' of *esse* by a pre-apprehension of Absolute *Esse*, the totality of being. As with Bernard Lonergan, knowledge, whether theoretical or practical, can never be described as "taking a look.")

If it is by the entire dynamic of human knowing, individual and communal, that human being enters into and embraces the other, then all the disciplines of human knowing become critical for the enterprise of transcendental love. The theoretical disciplines oriented to what *is*, ecology, economics, history, anthropology, psychology, sociology, political science, must serve the practical exercise of love as oriented in hope to the future. Indeed, a prophetic call that is responsible to the complexities of our situation today must be informed. As we will see, a prophetic theology can provide such an informing. Even so, as Rahner has pointed out, we can never wait until all the facts are in before making a decision, before responding to the charismatic summons of God which comes to us in and through the multi-faceted dimensions of our experience. The situation of the historical moment demands a response.

If we have understood Rahner correctly concerning the dynamic of love and the relationship of knowledge and love, certain things can be said about the relationship of theory and praxis. In regard to the fundamental dynamic of human knowing, praxis, understood as orientation to empirical reality, has a certain primacy. Rahner is in keeping with the spirit of Thomism in his insistence upon sensibility as the a priori condition for being immersed in the other. There is no knowledge except through the medium of matter. Consequently, all our coming to knowledge, theoretical as well as practical, happens through the material of world and history.

Furthermore, if we understand the relationship of knowledge and love, we realize that within knowledge, whatever the kind, speculative or practical, there is an element of freedom and therefore praxis as committed involvement. This, as we have seen, is most dramatically the case with practical knowledge and in particular prophetic knowledge. Theoretical or speculative knowledge, which informs concerning what *is* and requires little commitment, can never provide the prophetic vision from which the call to act is derived. Rather, it is out of committed involvement in the present configuration of things and in openness to the absolute future, that the prophetic vision arises. Certainly a theoretical reason is an element in that envisioning, but it is not the primary motive force or ingredient. Transcendental love oriented to and participating in the other, transcendental faith envisioning within and out of the configurations of a particular context, and transcendental hope reaching into the future, God's future, for the new reality that is called for, are the basis for a prophetic word and decision.

Consequently, it is agapic or transcendental love that enables the church to participate in the world in such a way as to be able to know the world (and itself) within the horizons of God's future and thus be able to speak the necessary word within the present situation. There is no question that the church must enter into the discussions of the various sciences. It must learn from the world. Nevertheless, the greatest potential for learning resides in loving, committed involvement within the present context which is a context of suffering and oppression. Without committed involvement with suffering others (our world is a world of others), all the theoretical knowledge which takes little personal, whole self commitment to achieve will tell us little regarding the necessary, timely, life-giving word that truly speaks to our present age.

This solidarity with the other grounded in transcendental love is often most clearly seen in individuals, groups, movements, and in local communities of faith. With this in mind we turn to a discussion of prophecy in the local congregation.

Prophecy in the Local Congregation

When prophecy is considered within the life of the church, ecclesial formulations are significant. Often discussions relating one aspect of the life of the church to the church as a whole treat the church abstractly and the impression is given that the church being referred to is the church catholic, interpreted often as the church "official." It is important, especially for a discussion of the prophetic element in the church, to give special attention to the church as congregation, as local community of faith. The individual congregation must be seen as the place of the charismatic summons of the Spirit. It is in the struggles of the community of faith to discover its unique mission; it is in its goal setting and decision making that the prophetic character of the church is realized.

Rahner has written of a "communal spirituality" as characteristic of the spirituality of the church of the future, a movement away from the "spiritual individualism" of the past. Rahner envisions a form of faith community in which there can be a communal discernment of spirits. He envisions community in which "the prayer to the Holy Spirit at the beginning of a consultation between Christians [is not] concretely and practically merely a pious opening ceremony, after which everything goes on as otherwise at a secular board meeting with the management making use of purely rational arguments ... "⁵ Rather, he sees the beginnings of a "communal lived spirituality" which will be the concrete ground for the prophetic perception of the congregation.⁶

The local congregation, furthermore, must view itself as a sign of God's reign, which is always breaking in anew and criticizing the present configuration of the church's life and mission and of the world. As a sign of God's reign, it must expect to be a sign that contradicts in the world. The local congregation has a sociocritical role. It must recognize that, in its response to the charismatic summons of God, it will increasingly come into conflict with the status quo both within itself and society. In its prophetic role the local congregation must also increasingly become aware of a global village; it must broaden its context so that when it addresses the issues of social justice of its neighborhood and nation, it does so within global horizons. As Rahner has pointed out on many occasions, the world has become small. Local injustice is a microcosm of global injustice. This means a special responsibility on the part of Christians and congregations to make connections in their addressing local and global social and political issues.

Prophetic imperatives for justice as grounded in a communal spirituality and as giving form to the mission and life of individual congregations can be viewed as a *necessary* aspect of being the church in the world, as sign of God's reign. The prophetic element in the church will necessarily express itself in social, political, and economic terms and will not fail to address a global village.

Also, within the local congregation, the 'priestly' or pastoral office must be seen, as Rahner has pointed out, not so much in terms of its cultic responsibilities but in terms of the prophetic element. Rahner has written of the need for "existential imagination" on the part of preachers; they must imagine them-

---

⁵Rahner, "The Spirituality of the Church of the Future," *TI* 20:151-52.

⁶Ibid., pp. 150-52. See also Rahner, *The Shape of the Church to Come*, trans. and intr. Edward Quinn (New York: Seabury Press, 1974), pp. 82-89.

selves in the life situation of their listeners.[7] It is clear, for Rahner, that such imaginings are important precisely because there is a prophetic discernment which perceives the timely word which must be proclaimed to *this* particular people in *this* place.

Finally, this ministry of the word cannot be viewed as limited to the pastoral office but must be given the opportunity to come to expression in the priesthood of all believers. Neither listening for nor hearing the 'word of the Lord' ends with a sermon but rather continues in the gathered community at prayer, in its sacramental acts, in its committee meetings, and in the community's activity in the world.

The power of the local congregation and the prophetic individual or group must not be underestimated as potential to change existing structures of church and society as the history of charismatic movements in the life of the church demonstrates. Nevertheless, the prophetic element is not confined to such expressions.

Prophecy within the 'Official' Structures of the Church

Rahner has noted various ways that the prophetic element can be seen in the ministry of magisterium and episcopé. It is, of course, in this representative ministry that the church as a whole can speak to the world as a whole. (This, at least in principle, would be the situation in a united church.) In any case, there are examples of prophetic witness in official expressions of the church. The document, *Gaudium et Spes* of Vatican II, has a prophetic character to it. A number of synods of bishops have sought to speak a concrete word to the age and society in which they reside.[8] What is the basis for such documents and statements which are not

---

[7]Rahner, *Shape of the Church*, p. 83.

[8]David J. O'Brien and Thomas A. Shannon, eds., *Renewing the Earth: Catholic Documents on Peace, Justice and Liberation* (Garden City, NY: Doubleday, 1977).

merely the reciting of universal theological principles but attempts to speak a word or imperative discerned for the social situation of the time, if not the prophetic dynamic which has been our concern? Lutheran and most Protestant churches do not have anything quite comparable, in a formal way, to the teaching office in the Catholic church (largely due to the provisional nature of the Protestant movement).[9] Nevertheless, they do have official structures and means by which church bodies as a whole take positions and make statements for the edification and 'direction' of their members. These structures need to be examined in order to determine their ability or inability to provide a truly prophetic word. This examination must be included in all theological discussions of the official ministry of the church, especially as these discussions are taken up in ecumenical forums. Indeed, the element of prophecy has particular significance for the ecumenical movement.

Prophecy and the Unity of the Churches

Much of the struggle for the unity of the churches has centered in a search for either unity in doctrine or unity in action (so, for example, *Life and Work* and *Faith and Order*, predecessor movements to the World Council of Churches). A great deal of attention, much of it quite necessary, has been given to resolving past confessional disputes. When results have proved minimal, especially early on in the ecumenical movement of this century, the other recourse has been unified effort in the arena of social action. Even here a unified witness has often eluded separated churches. In recent years the term "spiritual ecumenism" has found a significant place in the ecumenical movement. There has been the awareness of a unity more original than either reflection or action can provide. Christians are baptized into Christ whether or not they entirely agree on the *meaning* of that baptism. They gather

---

[9]See Paul C. Empie, T. Austin Murphy, and Joseph A. Burgess, eds., *Teaching Authority and Infallibility in the Church: Lutherans and Catholics in Dialogue VI* (Minneapolis: Augsburg, 1978).

at the table of the Lord; they know a common bond of fellowship in Christ and a common call to mission; there is an underlying unity regardless of the diversity and division in the reflections or actions that flow from that basic reality. It has seemed to many that that is the starting point.

Such a starting point does not take away the necessity of dialogue on doctrinal matters or the struggle for common witness in action. The question remains as to what gives adequate expression in reflection and action to the underlying reality and what finally is sufficient for unity. After all, we only recognize each other through our expressions of that underlying ecclesial and Christic reality; the expressions do matter. What is sufficient for tangible, embodied unity in the way of confessional agreement and witnessing action remains the predominant question.

Rahner believes that bilateral and multilateral dialogues, the work of the Faith and Order Commission of the World Council of Churches, and the work of theologians in general have brought us to the point where the unity of the churches is an "actual possibility."[10] Above all he believes that separated churches must embrace a tolerance toward diverse traditions on many 'peripheral' matters of faith and that remaining disagreements between mainline denominations can exist in a real, tangible, recognized unity of the churches. Given the historical and contextual nature of confessional documents, the inability of theologians, in the face of the explosion of knowledge and the specialization of disciplines, to adequately address each other, and the tremendous diversity of viewpoints and frames of reference; given this situation, it is simply impossible to expect a unity on the level of reflection beyond that which is most basic to the faith.

Consequently, one of the theses presented by Karl Rahner and Heinrich Fries in *Unity of the Churches* is that

---

[10]See Heinrich Fries and Karl Rahner, *Unity of the Churches: An Actual Possibility*, trans. Ruth C. L. Gritsch and Eric W. Gritsch (Philadelphia: Fortress Press and NY: Paulist Press, 1983).

Nothing may be rejected decisively and confessionally in one partner church which is binding dogma in another partner church. Furthermore, beyond Thesis I ["The fundamental truths of Christianity, as they are expressed in Holy Scripture, in the Apostles' Creed, and in that of Nicaea and Constantinople"] no explicit and positive confession in one partner church is imposed as dogma obligatory for another partner church. This is left to broader consensus in the future.[11]

The potential of this approach is found in the fact that it sets churches free to continue dialogue over truth within a unified church (such dialogues go on within individual denominations anyway) but no longer as a way to achieve unity, but for the sake of truth and for the further expression of unity. The dialogues would take place in a unified church finally capable of speaking to the world as one.

Of particular concern for our discussion is the position Rahner gives to the doctrinal and confessional discussions. Rahner has consistently called the church to the central core of the Christian faith, the revelation of God in Christ and those dogmas that give expression to that reality, the Trinity, incarnation, and grace. All other confessional expressions must flow from this core. Those confessional stances that are of a peripheral nature or which have come to expression within separated traditions and histories, cannot carry the same weight, and in ecumenical discussions, must not be made requirements for unity. If the churches were to radically embrace such an approach, tremendous avenues toward unity would open up. That this has not been sufficiently recognized may be due in large part to those sociological and institutional factors that always have a capacity for resisting sound theology.

Rahner is not alone in recognizing that the present state of ecumenical discussion is such that it is time to begin making actual that which is an actual possibility. The question remains how and the 'how' is a process, the end of which cannot be clearly seen. Nevertheless, there are some clues concerning direction.

---

[11]Ibid., p. 7.

The *Baptist, Eucharist, and Ministry* (*BEM*) statement before the churches is especially significant for the response it has received from the churches. It has been received as a kind of watershed. It is challenging churches to move beyond rigid confessional positions, to see how far they can go in recognizing the apostolic faith in this common statement. Churches are responding seriously to this challenge. Furthermore, *BEM* has renewed discussions on the question of 'reception'; the question of how Christians and churches receive a confessional statement as a true or adequate expression of the faith they know and live.[12] The need has been voiced for a 'spirituality of reception', an openness to reform and to new possibilities in decision making.[13] There is good reason why *BEM* and the discussions and responses related to it have on so many occasions been referred to as a kairotic moment in the ecumenical movement.

It is with this in mind that I would like to move the discussion to the question of prophecy in relation to ecumenism, for it is in the discernment of the kairotic word or call that true movement, true coming-to-be can take place. To the extent that the churches seriously and intentionally give room to the prophetic dynamic there can be expected steady movement toward the unity of the churches.

A greater attention to the prophetic dynamic by the churches would mean, first of all, an intentional orientation to the *future* so that confessional documents would be viewed as provisional steps along the way, a means by which churches check their bearings but not the predominant or sole means by which the present is determined. A church which is future oriented, learning to view things from horizons formed by a stretching out to (a pre-apprehension of) the Absolute Future, is a church which has the capacity not

---

[12]See William G. Rusch, *Reception: An Ecumenical Opportunity* (Philadelphia: Fortress Press, 1988) and Max Thurian, ed., *Ecumenical Perspectives on Baptism, Eucharist and Ministry* (Geneva: World Council of Churches, 1983), pp. 140-74.

[13]Rusch, *Reception*, p. 64.

only to see the new possibilities, but to discern which among them is the way of the future. Such a Spirit-guided church can let go of provisional expressions of the past for the new direction which makes contemporary God's revelation in Jesus Christ. It expects prophetic signs and is constrained to discern them. If there are already examples of unity in the form of ecumenical communities, they are not simply dismissed as fringe groups but may be viewed as signs of the church's future and as calls into that future. The discernment of the kairotic word or moment becomes crucial in a future-oriented church; the kairotic word is viewed as a living and active word.

What would happen to ecumenical discussions if questions were framed not so much in terms of resolution of past confessional stances, but in terms of what is necessary for our time? For example, regarding the question of the tripartite structure of the church's ministry, instead of asking whether particular church documents or teaching permit a tripartite ministry (or allow for the possibility of living without it), why not ask whether it is necessary *at this time* (regardless of past experience) for the church to be more fully the church. The question becomes one of *calling*. Are we called at this time to embrace this aspect of church structure or decision making? By putting the question in this form we place it before practical reason, and graced, faith-filled practical reason has opportunity to exercise discernment. Rather than a preponderance of emphasis upon theoretical reason and deduction from past documents, an emphasis is given to a practical and future-oriented knowing. The possibilities for *movement* toward unity become clear.

The second factor which must be considered in relation to the ecumenical movement, as we have seen with all else involving the prophetic dynamic, is the element of contextuality. A faith-filled practical reason exercises discernment within particular historical configurations. How those historical factors are experienced and known is extremely critical. It is significant that the divisive issues lifted up by predominantly white European and

European-American churches have been primarily dogmatic in nature while Third World churches have directed the world-wide church community to social, economic, and political divisions? African-American church representatives, addressing the issue of unity, point to racism and classism as the major barriers. Blackness (understood as identification with Jesus, the "Oppressed One of God," in "faithfulness through suffering"), "is one of God's gifts for the realization of the unity of the church and humankind at this critical stage of history."[14] Indeed, the growth in recent years of the number of churches of color represented in the WCC holds promise for addressing the issue of unity in a manner which directs the churches to the necessity of unified acts of confessing, not only in word but in deed. What we must see is that the fundamental divisions in our world are also the fundamental divisions in the church, and when those divisions are addressed, not merely by reflection but by prophetic word and action, and therefore in the act of confessing, then the church's unity is expressed in the only way it can finally be expressed and that is in identification with the crucified and risen Christ. This realization also leads to a recognition that the church finds unity in mission.

The third factor, therefore, for a prophetic church in relation to the ecumenical movement has to do with its mission. The church must be one for the sake of the world; consequently, the prophetic impulse even as it involves ecumenism is not merely related to the internal development of churches moving toward unity, but rather is oriented to the necessary action and word directed to the world. In a world of oppression and hunger, what word must the one church speak and live? It is in confessing Christ in the present; it is in the necessary word and action for this time, in this age, that the unity of the church can most profoundly

---

[14]David T. Shannon and Gayraud S. Wilmore, eds., *Black Witness to the Apostolic Faith* (Grand Rapids, MI: William B. Eerdmans for Commission on Faith and Order, National Council of Churches of Christ in the U.S.A., 1985), pp. 64-65.

be realized.[15] The world does not need a divided church; it does not need a divided word. A church that is seeking to express the one word, the timely word, is a church being constrained to unity for the sake of the world.

A Prophetic Theology

Finally, it must be recognized that there is a prophetic element in theology itself. The church in its reflection upon its faith cannot exclude this prophetic element. It would seem, however, that speculative theology would, by its very nature, provide little room for the prophetic dynamic, at least as a major component of its method, since it is concerned with interpreting the universal or essential meaning of revelation (though its reinterpretation for each age may involve something of the prophetic). Practical theology, however, presents other possibilities. Rahner has made the point that practical theology is a discipline in its own right with its own method and is not merely dependent on speculative or theoretic theology.[16] This, of course, follows from Rahner's understanding of the relationship of those two basic modes of human self-realization, namely, the modes of knowledge and freedom or theoretical knowledge and practical knowledge. As we have seen, practical reason and prophetic perception are not merely the result of rational deduction from the theoretical and conceptual grasp of essential human reality. Rather, practical reason, while including a rational or theoretical element, nevertheless, operates in its own peculiar mode which involves the reaching out to being as good, to be valued, willed, welcomed, loved. It is oriented to the future, to what ought to be, to what is to come into

---

[15]Ulrich Duchrow, *Conflict over the Ecumenical Movement: Confessing Christ Today in the Universal Church*, trans. David Lewis (Geneva: World Council of Churches, 1980), pp. 298-359.

[16]Rahner, "Practical Theology within the Totality of Theological Disciplines," *TI* 9:102.

being, whereas speculative reason is primarily concerned with what is. As with theoretical reason, practical reason is grounded in human transcendentality so that its reaching out to conditional being is conditioned by its anticipatory grasp of being in its totality in that infinite openness which is the valuing and love of God. We have noted the two basic aspects of practical reason, namely the grasp of an essential ethics and the grasp of individual concrete imperatives. A practical theology can also be expected to express these aspects of practical knowing. This means that within practical theology there ought to be a discipline that could be described as 'prophetic theology'. Rahner seems to have this very kind of discipline in mind when he writes of the need for a "practical ecclesiological cosmology."

In "Theological Reflections on the Problem of Secularization," Rahner sees the need for a theological discipline which relates the church to the secular world in the concrete, present situation.[17] Such a discipline would involve a theological interpretation of the contemporary situation. Because its subject matter, in part, is not 'revealed' (since it involves knowledge of the secular world) it would be partially dependent on the secular sciences, although it would not be merely an application of such sciences, but would involve a theological perspective. Rahner makes the point in the *Handbuch der Pastoraltheologie* (II/1), that practical theology must concern itself with the present situation in the church and this means something more than common everyday experience; it rather involves a systematic scientific reflection.[18] The question of norms and imperatives for this present situation of the church, however, involves a theological perspective which goes beyond what can be obtained by a secular scientific analysis. This theological perspective and task, though, cannot be supplied by dogmatic theology because of its abstract nature (otherwise one is simply involved in casuistry). Rahner believes the theological

---

[17]Rahner, "Problem of Secularization," *TI* 10:337-41.

[18]Rahner, *Handbuch* II/1, pp. 181-88.

character of this practical theology which relates the church to the contemporary situation of the world can be grasped by reflecting on the activity of the church in the here and now. The church acts as supernaturally borne by the Spirit, by a kind of faith-instinct. Rahner writes of a "supernatural existential logic of Christian decision" which is true not only for individual Christians but also for the church. This logic must also be reflected in a theological discipline which relates the church to the present situation.[19]

This is Rahner's point also in "Theological Reflections on Secularization," concerning a "practical ecclesiological cosmology":

> A further point is that this relationship [the church to the secular world] entails, as one of its characteristics, an element of prophetic decision. In other words, it is totally incapable of being interpreted as a mere combination of two elements alone, namely a theoretical ecclesiology and a recognition of the situation.[20]

This scientific cosmology or what I am calling 'prophetic theology', while not itself producing prophetic imperatives, nevertheless "could pave the way for them and provide the scientifically and critically informed conscience leading to them, and at the same time the encouragement necessary for concrete action."[21]

Rahner points out that this 'prophetic theology' does not yet

---

[19]Ibid., pp. 185-86. This is also expressed clearly in Rahner, *Theology of Pastoral Action*, trans. W. J. O'Hara (New York: Herder & Herder, 1968). In this translation of "Grundlegung der Pastoraltheologie als praktische Theologie," *Handbuch* I/2, Rahner states:

"In formulating maxims regarding the future life and action of the Church, to the extent that it goes beyond what can be deduced from dogmatic ecclesiology and from a methodical, sociological, and theological analysis of the present time, practical theology itself becomes free evaluation, decision, a part of the free historical activity of the Church and, if the conclusion is correct, a piece of prophecy, a charismatic summons from the future as God wills it. Complete separation between theology as a scientific branch of study and as decision or prophecy is impossible for historical man, who can never step outside the course of his own history" (p. 57).

[20]Rahner, "Problem of Secularization," p. 338.

[21]Ibid., p. 340.

have a name, for it does not yet exist in a formal, identified fashion. He points to *Gaudium et Spes* as an example, however, of a document that would correspond to the concerns of the theological discipline he has in mind.[22] There is another kind of theology which is being done today which I believe, at least in part, expresses the prophetic element and something of the theological discipline Rahner has conceived (although Rahner himself does not mention it in this way), and that is liberation theology. It seems to me that liberation theologies tend to be something of a hybrid between the way speculative theology has traditionally been done and a new kind of practical theology.[23]

Liberation theology has principally directed our attention to the historical context of our ethical decisions. It is noted for its turn to *praxis*, for its giving primacy to the practical over against the theoretical. Liberation theologians have called into question the traditional manner in which theology has been done with its emphasis on theoretical reason and have directed theology's attention to the lived faith, including its social and political context, as the basis from which theological reflection must arise.[24] It has held that the gospel cannot be truly grasped without a prior commitment to the poor and oppressed and to the struggle for liberation. Such a turn to praxis makes possible a critique of the ideological trappings of traditional theology and makes one open to the new call of God in the present historical context. Furthermore, the emphasis on praxis has involved a theological analysis and interpretation of the contemporary situation of the church. Much

---

[22]Ibid., p. 339.

[23]I realize that there are many liberation theologies, and there is always some problem trying to find a common denominator which can truly speak to all such theologies in question. In addition my own reading in this area is somewhat limited. Nevertheless I venture some tentative observations and impressions.

[24]In Gustavo Gutierrez's *A Theology of Liberation: History, Politics, and Salvation* (trans. and ed. Caridad Inda and John Eagleson [Maryknoll, NY: Orbis Books, 1973]), "praxis" includes the Christian's relation to God and neighbor, the church in its concrete historical situation, and in fact human history.

attention has been given to the question of discerning the 'signs of the times', and liberation theologians have taken up the question of the nature of Christian imperatives for action which can never simply be deduced from general principles.[25]

What is particularly important to us is that, regardless of the way liberation theologians formulate theological method and the nature of discerning the call to action for our times, their turn to

---

[25]This can be seen in a discussion by Juan Luis Segundo (*The Liberation of Theology*, trans. John Drury [Maryknoll, NY: Orbis Books, 1976], pp. 172-73; see especially chap. 6, "Ideologies and Relativity," pp. 154-81) on the question of making decisions in a specific historical context, decisions that cannot be deduced entirely from past revelation. Segundo's approach to the problem involves the recognition of the relativity of historical situations. Past revelation cannot spell out the mode of action for the present concrete situation. Rather, we are left with our imagination and creativity to determine by what means love effectively brings about the good of the other including the larger community. The principle Segundo operates with is that of the end justifying the means. The morality of the means "must be studied in the context of a given historical situation in order to determine which means represents the richest and most promising possibilities of love." The historical situation and an analysis of it become a primary focus in determining the mode of action. Segundo's concern is that we do not simply rest with general principles deduced from past revelation which can never provide an absolute call to action which specifically takes up the needs of the present. Segundo calls us to risk specific forms of action and to respond to them as imperatives. This concern mirrors Rahner's and yet Segundo has not taken us much farther than traditional theology for grasping the nature of this discernment of imperatives for the times in which we live. More attention must be given to the nature of the human creativity and imagination of which Segundo writes.

The question of *how* we choose among various alternatives presented to us by the historical situation has been raised by others. José Míguez Bonino's answer to this question (*Toward a Christian Political Ethics* [Philadelphia: Fortress Press, 1983], pp. 107, 106) involves a recognition of the dialectic between reality and consciousness and between praxis and theory and the assumption that the fundamental criterion for action is commitment to the poor. (He also gives a basic ethical guideline for the situation of conflict that is present in any radical social change: "the maximizing of universal human possibilities and the minimizing of human costs.") Our concern, however, has been with the possibility of a number of options for commitment to the poor and we have wondered about a "charismatic imperative" that assumes one specific call to action among other alternatives. Bonino recognizes that the necessary discernment for such an imperative has "a prophetic dimension to it that eludes thoughtful analysis." The concern of this work has been to give a "thoughtful analysis" of this prophetic dimension.

praxis has meant the involvement, within theology, of a prophetic kind of decision making and imperative. I believe a good example of this, an example of what Rahner calls a "practical ecclesiological cosmology," can be seen in José Comblin's *The Church and the National Security State* which combines a theological interpretation of the present situation in Latin America with a mission and strategy which can be the material basis for prophetic imperatives. Comblin makes the point that "the theology of liberation tries to enlighten and to guide the Church toward pastoral practice, a geopolitics, and a strategy of liberation."[26]

This 'new' way of doing theology which I am calling a 'prophetic theology' must be more clearly defined by careful attention to the dynamic of practical reason in the human person and its relationship to theoretical reason. A 'prophetic theology' does not have to view itself as replacing the 'old way' of doing theology but of developing a necessary discipline in its own right, particularly needed for our times, in which careful scientific analysis of the world situation must be coupled with a theological perspective of the church's and theologian's own discernment of the 'signs of the times', a discernment which involves this prophetic dynamic as we have described it in this work. As Rahner has pointed out, practical theology has not yet been sufficiently defined in its method, much less this discipline within practical theology which I have called 'prophetic theology'. I believe that as this defining is accomplished it will become clearer that many liberation theologies cannot be critiqued by the criterion of the method of speculative theology, and the distinctive contribution of liberation theologies may also, therefore, become clearer.

The recent difficulties of the teaching office of the Roman Catholic church with liberation theology can be seen partially in this light. While the predominant problem may revolve around the question of ecclesial authority, nevertheless, a conflict can be seen

---

[26]José Comblin, *The Church and the National Security State* (Maryknoll, NY: Orbis Books, 1979), p. 217.

also between a traditional speculative theological approach and an approach defined by the 'turn to praxis'. Difficulties arise when in liberation theology imperatives or strategies for our times are treated (by either liberation theologians or official theologians) almost as if they were principles of the gospel or directly deduced from the gospel as applicable to today's situation. The teaching office of the church by its traditional nature is inclined to view such theologies in this manner, as dealing with timeless and essential truths, when in fact many of the concerns of liberation theologies are precisely with timely and existential truths, the situation of the church and its mission in *this* age. It seems to me certain difficulties could be cleared up if we fully recognized the existence of a practical as well as theoretical method and the significance of a prophetic theological discipline which is concerned to address the question of the situation and mission of the church in the world today.

Clearly there is a need for a recognition of prophetic theology as a distinct theological discipline, a necessary part of the church's reflection. The prophetic element in the church would then be included not only in the charismatic decision making of the local congregation, the calls to action of individuals and movements, the existential word of the preacher, the timely directives of presbyter and episcopé, but also in the practical reflections of the prophetic theologian.

Selected Bibliography

Works by Karl Rahner

Rahner, Karl. *The Christian Commitment: Essays in Pastoral Theology*. Translated by Cecily Hastings. New York: Sheed & Ward, 1963.

_____. *The Christian of the Future*. Translated by W. J. O'Hara. New York: Herder & Herder, 1967.

_____. *Encounters with Silence*. Translated by James M. Demske. New York: Newman Press, 1960.

_____. "Experiencing the Spirit." In *The Spirit in the Church*, pp. 1-31. Translated by John Griffiths. New York: Seabury Press, 1979.

_____. *Foundations of the Christian Faith: An Introduction to the Idea of Christianity*. Translated by William V. Dyck. New York: Seabury Press, 1978.

_____. *Free Speech in the Church*. Translated by George Lamb. New York: Sheed & Ward, 1960.

_____. *Gefahren im heutigen Katholizismus*. Einsiedeln: Johannes Verlag, 1950.

_____. *Geist in Welt*. Munich: Kösel, 1957.

_____. *Grace in Freedom*. Translated and adapted by Hilda Graef. New York: Herder & Herder, 1969.

231

Rahner, Karl. *Grundkers des Glaubens: Einführung in den Begriff des Christentums.* Freiburg: Herder, 1976.

_____. *Hörer des Wortes.* Revised and edited by Johannes B. Metz. Munich: Kösel, 1963.

_____. "Listening to the Word." Unpublished translation by Joseph Donceel of *Hörer des Wortes.*

_____. *The Love of Jesus and the Love of Neighbor.* Translated by Robert Barr. New York: Crossroad, 1983.

_____. *Meditations on Freedom and the Spirit.* Translated by Rosaleen Ockinden, David Smith, and Cecily Bennett. New York: Seabury Press, 1978.

_____. *Meditations on the Sacraments.* New York: Seabury Press, 1977.

_____. *Nature and Grace: Dilemmas in the Modern Church.* Translated by Dinah Wharton. New York: Sheed & Ward, 1964.

_____. *On Heresy.* Translated by J. W. O'Hara. New York: Herder & Herder, 1964.

_____. *On Prayer.* New York: Paulist Press, 1958.

_____. *Opportunities for Faith: Elements of a Modern Spirituality.* Translated by Edward Quinn. New York: Seabury Press, 1975.

_____. *The Practice of Faith: A Handbook of Contemporary Spirituality.* New York: Crossroads, 1983.

_____. *The Priesthood.* Translated by Edward Quinn. New York: Herder & Herder, 1968.

_____. *Quaestiones Disputatae.* Vol. 1: *Inspiration in the Bible.* Translated by Charles H. Henkey. New York: Herder & Herder, 1962.

_____. *Quaestiones Disputatae.* Vol. 2: *On the Theology of Death.* Translated by Charles H. Henkey. New York: Herder & Herder, 1961.

Rahner, Karl. *Quaestiones Disputatae.* Vol. 4: *Visionen und Prophezeiungen.* Freiburg: Herder, 1958.

_____. *Quaestiones Disputatae.* Vol. 5: *Das Dynamische in der Kirche.* Freiburg: Herder, 1958.

_____. *Quaestiones Disputatae.* Vol. 9: *The Church and the Sacraments.* Translated by W. J. O'Hara. London: Burns & Oates, 1963.

_____. *Quaestiones Disputatae.* Vol. 10: *Visions and Prophecies.* Translated by Charles H. Henkey and Richard Strachen. New York: Herder & Herder, 1963.

_____. *Quaestiones Disputatae.* Vol. 12: *The Dynamic Element in the Church.* Translated by J. W. O'Hara. Freiburg: Herder, 1964.

_____. *Quaestiones Disputatae.* Vol. 13: *Hominisation: The Evolutionary Origin of Man as a Theology Problem.* Translated by W. J. O'Hara. New York: Herder, 1965.

_____. *Schriften zur Theologie.* 15 vols. Freiburg, Einsiedeln: Herder, Benziger, 1954-83.

_____. *Servants of the Lord.* Translated by Richard Strachan. New York: Herder & Herder, 1968.

_____. *The Shape of the Church to Come.* Translated with an Introduction by Edward Quinn. New York: Seabury Press, 1974.

_____. *Spirit in the World.* Translated by William V. Dych. New York: Herder & Herder, 1968.

_____. *Spiritual Exercises.* Translated by Kenneth Baker. New York: Herder & Herder, 1965.

_____. *Theological Investigations.* 21 vols. Translated by Cornelius Ernst, Karl H. Kruger, Boniface Kruger, Kevin Smith, David Bourke, David Morland, Edward Quinn, and Hugh M. Riley. New York, Baltimore: Helicon, Herder, Seabury, Crossroads, 1961-88.

_____. *Theology of Pastoral Action.* Translated by W. J. O'Hara, and adapted for an English-speaking audience by Daniel Morrissey. New York: Herder & Herder, 1968.

Rahner, Karl. *The Trinity*. Translated by Joseph Donceel. New York: Herder & Herder, 1970.

_____, ed. *Encyclopedia of Theology: The Concise "Sacramentum Mundi"*. New York: Crossroad, 1982.

_____, ed. *Handbuch der Pastoraltheologie: Praktische Theologie der Kirche in ihrer Gegenwart*. 5 vols. Freiburg: Herder, 1964-72.

Rahner, Karl; Ernst, Cornelius; and Smyth, Kevin, eds. *Sacramentum Mundi: An Encyclopedia of Theology*. 6 vols. New York: Herder & Herder, 1968-70.

Rahner, Karl, and Fries, Heinrich. *Unity of the Churches: An Actual Possibility*. Translated by Ruth C. L. Gritsch and Eric W. Gritsch. Philadelphia: Fortress Press and New York: Paulist Press, 1985.

Rahner, Karl, and Imhof, Paul. *Ignatius of Loyola*. Translated by Rosaleen Ockenden. New York: Collins, 1979.

Rahner, Karl, and Vorgrimler, Herbert. *Dictionary of Theology*. 2d ed. New York: Crossroad, 1981.

Biblical and Phenomenological Studies on Prophecy

Aune, David E. *Prophecy in Early Christianity and the Ancient Mediterranean World*. Grand Rapids: Eerdmans, 1983.

Brueggemann, Walter. *The Prophetic Imagination*. Philadelphia: Fortress Press, 1978.

Campenhausen, Hans von. *Ecclesiastical Authority and Spiritual Power in the Church of the First Three Centuries*. Translated by J. A. Baker. Stanford, CA: Stanford University Press, 1969.

Carroll, Robert P. *When Prophecy Failed: Cognitive Dissonance in the Prophetic Traditions of the Old Testament*. New York: Seabury Press, 1979.

Clements, Ronald Ernest. *Prophecy and Covenant*. Naperville, IL: A. R. Allenson, 1965.

Clements, Ronald Ernest. *Prophecy and Tradition.* Oxford: Basil Blackwell, 1975.

Coats, George W., and Long, Burke O., eds. *Canon and Authority.* Philadelphia: Fortress Press, 1977.

Coggins, Richard; Phillips, Anthony; and Knibb, Michael, eds. *Israel's Prophetic Tradition: Essays in Honour of Peter B. Ackroyd.* Cambridge: Cambridge University Press, 1982.

Crenshaw, James L. *Prophetic Conflict.* New York: Walter de Gruyter, 1971.

Eissfeldt, Otto. "The Prophetic Literature." In *The Old Testament and Modern Study: A Generation of Discovery and Research*, pp. 115-61. Edited by H. H. Rowley. Oxford: Clarendon Press, 1951.

Ellis, Edward Earle. *Prophecy and Hermeneutic in Early Christianity: New Testament Essays.* Tübingen: J. C. B. Mohr, 1978.

Emerton, J. A., ed. *Prophecy: Essays Presented to George Fohrer on His Sixty-fifth Birthday, 6 September 1980.* New York: W. de Gruyter, 1980.

Fuller, Reginald H. *The Foundations of New Testament Christianity.* New York: Charles Scribner's Sons, 1965.

Heschel, Abraham J. *The Prophets.* 2 vols. New York: Harper & Row, Torchbooks and Colophon Books, 1967.

Hill, David. *Prophecy in the New Testament.* Atlanta: George Knox, 1979.

Knight, Harold. *The Hebrew Prophetic Consciousness.* London: Lutterworth, 1947.

Koenig, John. *Charismata: God's Gifts for God's People.* Philadelphia: Westminster Press, 1978.

Lindblom, J. *Prophecy in Ancient Israel.* Philadelphia: Fortress Press, 1962.

McKane, W. "Prophecy and the Prophetic Literature." In *Tradition and Interpretation: Essays by Members of the Society for Old Testament Study.* Edited by G. W. Anderson. London: Clarendon Press, 1979.

Orlinsky, Harry M., ed. *Interpreting the Prophetic Tradition.* New York: KTAV Publishing House, 1969.

Pangopaulos, J., ed. *Prophetic Vocation in the New Testament and Today.* Leiden: Brill, 1977.

Robinson, Theodore H. *Prophecy and the Prophets in Ancient Israel.* London: Duckworth & Co., 1923.

Schweizer, Eduard. *Church Order in the New Testament.* Translated by Frank Clarke. Naperville, IL: A. R. Allenson, 1961.

_____. *The Holy Spirit.* Translated by Reginald H. Fuller and Ilse Fuller. Philadelphia: Fortress Press, 1980.

Society of Biblical Literature. *Semeia.* Vol. 21: *Anthropological Perspectives on Old Testament Prophecy.* Chico, CA: Scholars Press, 1982.

Theological Dictionary of the New Testament. 10 vols. Edited by Gerhard Kittel. Translated and edited by Geoffrey W. Bromiley. Grand Rapids: Eerdmans, 1964-76. S.v. προφητητες," by Gerhard Friedrich.

Westermann, Claus. *Basic Forms of Prophetic Speech.* Translated by Hugh Clayton White. Philadelphia: Westminster Press, 1967.

Widengren, G. *Literary and Psychological Aspects of the Hebrew Prophets.* Uppsala: Lundequistska bokhandeln, 1948.

Wilson, Robert T. *Prophecy and Society in Ancient Israel.* Philadelphia: Fortress Press, 1980.

Other Works

Aquinas, St. Thomas. *On Being and Essence.* Translated, with an Introduction and notes by Armand Maurer. Toronto: The Pontifical Institute of Mediæval Studies, 1949.

_____. *Summa Theologica.* Vol. 45: *Prophecy and Other Charisms.* Blackfriars in conjunction with New York: McGraw-Hill, 1970.

_____. *Summa Theologica.* Vol. 2: *Existence and the Nature of God.* Translated by Timothy McDermott. Blackfriars in conjunction with New York: McGraw-Hill, 1964.

Bacik, James J. *Apologetics and the Eclipse of Mystery: Mystagogy According to Karl Rahner.* Notre Dame: University of Notre Dame Press, 1980.

Barth, Karl. *Church Dogmatics.* Vol. 4, Part 3: "The Doctrine of Reconciliation. Jesus Christ, the True Witness." Edited by G. W. Bromiley and T. F. Torrance. Translated by G. W. Bromiley. Edinburgh: T. & T. Clark, 1961-62.

Bonhoeffer, Dietrich. *Ethics.* Edited by Eberhard Bethge. Translated by Neville Horton Smith. New York: Macmillan, 1955.

Bonino, José Míguez. *Toward a Christian Political Ethics.* Philadelphia: Fortress Press, 1983.

Braaten, Carl E. *The Future of God: The Revolutionary Dynamics of Hope.* New York: Harper & Row, 1969.

Bresnahan, James F. "An Ethic of Faith." In *A World of Grace: An Introduction to the Themes and Foundations of Karl Rahner's Theology,* pp. 169-84. Edited by Leo J. O'Donovan. New York: Seabury Press, 1980.

_____. "The Methodology of 'Natural Law' Ethical Reasoning in the Theology of Karl Rahner and Its Supplementary Development Using the Legal Philosophy of Lon L. Fuller." Ph.D. dissertation, Yale University, 1972.

_____. "Rahner's Christian Ethics." *America,* October 31, 1970, pp. 351-54.

Buckley, James Joseph. "Karl Barth and Karl Rahner on the Christian Community: Analysis, Comparison, and Assessment." Ph.D. dissertation, Yale University, 1977.

Bulst, Werner. *Revelation.* Translated by Bruce Vawter. New York: Sheed & Ward, 1965.

Burke, Ronald. "Rahner and Revelation." Ph.D. dissertation, Yale University, 1974.

Callahan, Annice. *Karl Rahner's Spirituality of the Pierced Heart: A Reinterpretation of Devotion to the Sacred Heart.* New York: University Press of America, 1985.

Carr, Anne. *The Theological Method of Karl Rahner.* Missoula, MT: Scholars Press, 1977.

_____. "Theology and Experience in the Thought of Karl Rahner." *Journal of Religion* 53 (July 1973): 359–76.

Comblin, José. *The Church and the National Security State.* Maryknoll, NY: Orbis Books, 1979.

Congar, Yves. *I Believe in the Holy Spirit.* 3 vols. Translated by David Smith. New York: Seabury Press, 1976.

Cooke, Bernard. *Ministry to Word and Sacraments: History and Theology.* Philadelphia: Fortress Press, 1976.

Copleston, F. C. *Aquinas.* Baltimore: Penguin Books, 1955.

Dulles, Avery. *Models of Revelation.* Garden City, NY: Doubleday, 1983.

_____. *Revelation Theology: A History.* New York: Herder & Herder, 1969.

Egan, Harvey D. *The Spiritual Exercises and the Ignatian Mystical Horizon.* Foreword by Karl Rahner. St. Louis: Institute of Jesuit Sources, 1976.

Eicher, Peter. *Die anthropologische Wende: Karl Rahners philosophischer Weg vom Wesen des Menschen zur personalen Existenz.* Freiburg, Schweiz: Universitätsverlag, 1970.

Fischer, Klaus P. *Der Mensch als Geheimnis: Die Anthropologie Karl Rahners.* Freiburg: Herder, 1974.

Fleming, David L., ed. *Notes on the Spiritual Exercises of St. Ignatius of Loyola.* St. Louis: Review for Religions, 1983.

_____. *The Spiritual Exercises of St. Ignatius: A Literal Translation and a Contemporary Reading.* St. Louis: Institute of Jesuit Sources, 1978.

Floristan, Casiano, and Duquoc, Christian, eds. *Discernment of the Spirit and of Spirits.* Concilium vol. 119. New York: Seabury Press, 1979.

Gilson, Etienne. *Being and Some Philosophers.* Toronto: Medieval Studies of Toronto, 1949.

Gilson, Etienne. *The Christian Philosophy of St. Thomas Aquinas.* New York: Random House, 1956.

Gutiérrez, Gustavo. *A Theology of Liberation: History, Politics, and Salvation.* Translated and edited by Caridad Inda and John Eagleson. Maryknoll, NY: Orbis Books, 1973.

Greiner, Friedemann. *Die Menschlichkeit der Offenbarung: Die transzendentale Gundlegung der Theologie bei Karl Rahner.* Munich: Chr. Kaiser Verlag, 1978.

Gustafson, James M. *Can Ethics Be Christian?* Chicago: University of Chicago Press, 1975.

Heidegger, Martin. *Being and Time.* Translated by John Macquarrie and Edward Robinson. New York: Harper & Row, 1962.

James, William. *The Varieties of Religious Experience.* New York: New American Library, 1958.

John, Helen James. *The Thomist Spectrum.* New York: Fordham University Press, 1966.

Kant, Immanuel. *Critique of Judgement.* Translated with an Introduction and notes by J. H. Bernard. London: Macmillan, 1914.

_____. *Critique of Practical Reason.* Translated with an Introduction by Lewis White Beck. Indianapolis: Bobbs-Merrill, 1956.

_____. *Critique of Pure Reason.* Translated with an Introduction by Norman Kemp Smith. Unabridged Edition. New York: St. Martin's Press and Toronto: Macmillan, 1929.

_____. *Foundations of the Metaphysics of Morals* and *What Is Enlightenment?* Translated with an Introduction by Lewis White Beck. Indianapolis: Bobbs-Merrill, 1959.

Kerr, Fergus. "Rahner Retrospective: I. Rupturing Der Pianische Monolithismus." *New Blackfriars* 61 (May 1980): 224-330.

_____. "Rahner Retrospective: II. The Historicity of Theology." *New Blackfriars* 11 (July-August 1980): 331-41.

Küng, Hans. *The Church.* Translated by Ray Ockender and Rosaleen Ockender. New York: Sheed & Ward, 1967.

Küng, Hans. *Why Priests? A Proposal for a New Church Ministry.* Translated by Robert C. Collins. Garden City, NY: Doubleday, 1972.

Lamb, Matthew L. *Solidarity with Victims: Toward a Theology of Social Transformation.* New York: Crossroad, 1982.

Latourelle, René. *Theology of Revelation.* Including a commentary on the Constitution "Dei Verbum" of Vatican II. Staten Island, NY: Alba House, 1966.

Lonergan, Bernard J. F. *Insight: A Study of Human Understanding.* New York: Harper & Row, 1957.

_____. *Method in Theology.* New York: Herder & Herder, 1972.

Lynch, Patrick Joseph. "The Relationship of Church and World in the Theology of Karl Rahner." Ph.D. dissertation, University of Chicago, 1980.

Marechal, Joseph. *A Marechal Reader.* Edited and translated by Joseph Donceel. New York: Herder & Herder, 1970.

Maritain, Jacques. *Creative Intuition in Art and Poetry.* The A. W. Mellon Lectures in the Fine Arts. Cleveland: World, Meridian Books, 1953.

_____. *Existence and the Existent: An Essay on Christian Existentialism.* Translated by Lewis Galantiers and Gerald B. Phelan. Garden City, NY: Doubleday, 1956.

_____. *The Range of Reason.* New York: Charles Scribner's Sons, 1942.

McCool, Gerald A., ed. *A Rahner Reader.* New York: Seabury Press, 1975.

Metz, Johann Baptist. *Faith in History and Society: Toward a Practical Fundamental Theology.* Translated by David Smith. New York: Seabury Press, 1980.

Moran, Gabriel. *Theology of Revelation.* New York: Herder & Herder, 1966.

Motzko, Maria Elisabeth. "Karl Rahner's Theology: A Theology of the Symbol." Ph.D. dissertation, Fordham University, 1976.

Muck, Otto. *The Transcendental Method.* Translated by William E. Seidensticker. New York: Herder & Herder, 1968.

Niebuhr, H. Richard. *The Meaning of Revelation.* New York: Macmillan, 1941.

Otto, Rudolf. *The Idea of the Holy: An Inquiry into the Non-rational Factor in the Idea of the Divine and Its Relation to the Rational.* Translated by John W. Harvey. New York: Oxford University Press, 1958.

Pannenberg, Wolfhart; Rendtorff, Rolf; Rendtorff, Trutz; and Wilkens, Ulrich, eds. *Revelation as History.* Translated by David Granskou. London: Macmillan, 1968.

Pelikan, Jaroslav. *The Light of the World: A Basic Image in Early Christian Thought.* New York: Harper & Bros., 1962.

Prenter, Regin. *Spiritus Creator.* Translated by John M. Jensen. Philadelphia: Muhlenberg Press, 1953.

Raschko, Michael B. "The Ontological Roots of the Relationship of Religion and Culture in the Thought of Paul Tillich, Karl Rahner, and Bernard Lonergan." Ph.D. dissertation, University of Chicago, 1982.

Schillebeeckx, Edward. *Ministry: Leadership in the Community of Jesus Christ.* Translated by John Bowden. New York: Crossroad, 1981.

Schleiermacher, Friedrich. *On Religion: Speeches to Its Cultured Despisers.* Translated by John Oman with an Introduction by Rudolf Otto. New York: Harper & Row, 1958.

Segundo, Juan Luis. *The Liberation of Theology.* Translated by John Drury. Maryknoll, NY: Orbis Books, 1976.

Speck, Josef. *Karl Rahners theologische Anthropologie.* Munich: Kösel-Verlag, 1967.

Synove, Paul, and Benoit, Pierre. *Prophecy and Inspiration: A Commentary on the Summa Theologica I-II, Questions 171-178.* Translated by Avery R. Dulles and Thomas L. Sheridan. New York: Desclee, 1961.

Szura, John Paul. "The Vocational Decision; Its Theological and Psychological Components: An Attempt at Integrating the

Theological Anthropology of Karl Rahner with the Psychology of Donald Super." Ph.D. dissertation, Fordham University, 1978.

Tillich, Paul. *Systematic Theology.* 3 vols. Chicago: University of Chicago Press, 1951-63.

_____. *Theology of Culture.* London: Oxford University Press, 1959.

Tracy, David. *The Analogical Imagination: Christian Theology and the Culture of Pluralism.* New York: Crossroad, 1981.

Underhill, Evelyn. *Mysticism.* New York: E. P. Dutton, 1961.

Wyschogrod, Michael. *Kierkegaard and Heidegger: The Ontology of Existence.* New York: Humanities Press, 1954.

Index